Reluctant Bureaucrats

The Struggle to Establish the National Endowment for the Arts

Charles Christopher Mark

D1736604

KENDALL/HUNT PUBLISHING COMPANY
2460 Kerper Boulevard P.O. Box 539 Dubuque, Iowa 52004-0539

Copyright © 1991 by Charles Christopher Mark

Library of Congress Catalog Card Number: 91–60261

ISBN 0–8403–6547–0

Printed in the United States of America
10 9 8 7 6 5 4 3 2 1

Dedication

To my children, Chris and Hilary, who were neglected during much of this period of my life which I regret enormously.

Contents

Preface

I haven't attempted to write a definitive history of the origins of the National Endowment for the Arts and the National Endowment for the Humanities. These pages depict much of the very early history, but had I consulted everyone who played a role and had access to every document, the pages would have been heavier and more dense.

I haven't attempted to write an autobiography of a portion of my life. Occasionally, I mention family or personal pain or pleasure, but only when I believe it makes the narrative more insightful of a situation or one of the characters.

I have attempted to write precisely the kind of book described by Charles Ives as his purpose in writing his book:

"Some have written a book for money; I have not. Some for fame; I have not. Some for love; I have not. Some for kindlings; I have not. . . . In fact, I haven't written a book at all—I have merely cleaned house."

Well, not quite. What has been written is put down with love and a desire to see President Johnson and Roger Stevens given their rightful place as seminal leaders in the progress the arts have made since the 1960s.

Prologue

Before lunging into the central, important story a bit of background is necessary. It is necessary to understand the times and the people involved to appreciate the chronicle of progress of the arts from 1964 through 1969; the years which brought about the National Council on the Arts and the National Endowment for the Arts.

My first job after majoring in literature and theatre at the University of Wisconsin was as a radio quiz program writer in Chicago. It's still embarrassing when watching drivel television quiz programs or playing parlor games that I know so many obscure facts about inconsequential events and people. (Roland Hill invented the gummed postage stamp. Benjamin Harrison was the last President to wear a beard).

After deciding the dulling future of radio quiz program writing was detrimental to a normal life, I went back to school and earned a masters degree in Community Organization. This qualified me to be a United Way executive and professional fundraiser which I was for four years.

While learning about the pressure points of communities and the techniques for organizing volunteers in graduate school, it occurred to me that with these techniques we wouldn't have gone bankrupt with a summer stock theatre we had imposed on the city of Madison, Wisconsin in 1953 and 1954.

I saw a valuable parallel between a welfare council and United Way campaign and an "arts council" and a "United Arts campaign." I foolishly mentioned this fanciful theory to an old friend, Prof. Robert Gard, and he told me an arts council already existed in Winston-Salem, North Carolina.

Purely out of intellectual curiosity I wrote for information. A week later I was telephoned by the president of the Winston-Salem Arts Council and recruited to be their executive director. I refused to apply because of commitments on my present job. A Ralph Burgard accepted the position.

However, my name and resumé were not circulating in a tiny circle of progressive communities examining their cultural life. A Junior League of America arts consultant named Virginia Lee Comer was sowing the seeds by organizing communities for purposes of cultural planning and fund raising. I received calls from Fort Wayne and someplace in Texas.

Then in the fall of 1957, the Saint Paul Council of Arts and Sciences wrote and asked me if I would be interested in applying for the directorship there. I decided something exciting was happening in communities all over the country and that I wanted to be part of it. I didn't get the St. Paul job after applying for it, but Winston-Salem hired me when Ralph Burgard left there for St. Paul.

I was the fourth person in the country to be employed as a professional arts council executive; St. Paul, Fort Wayne, and Cincinnati were the only other cities to have professional directors.

After three and a half years of pioneering in Winston-Salem I was lured to St. Louis by a larger salary and bigger challenge to found the St. Louis Arts and Education Council. Three years there were a struggle that ended with a front page debate which I knew I would lose.

And then the phone rang.

Roger Stevens' family was from Ann Arbor, Michigan. His father suffered financial ruin a year or so before the famous crash of 1929 when Roger was a student at Choate, the exclusive prep school. He had been accepted at Harvard for the coming year. Choate allowed Roger to graduate through a scholarship, but Harvard was out of the question. The University of Michigan had almost no tuition in those Depression years, but student life was still extremely difficult with no income or family support and Roger left after a semester or two.

Reading was always his passion and through the next few years of odd jobs he read his way through the Detroit Public Library. In mid-Depression he developed a concept in real estate that began to give him an income and confidence in his ability to make money. He married the girl of his dreams and was able to make a trip around the world as a honeymoon while most people were struggling to survive.

He served as a naval officer during the war and afterward moved his real estate business to New York. Roger Stevens became known as the man who bought the Empire State Building in the early 1950s at the same that he began producing Broadway plays. At the time this story begins he had produced more than one hundred plays of high standard.

Roger Stevens came to Washington not only respected by politicians and bureaucrats for his accomplishments of rising from gas station jockey to respected financial wizard, but also as a highly successful political fund raiser. He became a friend of Adlai Stevenson and raised money for his 1952 campaign, and in the 1956 election was fundraising chairman for the Democratic Party. In the 1960s he always seemed surprised when Senators and Representatives greeted him with respect and gratitude because he had raised millions of dollars for Democratic campaigns.

President Kennedy was responsible for luring Roger Stevens to Washington because of Adlai Stevenson's support of Kennedy during the campaign and Roger's support of Stevenson in other campaigns. When asked what appointment he would accept in the Kennedy Administration—an ambassadorship, a place on a commission or federal board—Roger chose the National Cultural Center because he understood both the arts and real estate. After the unforgettable tragedy in Dallas Roger was instrumental in changing the National Cultural Center into a memorial as a Kennedy Center for the Performing Arts.

I was in St. Louis trying to prop up a wobbly new arts council, Roger was being tapped on the shoulder by a persuasive president to be his "can do" assistant charged with establishing a program of federal aid to the arts.

And then the phone rang.

Introducing the Times

The arts in America historically have been of Europe, by a small cadre of European immigrants, for a slightly larger group of European immigrants; the latter group being more senior in time spent in this country and proud of it. The smaller group performed for the larger group and the larger group supported the smaller group.

To illustrate the point, only three examples are necessary. In the early and mid 19th century, American actors pretended to be English in accent and ancestry in order to attain respect with patrons of the arts. During World War I, neither the conductor, who was European, nor the trustees, who were blue blooded Americans, could persuade the musicians of the Boston Symphony Orchestra to play the Star Spangled Banner before each concert. Most of the orchestra players were imported from Germany and sympathetic to the other side of the conflict. A U.S. artist didn't win a Nobel Prize in Literature until 1930 (Sinclair Lewis). By the 1960s, however, our arts culture was beginning to change into something more native.

Arts organizations were being established in cities and towns across the country after World War II. A virus called "Major League City" had infected nearly every metropolitan area. The American Symphony Orchestra League boasted that orchestras numbered 1500, an aggregate figure which included college and amateur orchestras. The major orchestras were beginning to compete for money with a small, but growing group of resident professional theatres being established in fertile but untilled soil in cities such as Washington, D.C., Houston, Texas, Minneapolis, San Francisco, Cleveland and Oklahoma City.

Dance and opera were beginning to gain commitments from a new generation. I remember doing a consultation for the Junior League of Tulsa, Oklahoma, and concluding the problem was that the sons and daughters of the cultural leaders were not content with the cultural life provided. They wanted more for themselves and their children. One mediocre opera, five over-rehearsed symphony concerts, and amateur theatre and ballet were not enough to satisfy them.

The once healthy road show circuit was dying, winter stock companies had all but disappeared except for Erie Playhouse and Barter Theatre, new art museums and other museums were being established while older museums were announcing they were closing certain days each week for lack of operating funds. It was the best and worst of times. A burgeoning interest in the arts that was unprecedented, at the same time financial resources were diminishing.

The Ford Foundation was pouring money into the arts, the Rockefeller Brothers Fund was in the middle of an elaborate study of the performing arts under the direction of a young dynamic woman named Nancy Hanks. The 20th Century Fund was undertaking a study of the economics of the arts. Perhaps fifty cities and a half dozen states had organized art councils, but few were firmly established as stable enterprises. Federal support was debated, and in some organizations put to a formal vote and defeated.

The arts were expanding while financial resources were becoming scarce. Something needed to be done to bring stability to the institutions which existed and to give encouragement to the newfound cultural interest and commitment. The country was poised for cultural progress. All that was needed was leadership of vision and courage to undertake the task. President Johnson and Roger L. Stevens, fortunately, were committed, capable, and unstoppable.

The phone was ringing.

▶ ─────────────────────────────────

Unemployed, and then . . .
Spring of 1964

In the beginning was the word and word was "You're fired." No one actually said those words, after all, this was a cultural organization where declaratory sentences are always avoided if possible. Instead, they said I obviously was ready for greater challenges than St. Louis could offer.

Two months, five days and three hours had gone by and greater challenges were in short supply. It was 1964. President Kennedy had cut taxes to stimulate the economy. The economy had been growing for a few months, but philanthropy lags behind the first blush of prosperity because pockets need to overflow before the large contributors pull their hands out with fists full of money. Consequently, the cultural explosion was at that moment a mere shot heard 'round the room.

For three and a half years I had pushed, pulled, yelled, cajoled, and whined, in an effort to establish a truly solid arts council and united arts fund campaign. In the end I was able to push hard enough for the conservative leadership to begin fulfilling their promises, but I in turn was pushed from the job the leadership had brought me to St. Louis to do. Robert Frost's words about miles to go and promises to keep weren't heeded in St. Louis; rather the leadership believed *IF* they had miles to go they wouldn't start the journey. But once started, they traveled steadily toward their destination.

What does a thirty-seven year-old man with a wife and two children to support do when he suffers from prolonged unemployment? In my case, I informed key people that I was available for other challenges immediately, and then sat back and waited. And waited. In the early 1960s employment services in the arts were limited and arts council jobs were extremely scarce. Actually, only approximately thirty American cities had community arts councils, most of them in smaller cities. In 1964, the sudden growth of regional theatres was two or three years from beginning. Ballet, at that time, had only an annual attendance of one million compared with the thirteen million today. People were just learning to love opera all over the country. Traditionally, and for good reason, arts councils were established only after a community had several cultural attractions to coordinate and support. One had to wait until enlightenment hit a community like divine intervention. This was a dry period.

Then Kathryn Bloom called. She and I had entered arts management at the same time in 1958. She was then the arts consultant for the Junior League and I was the executive director of the Arts Council of Winston-Salem. She was now Director of the Arts and Humanities Branch of the U.S. Office of Education.

"Are you really leaving St. Louis?"

"As soon as I have somewhere to go."

"Is there any . . . I have to ask this for a number of good reasons, and the answer is important, so let me ask you pretty directly. Is there any—scandalous reason for leaving. You didn't do anything illegal or blatantly immoral, did you?"

"Nothing memorable."

"Then you just resigned. Nothing in the papers of note?"

"Nothing memorable, really."

"Okay. How would you like to work in the White House with Roger Stevens?" She said this as if she was inviting me to have an Egg McMuffin.

I knew Kathy was no jokester; she didn't even smile often. When I made her laugh I felt guilty because I thought it somehow painful for her.

"You're not serious?"

"Yes. I am serious," she said in her manner that could only be serious. "I had lunch with Roger Stevens. You know he's been appointed by President Johnson to be Special Assistant for Cultural Affairs, don't you?"

"I hadn't heard." So much for my grasp of politics and current affairs at that time.

"He said he would like to know what the country was thinking about federal aid for the arts and to have someone who knew the grassroots arts people and have that person do a survey."

"But he doesn't like me. I opposed that television scheme he had for the National Cultural Center." (The Center later became the Kennedy Center for the Performing Arts as a memorial to the assassinated President.)

"We talked about that. But first, I said I could get a six month consultancy for someone. I could tie it into education somehow, but the person would actually be working for him. I informed him that most of the people in the White House were actually paid by some other agency, that to be attached to the White House was a great honor. He said he wouldn't know because he wasn't taking any salary."

"Can you really do that?"

"You'd be amazed what's done in Washington. So, he liked the idea of free staff and we started suggesting people for the job. He suggested one or two that I didn't think could do the job; you know provincial New York types. Then I suggested you. You know what he said? He said, 'Why should I hire my enemies?' "

"Bingo!"

"No. Wait. I looked him right in the eye and said, Because he was right about that television scheme of yours, wasn't he? And isn't that proof he knows the grassroots. He looked thoughtful for a minute and then said you had been right. The man is intellectually honest. He wanted you because you disagreed with him and you were right, not because you were a 'yes' man."

"I thought it was a bad idea and I told him so. That's all."

"Anyway, he said he wanted you and I cleared it with my boss this afternoon. So?"

"So, what's the job?"

"I guess he wants you to go around the country and feel the pulse of the cultural grassroots leadership. It's only for six months and no promises after that."

"I'm used to that. But you mean you're offering me a job for six months working with Roger Stevens in the White House." I had to be certain. "Would I have to move to Washington?"

"I'll tell him you accept, if you can work from St. Louis."

"Tell him I'll move if he insists."

She actually laughed. "I take it you want the job?"

"It's too good to be true."

"I think you will be a help in Washington. I'll get back to you in a few days."

That was it. A two minute conversation that turned a man from abject poverty, a thing to be scorned, into an envied member of the community. In my case, I was transformed from an obscure, unemployed art executive into the consultant to the man who was the advisor on the arts to the President of the United States. My thoughts now were careening around the fantasies of Potomac fever; I saw myself entering the famous portico with Marine guards holding the door for me, sitting in a high-ceilinged office with Roger Stevens surrounded by Federal period furniture, making plans for the cultural future of the great nation. President Johnson would of course drop in from time to time to see how we were coming along with our plans.

After fifteen minutes of adjusting my active imagination from a soup kitchen attitude to a White House Mess frame of mind, I told my wife. She wisely warned me of my tendency to conduct all my personal business in public. I not only washed dirty and clean linen in full view of friends and neighbors but I usually added some bleach to make my linen theatrically brighter. However, this time I was able to completely restrain myself by simply believing it would not happen, if I told anyone. President Johnson would not personally place my hand on a Bible, if I told a soul.

Kathy Bloom called in a day or two to tell me Roger Stevens had given final approval to hiring me and her boss, Commissioner Keppel, had also agreed. Technically, she said, I would be consultant to the Commissioner of Education in the Department of Health, Education, and Welfare. This would be the first of several long and meaningless titles I would hold before finally re-entering civilian life.

At this time, I had actually met Roger Stevens only once. He had accepted the appointment from President Kennedy to be chairman of the National Cultural Center. In

1962 I was in St. Louis trying to establish the Arts and Education Council. Roger Stevens had the idea he could raise the private money needed for the National Cultural Center through closed-circuit, televised, star-studded galas. These television galas had successfully raised large sums for Adlai Stevenson when Roger Stevens was fundraising chairman of the National Democratic Committee; it had been his idea. It was paramount that he organize the major cities and St. Louis was a key city for him.

At the 1962 annual conference of community arts councils and symphony orchestras in Detroit, I was given a message by the desk clerk to call someone named Roger Stevens. When I called I thought he was either awakened from a sound sleep or was drunk, so unenunciated were his words. During the next five years I became an expert at understanding his famous soft, slurred speech.

"'lo."

"Mr. Stevens?"

"gh."

"I had a message to call you. My name is Charles Mark."

"Oh . . . Yeah . . . I need to talk to you. When can we meet? Right now?"

"No. I've got a panel to moderate. Why don't you come up to the hospitality suite for a drink around five-thirty?"

"Fine." The phone went dead.

When we met we argued for what seemed to be hours. I was in opposition to the idea because I believed in gimmick-free fundraising; no bake sales, no gala balls, just hands out asking and receiving. I thought the arts needed to be established as a worthy community cause like schools, the United Way, and hospitals, not always attached to the rich and socially prominent. Secondly, the artists Roger Stevens promised were annual visitors to most major cities. People who could afford $100 for a ticket weren't going to sit in a movie theatre and watch these familiar artists in black and white on a fuzzy screen. Besides, at that time no one in the country as a whole was interested in helping D.C. build a cultural center no matter what it was called. Every city had the Oedifice complex and splitting any profit 50-50 with Washington was not appealing when funds were so difficult to raise for the arts.

In 1962, Roger Stevens was virtually unknown outside of New York theatre circles and political organizations. No one knew how he happened to be at our conference, or how he knew whom to contact. I knew of his reputation as a Broadway producer, but I didn't realize the extent of his high standards and perceptive artistic judgment during the 1950s until later in our relationship. I didn't know then of his real estate triumphs or his political activities.

I never met anyone before or since who was as singular of purpose as Roger Stevens. I had worked with some extremely successful and powerful people, but none of these people resembled this man who could persist so constantly in an idea. The first impression of him is his seeming inability to speak clearly. He is extremely articulate, but he speaks softly and seems to have an uncoordinated tongue, giving the impression he isn't actually expressing himself. The truth is he knows exactly what he wants to say and what he wants to accomplish and pursues those goals with bulldog tenacity. His pale blue eyes may be wandering around the room and never rest on the person with whom he is dealing, but his mind is three steps ahead of the opposition.

Roger Stevens believed St. Louis a key city in his plan because it was a large metropolitan market and a place known to be consciously making an effort to upgrade its cultural image. Also, since I was organizing the cultural leadership, it would be a comparatively easy city to mobilize. Few major cities at that time were organized for the arts.

After a three hour marathon session on the subject of closed-circuit television fundraising, he asked to meet me for breakfast where we continued the argument. We continued to disagree. But he didn't give up. Over the next year he sent at least three different people to St. Louis to promote the television idea. The first attempt came through a close friend of mine whom I couldn't refuse. I was asked to host a meeting of my leadership at the arts council so this woman could present the project. The woman was Selwa Roosevelt, who later became Chief of Protocol under President Reagan. She wasn't able to answer basic questions about the proposed television program and my people voted it down without any comment from me. Apparently, other people were sent to town with the same results and instead of admitting their failure they would report to Roger Stevens that I had interfered. I then wrote to him and suggested he keep his inefficient people away. It was largely because of this heated correspondence that led to his remark about enemies.

Now I was going to work with him on a larger project, at least that was the promise. But a promise didn't put money in the bank.

Roger Stevens, planning session.

A Six Month Suspenseful Sentence
Summer of 1964

When July rolled around and no final word of the appointment had been mentioned, I wasn't fun to live with.

I decided I had to do something to ease the tension. How about a trip to New York to see the 1964 World's Fair? I could think about highways, for which attractions would it be worth standing in line, how much to spend, and the pleasant but predictable conversations with my parents-in-law. As I planned the trip, thoughts of unemployment diminished substantially from 10,000 times a day to about 5,000 times. Was I making a mistake to trust in the casual word of Roger Stevens? Should I perhaps be applying for other jobs? When we left St. Louis I called Roger Stevens offices in New York and Washington and left the phone number of my in-laws in Far Rockaway.

Literature abounds with material on Jewish mothers, but little has been recorded about the relationship of Jewish mothers-in-law to their gentile sons-in-law. What kind of family is his where no one shows concern by yelling and telling each other how to improve?

All of this attitude is reflected in a certain reserve, a certain distrust, a skepticism bordering on persistent disbelief. Everything the son-in-law says or does is greeted by the same set of the mouth and nervous folding of the hands at the waist like a lieder singer making a debut. Often this pose is accompanied by a tentative "hmnnn" and a vague nod of the head.

We were in residence in New York for about a week when upon returning from the Fair one afternoon I was greeted by my mother-in-law on the front porch. Her hands were in the nervous singer's position and her mouth was poised to spit. I knew I was responsible for something.

"You got a call while you were gone," she said. She could get real meaning into a monotone.

"Yes?"

"They *said* it was the White House."

"Oh, good. It may be good news."

"Hmnnn." Facial expressions like hers must have been common among the people when Jesus walked on water or fed the multitude with a couple of fishes.

My wife's parents were abnormally circumspect about not appearing to interfere in my business or social life. They usually left for the farthest corner of the house when I happened to receive a phone call while they were present. Afterwards, I would have to retrieve them from the back bedroom or from the screened porch, even in winter.

But this time, my mother-in-law stood beside me as I dialed to make certain I was calling the number she inscribed on the pad beside the kitchen phone. She then moved two feet away and began polishing a glass with a dish towel, holding the towel and glass in the telltale waist-high position. She polished and polished and I strained to keep from gloating.

The operator said "White House" quite distinctly.

Ignoring her, I said "Is this the *White House?*"

The operator said it was again. "Roger Stevens office, please, in the *White House.*" While she was ringing his office, I couldn't resist saying to a dead line, "That's right. Roger Stevens, Special Assistant to President Johnson on the Arts."

"Are you in New York?" Salutationless as always.

"Yes. A little family vacation before I start work for you."

"Uh . . . I'll be in New York tomorrow. Could you drop in around . . . two? No. uh . . . eleven?"

"Is the appointment coming through soon, do you know?"

"Idunno. It should. Soon. I need to get moving, and there's no damn money here."

Glancing at the mother of my wife, I said, "In the *White House?* That's ridiculous."

"You'll learn a lot about the government in the next six months, my boy."

"I'm sure," was my snappy reply. Then, silence stretched until Christmas before I said I would see him the following day in his office. Immediately, the line went dead, leaving me to offer a friendly good-bye to a low hum. I didn't know where his office was in New York, but I had been too embarrassed to ask.

"So that really was the White House calling you?"

"Uh huh. It looks like I'm going to be a consultant in the White House for Roger Stevens."

"The Textile man?"

"No, the theatrical producer. You know, 'West Side Story?' That was one of his." I left her still polishing the glass and went to tell my wife the news.

From that moment on I never saw the set mouth and the hands locked at the waist like she was holding up her slacks. From then on she believed every syllable I uttered and loved to say to her friends, "my son-in-law in the *White House* says . . ."

I felt then, for the first time, it was really going to happen. I was going to work with Roger Stevens on the planning and the beginning of a federal arts program. I was going to meet him to talk about my role. I might even have a small influence on the course of the arts in this country some day. We might bring the idea to fruition, and I might get a permanent job in administering the program and the sky might fall, and it might rain dimes in July. I felt almost confident for the first time.

Roger Stevens address turned out to be the Squibb Building, where I arrived fifteen minutes early. F. A. O. Swartz occupies the ground floor so I browsed until the appointed minute. Upstairs, I found no receptionist and several empty desks, but I heard the unmistakable soft voice of Roger Stevens off to my right. As I approached the sound I passed an attractive woman who looked familiar. When she smiled I realized it was Kim Hunter. Around a corner in a small anteroom sat an attractive woman typing furiously. One could hear that he was winding down a phone call. She waved me into his office without missing a beat at the IBM. He put down the phone with one hand and gestured me into a side chair with the other.

He put his feet on the desk and his hands behind his head. It was the first time I had actually seen him since the argument about the television idea more than a year earlier. He didn't seem to be remembering the past; his eyes were bright and he was smiling. It was his Saturday morning relaxed mood which I came to know well over the next five years.

I don't remember the conversation that morning, except that it was more philosophical than I wanted it to be. I wanted to talk about my particular assignment, and my future. Instead, he kept asking me questions about how I thought the arts should be supported in this country, and what I thought would be the best way to administer a federal arts program. I do remember saying that the greatest obstacle to getting federal aid through the Congress was the fear of government control of the arts. It wasn't a profound observation, but he seemed pleased with me.

He said, "I know, it's Helen Thompson and that damn Symphony League of hers. They think President Johnson's going to choose all the operas the Met puts on."

"I think Helen is personally in favor of federal support, but the trustees of the symphony orchestras aren't. She's only reflecting an attitude that is prevalent among the rich supporters on the boards of the orchestras."

"Well, that's one of your jobs, to get out and convince these people that we aren't going to dictate artistic taste or anything else to anybody."

He definitely said "we"; did he mean him and me, or the Johnson Administration's imperial "we."

"When you come on board, that is."

I still felt I was in mid-air between the dock and the deck of the ship and not certain whether I would land on board or in the water.

He asked me some other question about the arts and my life. Then, suddenly, he jumped up and left the office, trailing behind him something about being late and we should get together as soon as the Office of Education cleared my papers.

I decided not to sit indefinitely in an empty office and wandered out to the woman who was still typing furiously. I introduced myself. Her name was Jean Bankier, Roger Stevens loyal assistant who had worked for him forever. She made no comment when she heard my name. I had hoped for "So you're the young man Roger has been excited about," or at least, "Yes, I'd heard you were coming aboard." I asked her if sudden departures were a common practice for the man.

"It doesn't mean he's bored with you. It sometimes means he's enjoying the meeting and forgets about his next meeting."

"He had another appointment?"

"Yes."

"Could we have lunch?"

"Can't."

I remember walking down Fifth Avenue toward Penn Station thinking about the meeting. I realized suddenly that it had been some sort of test. Perhaps he wanted to verify that I was the same person he remembered from our one encounter. He asked me questions to see if my thoughts were compatible with his. I hoped I hadn't said anything too stupid and failed.

Apparently I hadn't, but still it was mid-August before the appointment came through. Kathy Bloom called to say I was officially on the payroll, but I would have to come to Washington to sign papers before I could be paid.

When I did appear in D.C. Kathy scheduled a meeting with Roger Stevens at her office. We had agreed beforehand that we would ask him what he needed done and then we would cloak the project in academic verbiage to make it acceptable to the Office of Education. His charge to me was simplicity itself: "Find out what the people in the country think about federal arts support. Are they against it? How would they like it to work? If at all?" This was my assignment and this was my baptism by fire. This was also the moment when I felt comfortable calling Roger Stevens by his first name.

Since I was officially employed as a special consultant to Francis Keppel, it seemed appropriate I at least meet him. The next day I did. I liked him. He was articulate without being glib, had an extremely fast mind, and an affable manner. He suggested I assume state arts councils were part of the proposed legislation and I examine the relationships which might exist between state universities and these presumed state arts councils. Such an investigation would leave me free to poke around generally and make valuable contacts in each state's cultural circles. Commissioner Keppel asked me to write a report he could use at the Congressional hearings when the legislation was introduced. He asked Kathy to be my supervisor and two of his aides to act as my contact point with him, if I needed contact. With that short meeting of the minds, I was off on a six month odyssey at seventy-five dollars a day, the maximum fee at that time, and sixteen dollars per diem, the maximum for hotel and food.

The administrative officer working with Kathy was extremely efficient with all the papers I was to sign and the rules I was to follow. I was assigned space in the Office of Education building on Maryland Avenue, but I couldn't find it without a guide dog. The bureaucratic code of corridors and compass directions that was supposed to make office finding easier only confused me. Rather than admit I was a failure at elementary office finding navagation, I kept coming to work in Kathy's office and saying my office was too lonely.

The government office numbering system is probably designed to confound the enemy in case of another invasion as was done in 1812. The confusing traffic circles which abound in D.C. were designed for mounting canons, so several streets could be defended simultaneously against advancing enemies.

The greatest gift given then was my own book of TRs. A TR means travel request, and with these little slips of paper one can write a ticket to any destination in the world and just sign one's name at the bottom. The airline or railroad will issue a ticket and use the TR to collect from the appropriate agency of government. To have one's own book of TRs is like having a personal federal flying carpet.

However, TRs do not a travel expert make. My first planned trip taught me that airlines fly east and west or north and south, but they seldom have routes in a circle. I learned on my first trip it is difficult to fly around a particular region, which I had planned, and I ended up spending endless hours in isolated airports re-reading local newspapers countless times. My next trip was across the northern tier of states with frequent stops and I spent less time on the ground making connections.

And there were other magical items in the federal government at my disposal because I had the support of powerful people. If I was Everyman just trying to obey orders, then Roger and Francis Keppel were the fates controlling my life. I didn't realize until much later that most United States employees are not turned loose in St. Louis with a book of TRs, a dictating machine, and a telephone number that connects with an unseen secretary in D.C. For the first few weeks I felt like Cinderella at the ball. I discovered less pleasant aspects of federal employment later.

Whenever one asks a question in government the answer is in the form of a regulation. How simple it must have been when G. Washington was President, Jefferson was Secretary of State, and John Adams was railing away as V.P. Whenever a Congressman or bureaucrat raised an objection, they could say, "We wrote the Constitution and this is what we had in mind." By 1964, however, it had become more complicated. We now have the Government Accounting Office (a kind of Congressional FBI), the Government Services Administration (a Janitor in a Drum filled with quicksand that owns all government physical property and maintenance contracts), and the Office of Management and Budget (the President's Jewish mother). The GSA and the OMB (then called the BOB) have regulations for everything from the kind of water carafe one could have on one's desk to the number of questions a federal employee can ask a civilian without official approval. (Below a certain grade level a plastic carafe is mandated, above that level a chrome one is approved. Any form that asks six or more questions of a civilian, must be approved by the OMB.)

My first perception of government employees in Washington was that seldom does one give an unqualified answer. Hesitation is universal, delay is an accepted procedure, compromise a method, and less than expected a standard result. Even the slightest doubt precipitated a negative response toward any proposal for creative action. These tendencies were probably first present in the Roman Empire bureaucracy and are inevitable because of the layers of authority imposed to assure reasonable honesty and integrity. Promotions ride on the fewest mistakes not on solid accomplishments. Inaction minimizes mistakes. Attentive passivity is revered and nit-picking travels as devotion to duty. The word "yes" rests strangely on most bureaucrats tongues because that word implies some kind of action or progressive decision. The words "maybe" and "but" are also used sparingly because they often connote a continued exploration of an issue at hand.

However, I learned at this time, and continue to believe until today, that government employees are hard working and dedicated. It is almost axiomatic that a government worker keeps long hours and plods forward doggedly because the paper work and the conflicting authorities make it necessary in order to accomplish anything at all. The forms to be filed are there because someone at some time suspected, or discovered, some person was taking advantage of a privileged position. The form's initiation led to a supervisor of that particular form and no one ever admits their job is not necessary, so the form stayed and the supervisor became implanted. The Congress and the Executive Branch see honesty not as a moral imperative firmly installed by parents and religious teaching, but a condition monitored through the careful scrutiny of printed forms. It is the firm belief of the OMB and the GAO that a dishonest person wouldn't dare fill in a form dishonestly; they presume such an act would cause the dishonest person to melt immediately into a puddle of acrid water. A single expense form, from the time that millions are printed by the Government Printing Office, then filled out in triplicate by thousands of employees, then checked by thousands of administrative officers for accuracy, filed by thousands of file clerks, declared useless and taken to be burned twenty years later by thousands of form-burners, costs the taxpayers billions of dollars. All that, in the futile attempt to keep employees from adding an extra $2 to their taxi fare while traveling on official business.

I had another problem bigger than the fear of filing; the fear of flying. It was undoubtedly a byproduct of childbirth; as my wife produced children my fear of flying increased until I was petrified of unscheduled, sudden falling while in an airplane. Since flying was a sometime thing before I took the vows of consultancy, I didn't worry about it much, but now I was ordered to fly 20,000 miles in the next six weeks. I persuaded my internist in St. Louis to prescribe the largest legal amount of Dramamine and off I went into the wild, blue yonder. Laced with Dramamine, I would arrive at a distant city in a semi-somnambulistic state, but not incoherent. After several meetings in which I was less than completely alert, I switched to the other effective prevention of air sickness, booze. Eventually, I conquered my fears and weaned myself from all chemical crutches. I decided that when the pilot's number is up, it is only kind of me to accompany him to that long runway in the sky.

There I was, sworn-in, laden with equipment and means, accredited and assigned a project. All I had to do was get started. Nothing could stop me now. I was on my way. Just get started. The only problem confronting me was that I didn't have the slightest idea of how to get started. I toyed with the idea of staying in my den in St. Louis and writing a report of pure fiction. I knew of one state arts council, the New York State Council on the Arts. It was only two years old. Maybe I could start there. I didn't know it then, but this was only the first of many assignments that led me where no one had ever trod before. The only way to handle such projects is as multiple choice exams were handled in college. You must have faith that the answers are there and just let instinct and logic intertwine in your unconscious until the right one appears. If one simply relaxes and merely accepts the tasks presented on a daily basis, confusion will eventually give way and a desperate solution will be temporized, right or wrong. But to paraphrase the old Chinese saying, "The longest journey begins with a single misstep."

Although I was completely serious about studying the relationship between proposed state arts councils and universities, I was secretly convinced that such relationships didn't actually exist at this time and probably wouldn't in the future. I learned the New York Council didn't go near the universities and that was all I had to hang onto at the moment. When I went to New York and opened the files there I found voluminous correspondence from all over the country on the subject of state arts councils. Hurrah. I found a direction and a way to use those TRs. I spent one whole day copying down the names and addresses found in those files.

Before I could begin flying around the country I had one task to perform for the troika of Kathy, Roger, and Commissioner Keppel. In a spasm of overconfidence I had promised them a statement of purpose that would explain what I intended to accomplish. I drew up the broadest possible statement and sent it off in multiple copies, and was surprised to have all three approve it as written. My final report six months later had little to do with that statement, but by that time I had learned to write nimble bureaucratic language. I wrote:

"If an occasional reader is so demanding as to examine the succeeding chapters only within the context of the above statement of purpose, let it be said now that he will not find this paper limited to these confines. Such an undertaking does not lend itself to precision. Conclusions do not always follow purpose, and fortunately, people do not think according to prescribed outlines. However, the more sympathetic reader will find an honest attempt to meet the demands of the objectives as well as a generous amount of additional information.

The above paragraph is proof positive it takes but six months to turn an average civilian into a language-fudging bureaucrat. The paragraph is also evidence that I found nothing about state arts councils and universities to report; instead, I learned a great deal about other trends, movements, and enthusiasms that were worth knowing.

By the end of November, 1964, I had spent considerable time in fourteen states, eighteen cities, and consulted with 120 people in the arts and politics. Those contacts proved invaluable during subsequent assignments such as lobbying the arts endowment legislation and when I was trying to establish state arts councils in most states. I spent December writing my report and reading about the arts and the social history of culture.

I had become convinced that the arts could not survive as vital in our society without some federal subsidy and that it could come about with careful planning of strategy. I was filled with self-importance at this time. I was convinced I stood in the dawn of a Golden Age for the arts in this country and that no one had ever had such an awesome responsibility for the future. I thought I somehow held the key along with Roger Stevens. If only I had a job when the six month appointment ran out.

My report identified twenty-six state arts councils, most of which were paper entities or loosely organized private alliances of cultural groups within the state. Others were patched into existence when someone in the state sensed the arts bandwagon was gaining momentum. Only four states had funded and functioning councils; New York, California, Missouri, and Utah. The funding for the four active councils ranged from $20,000 in Missouri to $562,335 in New York. Illinois was perched to become the fifth funded council. The nation was truly in the process of inventing a new kind of institution to serve the arts; a public agency with status within the state government. I reported this phenomena to the Commissioner of Education, but I also reported that university involvement with this movement was almost nonexistent in most places, slight in some places, but dominant in none. However, everyone involved knew at the beginning the educational component was only an excuse for the grassroots exploration I was undertaking

It was now January, 1965, and my contract was about to expire in a month along with my salary. Keppel and Kathy would keep me on, they said, but the U.S. Government has a peculiar rule that allows consultants to work only six months out of every twelve. I was ineligible to be hired under a new contract until August of 1965. Somehow the specter of unemployment didn't bother me this time. My vision had increased considerably during those six months. Hopefully, I had made a small contribution to the progress of the arts, and I was probably more valuable to my field because of everything that had happened. Still, I was out of work again. Roger had been working toward making me part of the federal arts scene, though neither of us knew it at the time. And as I had said before, it is obviously better to be out of work from the White House than from St. Louis.

The National Council on the Arts Act
The Same Summer of 1964

While I was flying around the country either doped or drunk, soliciting information and attempting to build a lobbying force for a federal program in the arts, Roger Stevens was busy on Capitol Hill trying to push an advisory National Council on the Arts through a reluctant Congress.

A bill to establish a National Council on the Arts had been introduced in the Congress periodically since the 19th century, but none ever became an actual reality. Presidents Buchanan (1859), Harrison (1891), and Theodore Roosevelt (1900) tried and failed. President Taft established the U.S. Commission of Fine Arts which oversees architecture in D.C., except for Capitol Hill. The Architect of the Capitol has jurisdiction there and that's how we happened to get the Rayburn Building and its cement cornucopias. Rep. Jacob Javits pushed an advisory council bill in 1949 and a similar one was introduced during the Kennedy Administration. The 1949 bill just died in committee, but President Kennedy's bill reached the floor, and ridicule. Rep. Smith of Virginia introduced an amendment which made poker playing an art form and the House laughed the bill out the door. When President Kennedy tasted defeat in his attempt to bring the arts into the federal stable, he reportedly said to hell with Congress and proceeded to create an advisory body on the arts through Executive Order. According to the story that persisted in those days, the Executive Order was on Kennedy's desk and unsigned when he was tragically assassinated in Dallas. Then, when President Johnson started into the unsigned orders he said that such a council should be the will of the people and not done on a president's signature. He then asked for someone to push it through Congress and supposedly Abe Fortas and Isaac Stern recommended Roger Stevens, pointing out that he had already persuaded the Congress to change the National Cultural Center to a living memorial to the late President. Shortly after that, on May 13, 1964, Roger Stevens was appointed Special Assistant to the President for the Arts. It was in August that I came on board.

President Kennedy and President Truman before him had thought about the needs of the cultural institutions of America, but did little about the situation. August Heckscher was employed as Special Consultant in the Executive Office of the President from 1962 to 1963, and he submitted an extensive report that was frequently quoted in the days before Roger Stevens struggled to make manifest that which everyone talked about, but didn't do much about.

It was to President Kennedy's credit that he actually did write an Executive Order for such a council, but it was eventually accomplished in a stronger position through President Johnson.

The Council bill that Roger was charged with establishing by legislative mandate was a fairly innocuous piece of legislation. It merely called for a 24-person advisory body that was to advise the President on how the federal government could assist the arts. The annual budget for "salaries and expenses" was set at $150,000, hardly enough to have staff and travel even in those days.

Roger was also responsible for raising the $15 million that Congress said had to be raised privately in order to receive the matching money from the Treasury for construction of the Kennedy Center. He was still involved in producing plays in New York and had several real estate deals that demanded his time.

At that time, Roger was not sophisticated about the workings of Capitol Hill. He had experienced a fairly smooth venture converting the National Cultural Center into a living memorial to a martyred President. It was a brilliant and dramatic idea. Even though the Kennedy family thought the matter should be studied, the Democratic Congress saw it as a great proposal. Republicans either agreed, or couldn't think of any reason to oppose it without appearing completely heartless. However, a national advisory council on the arts was a different matter. In the spring and summer of 1964, the Congress was not in any mood to create a new agency no matter how modest and inconsequential. In those days, the arts were still the last ignorance a "real" man could boast of in public. President Johnson was too busy with other legislative programs to apply much pressure and though the Senate was more than supportive, the House had no members who were willing to lead a real fight for it. Consequently, the bill languished in the Committee on Rules under the Chairmanship of the conservative Judge Smith of Virginia.

The Stevens approach at that time was the same straightforward, casual, businesslike method he had used to push the Kennedy Center. He was met with yawns of apathy, shrugs of indifference, and the full attention of deaf ears. He was greeted by Democrats in the House with warmth and respect; he had raised enormous amounts of money for the Party, but the members couldn't find enthusiasm for his bill. The almost unanimous excuse offered was that the bill was stuck in Judge Smith's Rules Committee and no one could force it out of his tightly closed pocket. They said, "If you can get it out of there, Roger, I'd be willing to support it, but . . . ." Eastern liberal Republicans were also willing to support it, if and when it could be pried out of Committee.

At that time, Roger had a secretary-assistant named Barbara Burns. When she came to work one morning she casually mentioned that her date the previous night had given her some information that might possibly be helpful. According to her dinner date, Rep. Smith's close friend was Robert Flemming of Riggs Bank, a man with whom Roger had been involved in several business deals over the years. As this sort of thing is sometimes done, Roger made an appointment with him on a business matter. At the appropriate time, he made mention of the friendship between the banker and the Congressman. The banker acknowledged the friendship and spoke warmly of the Judge.

"Well," Roger said, "Judge Smith is holding a little, unimportant piece of legislation that doesn't amount to anything at all, really. There's no money involved, so to speak. It's just nice to have."

"What is it?"

"It's a bill to establish a National Council on the Arts as an advisory body to the President. The cost is $150,000 a year; you know, it's nothing."

"That's nothing."

"That's right. But would you do a big favor for me and talk to Judge Smith about letting the bill come out of committee. It doesn't require any hearings or anything. I've got bi-partisan support for it, if I can get it to the floor."

"If you'll dictate a letter right now, I'll sign it."

Such are some of the folkways of Washington, and sometimes history is made that way, or at least helped along.

Roger Stevens felt victorious and assumed the rest of the assignment was simply routine procedure. The bill was released from the Committee on Rules without recommendation and placed on the agenda for a vote on a Thursday afternoon. The day before the vote Abe Fortas called and told Roger not to let the bill come up for a vote.

"You don't have the tickets," he said.

"You mean the votes?"

At the time, Roger had not heard about the habits of lawmakers in Washington. "Everyone up there said they would vote for it, if it ever came out of committee."

"On a Thursday afternoon?"

"What difference does that make, Abe?"

"Only the difference between victory and defeat. Most of your supporters are Easterners, aren't they?"

"Some midwest; big cities mostly."

"Well, Easterner Democrats and Republicans go home Thursday afternoon and don't come back to Washington until Monday morning."

Another obstacle to smooth sailing through the halls of Congress was the inevitable end of the session and the Democratic Convention that was about to convene in Atlantic City. Once the Congress adjourns at the end of a session all proposed legislation dies. The convention was only a couple of weeks away and already House members were defecting for political fence mending or building back home.

It should be noted here that Abe Fortas was a consistent behind the scenes advocate of a federal arts program. He had the ear of President Johnson regularly and used his influence on Roger's behalf on several occasions. With this essential information, Roger managed to have Rep. Frank Thompson, who was to lead the floor fight, postpone and re-schedule. Thompson boasted to Roger that he was responsible for getting the bill out of Judge Smith's Rules Committee; Roger didn't tell him about the banker's letter. Thompson said he would try to re-schedule before adjournment, but that President Johnson had ordered certain legislation passed before the convention and they were way behind on that agenda.

George Fellman had been active in national business circles and government posts for a number of years and was a business friend of Roger's. Fellman invited Roger to dinner to introduce him to Speaker of the House John McCormack. Roger was delighted at the opportunity of widening his acquaintances among the more powerful political personages and for pushing the bill. At dinner, Roger mentioned the problem of adjournment and the looming convention and how hard he had worked to get the bill to this point and hated to start all over next session. The Speaker called the Majority Leader, Carl Albert, the next day, who called Rep. Thompson and told him the arts council bill would be considered for a vote on August 20th. Thompson called Roger and told him how he had pushed through a re-scheduling. The bill passed on August 20, 1964, by a vote of 213 to 135, one of the last pieces of legislation to pass before the Congress adjourned to nominate Lyndon Johnson for President.

The Senate passed the National Council on the Arts bill without debate by a voice vote.

The National Council on the Arts, P.L. 88-579, which President Johnson was pleased to sign into law in August of 1964, instructed the President to appoint 24 persons for the purpose of advising the government on the arts. Specifically,

> *"The Council shall (1) recommend ways to maintain and increase the cultural resources of the United States (2) propose methods to encourage private initiative in the arts (3) advise and consult with local, state, and Federal departments and agencies, on methods by which to coordinate existing resources and facilities, and to foster artistic and cultural endeavor and the use of the arts, both nationally and internationally, in the best interests of our country, and (4) conduct studies and make recommendations with a view to formulating methods or ways by which creative activity and high standards and increased opportunities in the arts may be encouraged and promoted in the best interests of the Nation's artistic and cultural progress, and a greater appreciation and enjoyment of the arts by our citizens can be encouraged and developed."*

To the best of my knowledge no one in or out of government ever was able to give a sensible explanation of exactly what the Council was supposed to do. Nevertheless, the Congress and a President had acted for the first time and we had an official body within the government that was supposed to help the arts in the entire country.

Other past legislation, such as the WPA art programs, was aimed at economic conditions of the artist. This legislation, broad as it was, recognized our cultural pursuits as a bonafide concern of the government.

The bill passed only two days after I began work on my project to scout the country for support. I phoned Roger when I read of the bill's passage and asked if there was anything else I could accomplish for him now that I had gotten the bill passed after only two days on the job. He laughed and said he thought the Congress was afraid of me.

Neither of us laughed when we read the bill closely.

National Council on the Arts members and spouses at swearing-in ceremony in the Cabinet Room of the White House.

▶ ─────────────────────────────

One Foot in the White House
Late Fall of 1964

One day in November when I had been on the job for four months, I was in New York for a board meeting of the Community Arts Councils, Inc. (Now known as the American Council for the Arts.) A new member of the board was a young woman who worked for the Rockefeller Brothers Fund, Nancy Hanks. On that day the autumn rains were falling. The meeting was held in the board room of the New York Philharmonic Hall at Lincoln Center. Roger Stevens had agreed to meet there to discuss my report for the Office of Education. My hidden agenda was to discuss my impending unemployment to see if he wanted to keep me around. If he didn't, I would be back playing job hunting roulette shortly after the first of the year. The election was then behind us and the President would be around for four more years at least, but that didn't mean I would.

The meeting yawned to a close just as Roger arrived. He and I sat in the fading gloom in the board room with the carpeting that looked like an elephant had come in and gotten sick right in the center of it. Roger squinted at my rough typing of the report that was hammered out in my den in St. Louis. I tensely watched his every expression as he read. He grunted a few times, nodded once, pointed out two grammatical errors, and generally looked like a manager whose team was twelve runs behind in the ninth. When he finished, he handed the report back to me.

"No, that's your copy. You'll get the finished copy from Kathy Bloom, but you can keep that until then."

"Can I?"

Roger Stevens sometimes had a strange reaction to gifts of pieces of paper with words on them. It seemed he was expressing surprise that he was being honored with this invaluable gift. Apparently, he had such a high regard for all forms of writing that he physically reacts to possessing someone's creativity. He carefully folded the draft report and put it in his pocket.

"Are we finished?" he asked.

I nodded, and before I could broach the subject of my near future he was across the room, scooping up his raincoat without breaking stride and was gone. I frantically retrieved my papers from the board meeting and stuffed them into my briefcase, struggled with my coat, and arrived at the elevator just as it appeared.

"Not quite finished. I wanted you to know I won't be around after the first of the year. I'll be on the street again. It's apparently illegal to be a government consultant for more than six months at a time."

He chuckled.

I waited for some comment in vain. "I could be a consultant to another agency; that's not illegal."

He didn't acknowledge the hint. He said, "There's always a way around things, isn't there?"

By then, we were outside the Philharmonic Hall and it was raining a light downpour or a muscular drizzle. Roger didn't seem to notice the rain any more than my earnest comments. He moved off at a fast pace along Central Park South. He neither invited me to walk along nor indicated I shouldn't. Since I was determined to resolve my ambivalent situation, I tagged along and tried a more direct approach.

"Have you liked the work I have done for you?"

"What? Oh, yeah. It's been very helpful."

"So, I was wondering if you _____ "

"What are you going to do next?"

That sounded like something someone would say to a divorced spouse. At that point I had nothing to lose, I thought.

"I know what I would like to do. I would like to work with you, if you want . . . want . . . me . . . to."

"Well, I got a little money now from the Arts Council bill. The President made me the acting Chairman of the Council. Congress gave me the money."

"Yes?"

Then came that little word that causes ulcers. "But." He continued, "if I hire anybody, it's got to be a speech writer. I've got some speeches and _____ ." He mumbled the end of the sentence into the rush hour traffic. Then he said, "You have to be crazy to drive in New York."

"Speech writer. I can do that. I can write. I've had a novel published and I write all the time on my job . . . speeches and . . . other things." I was happy he didn't need a legal counsel.

"Would you send me a copy of your novel? And some other things? I read plays and novels and things every morning because I don't sleep much. I get up at four o'clock and read."

"I'll send it. And some other things. Right away. Then, can we talk again? I hope?"

Suddenly he stopped. In front of the Essex House, he stopped. I thought he was leaving me there and wanted to say good-bye but then I realized he had suddenly understood that he was talking to a desperate man with an employment problem and a wife and children. I now had his full attention. Lesson number 35 was now engraved on my consciousness; one needed to talk directly to Roger Stevens and not be subtle or vague. He responded to direct questions with direct answers and to indirect questions with vague answers.

Off he went again, down Central Park South, ignoring the rain and me. We walked briskly in silence, but from somewhere came the feeling he was thinking about me and my situation. I didn't want to break the magic mood. We arrived at the Squib Building and the brightly lighted windows of F.A.O. Schwartz.

"Be sure to send me your writing. But don't worry, we'll work something out." Without the usual phrases that indicate a conversation is ending, he disappeared into the doorway.

Back in St. Louis I bundled up a CARE package of my most careful writing and my novel, shipped it, and waited. Two weeks later the phone rang.

No salutation. "I read your stuff. Why don't you meet me in Washington in my office next Friday morning around ten."

"I'll be there." The line went dead.

The possibility of a writing job with this man seemed so remote, and at the same time frankly, it scared me.

But I did appear that Friday morning. Again, it was raining. This was my first visit to the White House office and I went to the White House proper. The pleasant guard smiled and told me that the Old Executive Office Building next door was also part of the White House and that was probably where I would find Mr. Stevens' office. (We were to learn more about the building when Richard Nixon had his secluded office there). I blushed at my ignorance and tried to look in control of my life as I walked the short distance across the lane dividing the two buildings.

The Secret Service guard at the desk at the EOB looked down his list of people who were cleared for appointments that day and then in a flat voice said:

"Mr. Mark, I have a message for you. Roger Stevens' plane crashed in New York."

"Oh, no." Those words were only partly in sympathy for a valuable life snuffed out in the charred and twisted metal of a horrible catastrophe. In that first moment, I selfishly thought about fate and me.

"But he left a message for you." A hint of a smile flickered across his face as if he enjoyed the drama of that first chilling message.

"Who?"

"Roger Stevens."

"He said to call him at his New York office."

"He's alive. In New York, At his office. Call him."

Most people seem to get weak and wobbly knees in times of shock or crisis, but my knees stiffened the moment I heard of Roger's plane crash. As I left the guard and went back out into the rain I walked like Charlie Chaplin. Why was it raining again?

Back at the hotel when I called him my selfishness had been overcome by true concern. I asked what had happened.

"Oh, that. Well, the weather was bad, but we took off anyway. Then the plane lost an engine out of the two we had. Everything on the East Coast was socked in, so we couldn't land anyplace safely. Finally, they let us come in at Newark. The dumb pilot didn't know how to land with one engine, so when he applied the brakes we spun around and skidded off the runway and tipped onto one wingtip. It was nothing."

"Are you now afraid to fly?"

"No. Now I figure I've had my crash and I can fly another million miles before my number comes up again."

"That's a good attitude."

"I'll fly down as soon as the weather clears. Stay where you are. Give me your number there. I'll call you when I leave."

I bought two books and holed up. The rain and fog continued until Sunday when Roger finally made it to Washington.

His office was across the corridor from Vice President Humphrey's suite. When we settled down he wanted to talk about everything, except the one burning subject. Finally, I asked about my writing. Did he like it?

"Oh, yeah, you can write. No doubt about that. And I need a speech writer. But I can only offer you a six month appointment and I definitely need you here in Washington."

"Okay."

"Would you move here for six months?"

"Yes. I'll sell my house in St. Louis, move my family and be here."

"Why would you want to do that?"

"Because I think we're going to have a federal program in the arts from my experience of the last six months traveling around, and it's a good idea to be in on the beginning. Second, I think you are the man to do it and I want to work with you."

After months of suspense, indecision, and federal footdragging, it was settled in a minute or two. We agreed on a January 1 starting date. I knew my wife wouldn't be too happy with my decision, though she had encouraged me to plot my way out of the St. Louis job.

The investigation for any appointment to the White House staff is carried out by both the Secret Service and the FBI. I cringed while filling out the endless application on which I had to list all addresses since 1937 and all jobs; these included a slaughter house, an ice company, working in a mental hospital among the 27 jobs I had taken during school days. Naturally, I listed as references only people who knew me as a sensitive, intelligent, responsible person.

We arrived in Washington after a cross country race with the moving van and checked into a motel. I was exhausted, but I called Roger about four o'clock to tell him I was available.

"Where have you been? I thought you were starting on January 1."

I reminded him that this was the first business day of the new year.

"Well, get down here. We've got work to do."

"You mean now?"

"If you can."

From my arrival day on January 3, 1965, until September I did not have one day away from the office and most days meant fourteen hours of work. I learned in the first week that Roger Stevens worked at all possible hours, on all possible days, with little drop in his energy. I learned that Saturdays and Sundays meant peaceful days of work with few interruptions and a chance to catch up on planning and details.

When one thinks of offices in the White House, even the Old Executive Building, one thinks of huge rooms, which this was, elegantly furnished, which most offices are not. Our suite of two rooms had high ceilings and lovely scroll work moldings, but the paint was faded. The draperies were early-Mussolini and the furniture was dark bureaucratic. The view from the large windows was of the courtyard, and the rug was just about two hard stomps from threadbare. Roger had hired a secretary, Luna Diamond, and she and I shared the outer office.

Nevertheless, working in the White House must be one of the strangest feelings in the world of employment. A number of divergent elements contribute to feelings that are in part contradictory. First, one feels self-important. Where do you work? Who, little me? I work in the White House. My title is Special Consultant on the Arts in the Executive Office of the President. I have a pass that allows me to walk into the secure home of the President of the United States anytime I want. Secondly, there is the overriding feeling of being involved in a nationally important, history making assignment. I didn't know if anything permanent would come of this undertaking, but I knew that President Johnson didn't have people sitting around because he wanted to solve their unemployment problem.

In my case, the undercutting feeling was that I was working in the power center of the free world, but that I was only needed for six months. Was there a money shortage, or was this some kind of trial period? Could the richest nation have a money shortage?

Perhaps the strangest feeling to which one never adjusts fully is that people take the White House very seriously. A letter on White House letterhead is read carefully, often framed, sometimes passed on to one's heirs. When an operator says "The White House calling," people tend to forget their names and will do whatever is asked. No matter at what level one works in the Executive Office of the President, that person is part of the most exclusive club in the federal world, even if one is completely isolated from all other members. People imagine that you chat with the President or at least the Vice President on a casual basis; maybe when you all take your coffee break. Certainly you see the Cabinet members daily. At that time I had never met anyone else who worked in the White House, except some of Vice President Humphrey's staff whom I met in the men's room and the Secret Service men who guarded Humphrey.

However, I soon learned that those magic words opened any door in Washington. At times it is an extremely powerful feeling.

(Years later, I read John Dean's book about his experiences in the Watergate White House. I felt great empathy for the man. He was simply told the White House did things differently from other places and he believed them. I might possibly have believed them, too. I wanted most ambitiously to succeed; I might have done anything I was told, IF it was not offensively immoral. I also believe most people in the government would undertake quasi-legal actions, if the White House said it was acceptable and routine. However, I do believe I would have questioned the Watergate abuses long before John Dean did, but that isn't the point.)

No past experience or habits can prepare one for this sort of situation; one is in a completely foreign atmosphere and forced to function as if it's a normal job. Yet, there is a sense that all actions have some sort of meaning beyond the action itself. Because everyone else is impressed by the source, one gets the feeling that the slightest misstep can mean an unintentional crisis, or worse, it can mean one's job. In a sense it's a cruel fate to be plucked from a quiet backwater position and thrust into such unfamiliar territory.

I was terrified of either making a mistake, or behaving in such an inactive way that I was useless. I had to keep telling myself I had something to contribute or I wouldn't be there. It would have been easier if Roger Stevens had assigned me to some cubby-hole and given me a theme for a speech to write for him. Instead, he was constantly asking me about this procedure or that problem. He would hand me letters from prominent people in the arts and then ask me if the subject of the letter made a good point. Whether he took my opinions seriously I didn't know. I decided to simply say what I thought and let my actions dictate my future.

The frustrating part was trying to get Roger to respond in some way. He never reacted much to anything I said or did. His face remained immobile and his comments were completely non-commital. Some years later he jokingly remarked that he thought he was successful in his real estate dealings because no one could read his placid face or understand his soft voice. In truth, I was experiencing complete euphoria half of the time and sheer terror the other half. Those first few weeks were an enormous strain, but also powerfully stimulating. I hoped it would last.

It was during those first weeks that I learned my first lesson about Washington behavior. A Congressional subcommittee hearing on our budget for the next year had been scheduled. On the day of the hearing, about two hours before the appointed hour, Roger appeared at my desk in hat and coat. He told me to call the subcommittee to tell them he wouldn't be able to appear and would they please re-schedule the hearing. I didn't know any better, so I called.

The clerk of the committee asked, "Is he sick?"

"No. I think he has a business appointment in New York . . . or something."

A long pause ensued.

"He wants it re-scheduled," I said dutifully.

I heard a deep breath being expelled. "Let me tell you a fact of life, fella. When the Congress sets a time for a hearing the witnesses appear punctually, prepared, and polite. Dying or a national emergency is the only excuse. Doesn't Roger Stevens know that? Are you new around here? I hope you are, because otherwise you win the hand-painted piss-pot for arrogance, and that's the last prize you're going to win in Washington."

Fictional characters are always gulping in crisis situations and I thought it a literary device, but I did gulp. I also saw my body being thrown down the steps of the EOB. "Yessir," I said, "I'm new around here. Very new. A few weeks is how long I've been here. I never worked for the government in my life until a few weeks ago. Roger Stevens is new, too. He is a special assistant to President Johnson, but we're just getting underway. We don't know all the fine points of these . . . things."

"Believe me, it's no fine point. You tell Roger Stevens when he once more graces our fair city that he should call the chairman of the committee and apologize profusely for the inconvenience he caused both the chairman and the busy and important members of the legislative branch of his government."

"Yessir, I'll tell him. And let me apologize to you. It must be inconvenient for you to re-schedule the hearing."

"We have not indicated in any way that we will, or even consider a request for a re-scheduling. You might just have to operate on last year's appropriation for this fiscal year."

Suddenly, my fumbling mind cleared. Until then I had been a timid neophyte trembling mentally while a voice verbally pistol-whipped me for a perfectly innocent error. Now, he was threatening the future of our enterprise, playing a power game with Roger Stevens and his assignment from the President of the United States. In that moment, I lost my timidity and found anger.

I said, "Roger Stevens has a direct order from President Johnson to become active as soon as possible. In order to do that the funds must be forthcoming. When should we tell the President the hearing will be re-scheduled?"

I surprised myself with my aggressive posture.

"I don't know. We'll have to look at the committee agenda and let you know."

His was a different tone of voice after my intense statement.

The lesson was clear. The two branches of the government have an adversarial relationship, but treat each other with exaggerated respect. Roger's cavalier attitude toward the hearing had violated the traditional respect and the clerk was punishing us for it. By invoking the name of the President, I had righted the imbalance and indicated we had no intention of being punished for the disrespect beyond a certain point. The clerk respected my stated position and withdrew from further confrontation.

Another lesson I learned from my first clash with Capitol Hill was that the term clerk is a complete misnomer. It wasn't until later in my federal career that I became completely knowledgeable about the power of so called clerks, but I did begin to understand that they were powerful people. Often they literally ran the committee. They dug into the issues, wrote the questions to be asked, wrote the testimony, and wrote the reports on the findings. I made a mental note to deal diplomatically with clerks from then on.

Thirdly, I learned from this incident that Roger Stevens could not serve as my guide through the federal jungle of procedure and protocol. Washington operates on protocol, politics, procedures, and the probable potential of agencies and people.

All those abstract and concrete rules came down on us suddenly about two weeks later. Because of the delay in the hearing, someone had time to scrutinize the National Council on the Arts Act of 1964. It was discovered that one word, one all-important word, had been inadvertently omitted from the printed text. Further examination showed that the word had not appeared in the bill when it passed, or when the President signed it into law. That word was "annually" as it applied to appropriations. The text said, "The Council shall have $150,000 to carry out its work," instead of "$150,000 *annually.*" This was undoubtedly a typographical error, because everyone involved intended to provide an annual appropriation, but no one could now change the wording. That amount wasn't even a comma in the federal budget even in those days, but it was the law and we were trapped by it.

We had only $50,000 for the current year. Roger had gotten that before I came to work. We were living on that money. That money was all there was and wasn't enough to finish out the year. Congress had appropriated one third of our lifetime authorization for less than one year. Even if we managed to secure our whole remaining $100,000 it wouldn't pay our salaries and expenses and then we would be extinct. Next year would be the end of the National Council on the Arts. The only course open to us was to try and push an amendment to the Act through the Congress during the next three months before we exhausted the current funds. Roger elected to try. Extinction would follow failure. But another financial blow would strike before then.

My Short Career as a Speech Writer
Winter and Spring of 1965

Everyone involved with the passage of the flawed bill which only allowed us $150,000 for the lifetime of the Council knew it was ridiculous, so Rep. Frank Thompson in the House and Sen. Pell in the Senate introduced an amendment to allow us more funds. Nothing was required of us at the moment, so we settled down to wait for passage and meanwhile devoted ourselves to work at hand. I was greatly heartened to hear Roger refer to "us" whenever he talked about the federal arts program, or the strange ways of democratic government. I interpreted the "us" reference to mean I had passed the probationary period.

The requests for speeches began arriving with almost every mail at an accelerated rate after the arts world realized what had happened. I was assigned the speech writing duties. He would tell me vaguely what he wanted to talk about and I would tackle the typewriter in the outer office. Luna Diamond would usually get my final draft for typing a few hours before Roger was to leave for the speech-making. When he returned I would naturally ask him how the speech was received, since I was anxious to learn and improve. He was always vague about the trip in general and the speech. Several times he admitted he didn't give the speech, because, he said, the meeting was different than expected so that the speech didn't fit the occasion. He was always complimentary about the quality of my work, and often talked about the content. After several of these avoidances he finally confessed he had never given one of my speeches.

"They're good speeches, but I just can't read all that purple prose in public. I'm sorry, but I can't. I'll have to find someone else to write my speeches."

Here we go again, back to unemployment. I wouldn't be on the job long enough to see bankruptcy in three months. Why hadn't he said something about the style? I was anxious to please and could have faded some of the purple prose to a mild violet. The answer is that Roger Stevens is a kind man who tolerates much from his staff because he doesn't want to hurt people. After confessing he needed a different speech writer he changed the subject to some immediate problem and never mentioned speech writing to me again. He never told me to find another job and he never said I had shown an aptitude for other kinds of work that were valuable to his mission. We just went on for another five years.

I was writing other material that apparently met with his approval. (Remember, I had learned to write bureaucratese while writing the report for Commissioner Keppel). Another kind of writing was added to my assignments. Every magazine faintly involved with the arts seemed to be upset with what had been wrought. Instead of seeing the federal action as a first step toward a sane federal policy on the arts the editors seem to find something sinister in this innocuous act. Some said it was too little and far too late. Others were certain it was an LBJ trick to win the support of artists without actually doing anything. The prevalent attitude seemed to be the fear of government interference with artistic freedom. How this toothless, impoverished agency was to interfere with anything was never stated, only that somehow the Constitution was threatened.

Roger wisely and patiently answered each article with a letter to the editor. I would write three or four drafts after he and I discussed the article in question. The third or fourth draft was usually acceptable. Then, too, personal letters were written to President Johnson about the Council, and to Roger, and these had to be answered. (Letters referred to us from within the White House were sent with a little red cardboard square attached. This meant the letter was to be drafted in 24 hours and sent back to the receiving source, usually to be signed by a machine pretending to be the President.)

It was then I discovered that Roger was the most talented editor I had ever known. It was painful to sit quietly while he composed a paragraph of prose for any purpose, because he always searched for the precise word to express the thought. Conversely, it was a lesson in effective editing to watch his lightning pen run through something another had written. He hated ambiguous writing.

In addition to answering this barrage of criticism in magazines and through the mail, we worked on draft legislation to create an agency that could actually aid artists and arts institutions. The chief drafter of the complex legal language was Livingston Biddle, a dedicated volunteer aide to Sen. Claiborne Pell. We would meet with Rep. Frank Thompson to discuss ideas, and then Biddle would draft the language. Technically, he wrote the bill as he later claimed when he was Chairman of the National Endowment for the Arts, but the ideas embraced in the legislation came from many sources.

There was, at that time, a private Commission on the Humanities that was issuing a report on the national needs of humanists. Every learned society in the country had contributed to the list of inequities suffered by the humanists of the country and enthusiastically endorsed the idea of a National Humanities Foundation similar to the National Science Foundation. With the scientists receiving nearly $1 billion in grants every year from their federal agency, the humanists envisioned a similar amount being given them to study philosophy, theology, literature, languages, and the like. The slogan of the Commission on the Humanities was "to redress the imbalance that exists between science and the humanities." That report, as issued, claimed all the arts but pushed them into a small corner of an elaborate humanities program. This of course was unsatisfactory because we had our own vision of a National Arts Foundation that would be the equal of the National Science Foundation. The universities were known to have fervent friends in Congress, and Rep. William Moorhead, who represented a district in Pittsburgh that was heavy with colleges and faculty residents, had introduced a bill establishing a national humanities foundation.

When Roger learned of the Moorhead bill he realized that the humanists might have the advantage of arriving on the floor for a vote before our arts foundation was ready and the arts would become a mere afterthought among the scholars and researchers. The arts were not even listed in the Index of Needs in the Commission on the Humanities Report. With alarm under control he made an appointment to meet with the American Council of Learned Societies. He said of the meeting years later, "This may have been the only time I threw the President's name around. I talked as if I knew what President Johnson wanted and it wasn't a foundation in which the arts were an afterthought. In a sense, I sandbagged them, which I hardly ever do, but the arts were in danger of losing out."

The strategy was reasonably effective. The members present began to talk in terms of cooperation and combining forces for a really comprehensive bill, but it wasn't until the official Administration bill was introduced that the humanists finally realized the arts were going to be no less than equal partners in any assault on the Congress.

The humanities problem loomed large but it was not the only one. Agreement among the principal Executive and Congressional Branch players was not present. Some strategists felt that the academic community of the country would not support an arts bill if the humanities were left at the gate. Others wanted the humanities as an umbrella with the arts program carefully spelled out under it. Also, some concern about the territorial rights of the old line agencies was present. Would the Smithsonian, for instance, welcome an agency that awarded grants to museums? Would the State Department's international cultural exchange program be threatened by a grant-making agency that could independently send artists and institutions overseas? Would these federal agencies secretly try to scuttle the bill?

The discussions, debates, and ideas flew around for weeks before finally everyone agreed it was time to submit some draft to the President by October 1. Roger proposed a meeting of all the people trying to construct the most effective bill along with Larry O'Brien, President Johnson's liaison with the Congress. All the principals agreed and the meeting was set for a Saturday morning in August in our offices in the EOB.

Senator Pell, Rep. Frank Thompson, Livingston Biddle, Roger Stevens, Larry O'Brien, and I were present. We discussed the various proposals for organizing an agency to serve (1) the arts, (2) the arts and the humanities, (3) the arts within the humanities or (4) the humanities within the arts. After everyone understood the problems and advantages, the focus fell on Larry O'Brien. He took a piece of paper from his breast pocket and slowly moved his finger down the paper. I realized he had a list of all the Representatives on one side of the paper and all the Senators on the other side.

After a silent minute that seemed much longer, he asked himself a question and answered it at once. "An arts foundation alone?" He made an "iffy" sign with his hand. After another tense minute or two, he repeated the process. "A humanities foundation without the arts?" He gestured with his thumb down. "An arts and humanities bill under one umbrella?" He turned his thumb up.

He then read a litany of do's and don'ts. Make the humanities an equal partner. Build in safeguards that protect the old line agencies from encroachment; words like "in this country" will satisfy the State Department's overseas program in the arts, he said. Don't try to sell art to the Congress; sell patriotism and our cultural heritage and future.

That basically is how we happen to have the structure for our federal arts and humanities programs under the Arts and Humanities Act of 1965. The legislation established two separate but equal endowments, one for the arts and one for the humanities under one totally useless and non-functional umbrella called the National Foundation on the Arts and Humanities. The British Arts Council was born of the days of the blitz, when concerts and plays boosted morale in the subway tunnels and bomb shelters of the cities. The Canada Council was established after arduous hearings from coast to coast by the Massey Commission at which artists, humanists, social scientists, and plain citizens were encouraged to offer advice on the structure and policies of a federal agency serving the arts before any political decisions were made. The basic structure of our federal program in the arts and humanities was hammered out during a rump session on a Saturday morning. In the final analysis, the three countries have remarkably similar programs, only the method for establishing them differed.

At least everyone was now supporting a single concept. Livingston Biddle was told to write a draft bill. The language was definite where it was meant to be definite and vague where it was intended to be vague. It contained the words "in this country" to please the State Department. It offered the states modest sums if the governors would appoint a state arts council, the price Sen. Jacob Javits asked for his support. Most important, the structure of the agency tied the arts and humanities together in such a way that supporting one cause meant supporting both; a strategy that worked perfectly later on in the long fight for passage through the Congress.

It should be noted that the section of the legislation pertaining to the state arts councils was not a favorite of everyone. No one really thought the states would pass legislation to establish arts councils as part of the state government. Possibly the governors could be persuaded to establish such an agency and give it token support. The reasoning was that the federal government was only partially enlightened about the concept of public support for the arts, how could anyone expect the less sophisticated state legislators to appreciate the subtle purpose of culture within their state?

Hearings Will Make It So
Continuing the Winter and Spring of 1965

Even though no official Administration bill existed at the time, hearings were scheduled in both Houses. What we had was a number of bills, a Javits bill, a Pell bill, and a Thompson bill; all were slightly different in organizational structure and the scope of the proposed agency. The joint hearings were to begin on February 23 and involve both Houses, which was unusual because the Senate and the House completely separate their work.

Officially, these hearings were titled "Joint Hearings before the Special Subcommittee on Labor and Public Welfare, United States Senate and the Special Subcommittee on Labor of the Committee on Education and Labor, House of Representatives, Eighty-Ninth Congress." And that's enough to scare anyone. Add to that the array of prominent members present and we had a major league team and title before us. Present that first day were; Senators Pell (D>RI) presiding, Yarborough (D>TX), Kennedy (D>MA), and Javits (R>NY); Representatives Thompson (D>NJ) Co-Chairman, O'Hara (D>MI), Carey (D>NY), Scheuer (D>NY), Griffin (R>MI), Findley (R>IL), Andrews (R>AL), and a non-committee member Moorhead (R>PA). Also in attendance was Sen. Gruening (D>AK).

As one might expect, a joint hearing takes twice as long to wade through the compliments the members pay each other and the prospective witnesses. All the members had to hold forth with introductory remarks about the important role he played in bringing the legislation to this point, and his hopes for particular provisions in the final version of the bill. The imbalance between the humanities and the sciences was mentioned prominently as well as the triumph of the National Arts Council legislation of the previous session. Sen. Javits reminded everyone that he introduced legislation for subsidy of the arts in 1949. Sen. Kennedy, since he was the new kid on the block stuck with the imbalance theme. Rep. Thompson was introduced as Co-Chairman and made only a short speech and introduced Rep. Moorhead as the champion of the humanities effort in the House. The overall impression was that all present had died and these were the eulogies.

I sat in the back of the room and felt awed by everything around me. I had never seen so many well known faces in one room in my life. My God, there's Charlton Heston. S. Dillon Ripley, the Secretary of the Smithsonian, just came in. Roger said the Librarian of Congress was going to testify, where is he? There's Francis Keppel, should I say hello or will that distract him? More people kept arriving as the verbal pats on the back poured forth from the politicians.

Roger was the first witness and he made the major points of the various existing bills lucid to the members. In his written opening statement he stated that none of the bills under consideration at present were the preference of the Administration, and that a President-approved bill would be submitted shortly. He pointed out that private foundations and corporations had not been funding the arts or humanities to any extent and federal aid would encourage greater participation by both these sectors. (This of course came to be one of the solid accomplishments of federal and state aid.)

In his opening statement, Senator Javits chided the President for not appointing the members of the National Council on the Arts as called for in the legislation that had passed six months ago. In his questioning of Roger he returned to that theme. He implied that further support for legislation would be somewhat less enthusiastic because the impression was that the President wasn't interested. Javits said, "And so I most respectfully but most strongly urge the President to at least appoint this Council with whom we can work and whose recommendations I think will be supremely important in respect to the type of legislation which we are to adopt." The other members seconded Sen. Javits' urging.

Sen. Javits then became interested in Roger's statement about state and community arts councils that he made in his opening remarks. He asked if there were any studies of these councils and their development. Roger answered, "Senator Javits, there has been a rather detailed study made by the Office of Education which is available for the committees. I think they plan to call as a witness later the gentleman who made that study."

Oh my god, he means me. Nobody told me I might be a witness. I decided to leave the room, pleading sudden illness, but several of Commissioner Keppel's staff turned and gave me the okay sign with thumb and forefinger. I didn't even have a copy of my report with me. Javits didn't seem too interested in the information once Roger quickly indicated a show of efficiency. He merely said "fine" and then went on to other questions.

Then before Sen. Javits could return to needling about the National Council on the Arts members, a messenger appeared at Roger's elbow.

Roger: I actually can now definitely state that our Council has been chosen and released to the press today.

Javits: Today?

Roger: Today.

Thompson: Would the Senator from New York like anything else done today?

Javits then asked that the White House news release be entered into the record.

"The White House announces the following people to serve on the National Council on the Arts. Mr. Stevens will be nominated to the Senate; Dr. Ripley will be a member ex-officio, and the other members are designated by the President for terms ending in the indicated years.

National Council on the Arts

Chairman, (sic) Robert L. Stevens, Special Assistant to the President on the Arts, New York City.

Class of 1970

Albert Bush Brown, head, Rhode Island School of Design, Providence, Rhode Island.
Paul Engle, poet, writer, teacher, Cedar Rapids, Iowa.
Ralph Philip Hanes, president, Community Arts Councils, Winston-Salem, N.C.
Rene d'Harnocourt, folk art, Modern Museum Director, New York City.
Oliver Smith, scenic designer, producer, painter, New York City.
Isaac Stern, musician, New York City.
George Stevens, Sr., film director, Los Angeles, Calif.
Minnoro Yamasaki, architect, Seattle and Detroit, Mich.

Class of 1968

Leonard Bernstein, composer, conductor, teacher, New York City.
Anthony A. Bliss, president, Metropolitan Opera, New York City.
David Brinkley, NBC News, Washington, D.C.
Warner Lawson, musician, educator, Washington, D.C.
William Pereira, architect, teacher, former movie producer, Los Angeles, Calif.
Richard Rogers, composer, producer, writer, South Port, Conn.
David Smith, sculptor, Boltons Landing, N.Y.
James Johnson Sweeney, writer, museum director, Houston, TX.

Class of 1966

Elizabeth Ashley, actress, Los Angeles, Calif.
Agnes deMille, choreographer, New York City.
Ralph Waldo Ellison, writer, lecturer, teacher, New York City.
Father Gilbert Hartke, clergyman, theatrical educator, director, District of Columbia.
Eleanor Lambert, fashion designer, head: Council Fashion Designers, New York City.
Gregory Peck, actor, Los Angeles, Calif.
Otto Wittman, art museum director, Toledo, Ohio.
Stanley Young, author, publisher, executive director, ANTA, New York City.
Ex-officio, Dr. S. Dillon Ripley, Secretary of the Smithsonian Institution."

The next witness was Commissioner Keppel. I knew if I was indeed to be a witness this would be the moment. He asked the committee for permission to add Kathryn Bloom as an additional witness because she was most knowledgeable about this project. Practically his first words referred to my study and I heard through a veil of sweat, "a study made by Mr. Charles Mark, who is here today, sir, if you care to question him, which shows that there are now 26 such councils in existence." He then offered my entire report for the record. Sen. Javits asked unanimous consent to enter it into the record. Had I known this would be the eventual fate of my work I would have been more careful with some of the more elusive facts. Consequently, I stopped breathing when Dr. Keppel made some salient points from my report, thinking momentarily he would swing around in his chair and ask me to come forward and elaborate on some statistics I could barely remember. But he didn't. They moved on to the humanities and education.

Most worrisome was the flat statement I had made in the report that 26 state arts councils existed. It was a technical fact, but the reality I had buried under mounds of bureaucratic verbiage was that only three of those 26 could be called functioning arts councils. The others were only extant because a piece of paper said so. In some cases I characterized certain minimal state appropriations to various cultural enterprises within the state as an actual council. Were I to be questioned by the professional inquisitors from their symbolic thrones, I wasn't certain I could continue to defend the paper councils as part of the great national cultural awakening.

The Keppel testimony entered the questioning phase and Sen Pell again brought up my work. Keppel asked Katherine Bloom to answer and she made it sound like I spent my life studying state arts councils, pointing out I had visited 17 states and talked with representatives of 14 active councils. By then, I was beginning to wonder why they didn't want me to testify; it didn't look all that difficult.

After Keppel testified, others took their turn and I stopped worrying. In fact, the hearings went on for ten sessions. The list of witnesses grew longer and the documents for the record continued to flow. Perhaps the basic structure of the eventual total agency was settled with Larry O'Brien on a Saturday morning, but Congress was making certain the record showed a real need and detailed the facts of artistic life.

After that first day, Roger sent me to cover the hearings he couldn't, or didn't want to bother about. I was at that time in complete awe of the political and artistic personages who appeared. I remember being fascinated by Robert and Edward Kennedy sitting together on the dais and the younger Kennedy having to explain over and over to Robert what the bill would mean to New York. Once I came from a hearing and said to Roger, "Guess who I sat next to today? Lillian Gish."

Roger gave me a sidelong glance, "How's she looking these days?" He seemed to know everyone in theatre and politics.

However, the important business of the moment was not the hearings on the Hill, but the shaping of the Administration's official position and writing a formal piece of legislation to send to the Congress. The idea of combining the arts and the humanities into one agency had been introduced shortly before the hearings. The priority was to submit an Administration bill as quickly as possible while the idea was current and revise it as necessary to please the maximum number of important people on the Hill and in the old line agencies. This was done by the President on March 10, five days after the hearings ended. The message accompanying the bill from President Johnson was more than we had hoped for:

> *"This Congress will consider many programs which will leave an enduring mark on American life. But it may well be that passage of this legislation, modest as it is, will help secure for this Congress a sure and honored place in the story of the advance of our civilization."*

With these words, which President Johnson repeated in a speech several months later after the bill had passed, the National Foundation on the Arts and Humanities legislation was submitted to the Congress of the United States. Never before had a President asked the Congress to pass such legislation. The chances of actually securing the establishment of a permanent agency were probably minimal. The Senate presented no problem, but unfortunately it takes both houses to pass a law. The House was not a home for the arts; not yet. The journey from here to passage was going to be a rough voyage, especially since Sen. Javits' pet provision concerning state arts councils was not included in the legislation as originally submitted.

Isaac Stern, Marian Anderson, Rudolph Serkin, Duke Ellington, and Robert Merrill, the musical brain trust, State Department meeting.

The Next Step
Summer of 1965

The period from March 10, 1965, when the Administration bill was introduced to September 15, when the House finally passed our bill, seemed to my innocent self to be the most important and chaotic, but at the time I didn't know what was to follow. It certainly never entered my mind that we were in the process of making history or national policy; I was clawing at each assignment and surviving in chaos. It was also a happy time in many ways for awhile.

Some time in March Roger hired a new speech writer, Diana Prior-Palmer. I was now thought to be general assistant to Roger. I never heard anyone, including myself, refer to my more lofty title of Consultant on the Arts in the Executive Office of the President. Diana was British, the daughter of a World War II general, and a fast talking, nervous woman of perhaps 35 years. She had an annoying habit of being positive and condescending in almost every situation, and like the Supreme Court she was often in error but never in doubt. On rare occasions she would spend the entire day lacerating herself over some error and the next day apologizing for being so self-deprecating. I don't remember why Roger hired her, or where she was before she took up residence in our office. I do know she didn't please Roger as a speech writer, though no one had to this point.

A short time later, Roger tried again and hired Frank Crowther. He was an ex-Marine, he said, had worked as an assistant to one or two Congressmen as a speech writer and came highly recommended by someone; I never discovered who. He turned out to be just the person to write excellent speeches, because his talent was that of vicariously being the person for whom he wrote.

Roger Stevens almost never fired anyone in those days. He would ignore them, almost ostracize them, take away all privileges and responsibilities, and if the employee didn't realize the situation he was in and was willing to live with indignity, he could survive for a long time. Theoretically, hundreds of people should then be drifting through life on Roger's payroll, but his severance system was ingenious. When some efficient employee pointed to the superfluous employee and recommended termination, Roger would agree, and charge the efficient one with the task of firing the idle one.

Since Frank wrote excellent speeches, he remained. Once he became identified with his employer he would fantasize that he was that person in all things. He somehow got his name added to Roger's White House limousine privileges and would call for a limousine to take him on personal errands. He told everyone he worked for the White House, when actually he was paid at first by Roger and then later by the Endowment. Later on, when Roger was out of town, Frank would spend hours at Roger's desk issuing orders to the staff. Everyone ignored his commands, but that didn't seem to bother him at all. He never tried to give me orders; I suppose he recognized my seniority.

Frank would phone the members of the National Council on the Arts and chat with them on a first name basis. In actual fact, he never had an assignment other than writing speeches for Roger, but that didn't prevent him from giving his opinion on programs and policies at any meeting he felt like attending.

I recall a phone conversation I overheard:

Frank: Greg Peck, please. (Pause) Hello Greg? This is Frank. (Pause) Frank. Frank Crowther. (Pause) Crowther, Greg. At the Endowment. C-r-o-w-t-h-e-r. Crowther. Roger Stevens asked me to call. . . . Hello, Greg?

Gregory Peck immediately called Roger and suggested Frank be fired for rising beyond his authority and not realizing it. I happened to be in Roger's office at the time; first overhearing Frank's end of the conversation from his office adjacent to Roger's and then Roger's conversation with Peck. When Roger hung up he turned to me and said, "That makes it unanimous. Now, every Council member has individually recommended that Frank be fired. All twenty-six." Roger had told Peck, and all the others, he would fire Frank when someone found him another speech writer as good as Frank. Frank remained almost four years.

Both Diana and Frank were hired in March, 1965, but before they could fill their desk drawers with cookies and hard candy, the White House Administrative Officer discovered a tragic flaw in our arrangements. He learned that Roger wasn't taking any salary. It was when Roger tried to add Frank to the payroll that the officer, Jim Sasser, discovered the problem. After World War II, when the Roosevelt "Dollar a Year Man" era ended, Congress forbade anyone from working for the government and not accepting the prescribed salary for the appointed position. Roger didn't need the $21,000 he was entitled to as Chairman, so he never filed for it.

Sasser was a smooth talking Southerner and a shrewd operator, so he wasn't about to break the news to Roger that he either had to accept the salary or resign immediately. He told me to tell him that if he accepted the salary it would have to be retroactive to the day of his appointment, and that meant we were almost out of funds. When I told him, Roger slammed down some papers on his desk, kicked a chair, stormed about the office for a couple of minutes, threatened to resign, said he would resign, and then sat down and calmly tried to work out a solution.

Sasser, who never let any political winds waft past his nose without doing a complete chemical analysis of them, had been in our office earlier in the month to offer us new draperies and rugs. He had learned somehow that the Administration was pushing our cause with hard legislation and thought being helpful would impress the President. What he didn't tell us was that the draperies and rugs would be charged to our inadequate budget. I realized at this late date that I should be paying attention to budget procedures; Roger was not a budget-watcher by nature. Asking more questions revealed that every piece of stationery and every phone call on the White House lines was charged to our budget as well.

After I dropped the iron shoe about his salary I let the other slip gently to the ground; the news about the stationery and the phone calls. In conclusion I informed him we had only $7,750 left in the National Council on the Arts budget and when that was gone, we were gone forever. (You remember the typographical error that left out the word "annually"). I remember distinctly Roger saying, "Here we are in the nerve center of the richest country this world has ever known and we don't have money for phone calls."

We both ranted for a few minutes and then settled down to find a solution. Roger decided Frank should come aboard on his personal payroll and Diana transferred to the same. Luna and I would continue to be paid by the White House budget. Roger would use his salary to pay Frank and Diana. The draperies and rugs were cancelled. If we used the phones sparingly and wrote fewer letters, we could squeak by. I told Sasser the solution and he indicated a few hundred dollars overspent could be absorbed within the overall White House budget through savings elsewhere. I had visions of the President announcing at a State dinner that no dessert would be served because the National Council on the Arts had run over their phone allotment.

And that's how the first and only year of the National Council on the Arts was financed.

Rudolph Serkin and Richard Diebenkorn, State Department meeting.

From Payroll to Post
Spring and Early Summer of 1965

We did squeak by to the end of the fiscal year, which in those days was the end of June, but then we had no more money. I don't know how Roger kept Diana and Frank on the job, but he seemed to worry more about me. I suppose it was because I had a wife and two children dependent on me. He sometimes worried about those things.

My third employer in the federal system was the Smithsonian Institution, following the Office of Education and the White House. When the Council budget ended, Roger called Dillon Ripley, Secretary of the Smithsonian, to ask if he had any unused places on his payroll. Ripley said he had some private endowment funds for special advisors. Roger suggested I would make a wonderful advisor to the Secretary of the Smithsonian and Ripley reluctantly agreed. Again, the power of the White House and the President's Assistant triumphs. My only contact with Ripley was to go to his office and fill out a W-2 form and sign a few other papers. I knew Ripley and would joke with him ever after about my advisory role and he always showed good humor about it. While I was in his office on the form-filling visit I asked one of his staff for a parking permit on the Mall. I was told to get lost. After three months Ripley called Roger to say he had enough advice from the phantom advisor and I was dropped from the payroll.

Again, Roger picked up the phone and used his influence. This time he elected the U.S. Commission on Fine Arts for my fourth employer and for my nonexistent services. I was officially Special Consultant to the Commission. This time I didn't even set foot in the door; everything was accomplished by mail. Roger warned that we had better work doubly hard to get our legislation passed because the Commission had set a deadline of three months on my employment and he didn't know where to turn for additional help for me. I reminded him that it would take some time for an actual appropriation to be received after the bill passed. He only grunted and changed the subject. This was August, 1965.

Looking back on those months from January, 1965, to the passage of the bill in September, I don't know why I worked seven days a week and 12 to 14 hours a day, except that I loved working for a cause I fervently believed in and would have done anything to see the health of the arts improved.

It was April of 1965 when Roger decided to call the first meeting of the National Council on the Arts. Though he had personally recommended the Council members appointed by President Johnson, he had not met several of them. He had asked a number of people whom he respected and taken their advice. One member had been the choice of Senator Pell (Albert Bush-Brown) and Senator Javits requested one nomination as the price of his support (Eleanor Lambert). After the official announcement of the members in February, 1965, Roger decided to visit those whom he hadn't met. He left on an extensive trip and gave me the assignment of thinking about what the Council should actually discuss and undertake when they first convened. No funds were available for anything, no mandate spelled out by Congress, no staff would be available after the end of June we thought, and yet the Council was to meet and supposedly accomplish something. Some of the busiest and most important people in the arts were being asked to serve under such circumstances.

I had no idea what such an august body would think about my concepts for the arts or what Roger wanted. My experience as a local arts council executive didn't seem to apply. The state arts council movement was the keystone to progress, I thought, but I didn't think the Council members would agree. I knew Roger didn't fully agree at that time. I put my ideas aside and studied the legislation and the other programs within the government, and I talked with everyone who would listen to me and possibly have some ideas about what the legislation meant. When Roger returned I presented him with what I thought was a cogent, candid and slightly inspirational statement as his opening remarks. His opinion was that I should try again. I did. He rejected the effort. I tried again. He rejected. I wrote 20 different approaches to what the Council might think about and he was negative about each one and offered few suggestions concerning what he wanted to say to that group. When I asked why he didn't have Frank Crowther write a speech for him, he said Frank didn't have experience with arts councils and I did. Finally, in desperation, I submitted my first draft as my twenty-first attempt. Roger read it while I sat across the desk from him, praying he wouldn't recognize it. "Now we're getting some place," he said. That was the speech he made to the Council. I never told him it was my first attempt resubmitted.

Roger had scheduled three days of meetings and receptions. The second part of my assignment, that of finding work for the Council seemed insoluble. Roger forbade me to plan a huge agenda, saying these people would have a lot of ideas and a full agenda would inhibit them. I secretly questioned whether these famous people would be willing to talk openly without any prior knowledge of the kinds of activity in which they had become involved. Together we planned the first morning's agenda and had nothing to fill the remaining two and a half days of meetings.

We were to meet in the White House proper in the Fish Room, as it was called at the time, because of a stuffed fish over the mantle. The room was just beyond the old press lobby at the extreme west end of the building. We would discuss the pending legislation and the pending revision of the copyright law. At sometime during the morning, when President Johnson was free, the Council would be welcomed by him. At noon we would walk across LaFayette Square to the Decatur House for cocktails and lunch courtesy of the National Trust for Historic Preservation and the Decatur House Council. Except for receptions, nothing else was on the agenda.

I didn't know what to do. I was convinced Roger would be embarrassed presiding over a group of distinguished people who didn't know what was expected of them. I realized the total stature of this group was far above any group I had ever worked with, but I also knew group behavior. First meetings are always sticky when the members don't know each other and they don't understand their assignment. Someone has to offer some guidance. I fretted about the dilemma for a couple of days and then decided to prepare a number of discussion papers without telling Roger.

April 9, 1965, was perhaps the single most dramatic and satisfying day of my career. Standing in the doorway of that White House conference room and greeting the members of the National Council on the Arts was the brightest moment of a journey I had begun when I left the security of the health and welfare profession in 1958 for the wild venture into this infant enterprise called arts councils.

All the Council members attended except architect Minoru Yamasaki and composer Richard Rogers. They were both ill. Out of the 22 members present I knew only two; Philip Hanes, of the well-known North Carolina family, was a close friend from my time in Winston-Salem, and Stanley Young, who was the director of the American National Theatre and Academy (ANTA), whom I had met several times on business.

Roger opened with our prepared statement. The pending legislation was on everyone's mind, so Senator Pell and Representative Frank Thompson described the bill and its status; the bill was at that moment in the hearings phase. After they finished their presentations a few questions were asked. Then, Philip Hanes began his well prepared anti-legislation attack. It was not unexpected. Phil had told us he would try to argue the case against the pending legislation, but it took Pell and Thompson by complete surprise. Roger let Phil present his elaborate material while the nervous tension in the room rose to greater heights. Several Council members attempted questions and rebuttal, particularly Isaac Stern, but Phil was better prepared and deflected all questions with his sincere argument.

His main contention was that a national advisory body such as the Council was needed and desirable. However, he was gravely concerned that once the federal government began subsidy of the arts, the business and industry support would dry up. He also thought the pending legislation placed too much power in the hands of the Chairman and might lead to government control of the arts. These views were widely held in the nation at the time by the more conservative art patrons. They were not simply the objections of a tiny minority. Eventually, Philip Hanes came to realize that government support at both the federal and state levels actually increased business and industry support for the arts. For the most part government grants had to be matched by nongovernment money and the grants have served as a seal of approval to corporations and businesses;

they also saw the advantage of receiving half the money free. Philip has publicly recanted many times since that historic morning. However, at the time he went on and on until finally Roger called for the next agenda item, which was the copyright law revision.

The Commissioner of Copyrights had treated my request to appear at the Council meeting in a perfunctory manner when I first called him. I didn't call on a White House line (remember we were saving our depleted Council funds) so he wasn't impressed. A few days before the meeting I called him to make certain of the details and I sensed his lack of enthusiasm, so I tried to impress him. I told him where we were meeting, that the President would appear, who the artists in attendance would be. I probably went too far because then he became extremely nervous and attentive. At the meeting his voice shook and he kept looking at the door as if he expected President Johnson to appear momentarily. When Agnes de Mille told him it was simply shameful that dance wasn't copyrightable unless it was written down, he apologized as if he had personally written and passed the law.

At about noon an aide interrupted to say President Johnson would meet us immediately in the Cabinet Room. We filed down the hall, past the Oval Office and into the Cabinet Room. The often photographed conference table with each Cabinet member's name at each place on a brass plaque had been moved aside to make room for all of us and the press. At the last minute, Luna had managed to get the wives of the Council members cleared through White House security and they were already there when we arrived. In the moments before President Johnson entered, Leonard Bernstein moved to the lectern and said, "I suppose you're all wondering why I asked you to join me here today." We laughed and some of the nervous tension disappeared.

The White House Administrative Officer swore in the members and then the President entered and spoke:

> "I believe that a world of creation and thought is at the very core of civilization, and that our civilization will largely survive in the works of our creation. That quality, as I have said many times before, confirms the faith that our common hope may be much more enduring than our conflicting hostilities. . . . Right now, the men of affairs are struggling to catch up with the insights of great art. The stakes may well be the survival of our entire society. So this great nation . . . is looking to this handful of extremely talented individuals . . . for ways in which the Government can maintain and can strengthen an atmosphere which will permit the arts to flourish and to become a part of everyone's life."

The press and photographers were present only during the formal segment of the meeting. After they were ushered out, President Johnson stood and talked informally to the members. He said, "It's important to meet, but it is more important to act." He asked for "instructive and dynamic" recommendations. He referred to the pending legislation and encouraged the members to lobby their Congressmen. He also said, "Nothing gives me more pleasure than taking a pen in hand . . ." (and signing legislation).

As he was leaving, he stopped to shake hands with all the wives. When he met David Brinkley's wife, he asked, "Why hasn't David brought you around?" She mumbled something I didn't hear. Then, he said, "Now that I've found you I'm not going to let you go. You're coming to the ranch with me this afternoon." She said she couldn't because of the children and baby-sitter problems. The President said he would send her home in a limousine to pack and supply a baby-sitter from the White House staff. He held her hand throughout this conversation and then took her through the door into his office. At the party that night at Roger's house I asked Brinkley about his wife and he said she had gone with the President to the ranch in Texas.

Roger hadn't mentioned any plans for the afternoon session, nor indicated my role at the meeting, but after the swearing-in session he gave specific instructions. The Council had gone back into session for a short time. They endorsed the pending bill and the revision of the copyright law. However, Phil Hanes began again with his anti-government sermon and Roger quickly recessed for lunch. During cocktails, Roger told me to tell Phil to keep quiet, that he had made his point and was only antagonizing the other members by continuing to press his points. I took Phil aside and told him. He thanked me and did as Roger recommended.

The cocktails and heavy lunch at the Decatur House served to diminish the energy of the group. They settled into a low key mood as Roger fell back on reciting the provisions of the Council law as passed: (1) the Council was to recommend ways to maintain and increase cultural resources; (2) encourage private resources; (3) advise and consult with local, state, and federal agencies on methods to improve the arts and foster projects; (4) conduct studies and make recommendations on how to create opportunities and increase appreciation for the arts among the American people.

This recitation only served to increase the sleepy mood of the members.

Roger surprised me by introducing an item we had barely discussed. This was the creation of advisory panels on all the arts with one member of the Council serving as chairman of each panel. He had said he wasn't certain it was a good idea and wouldn't introduce it at this first meeting. But there it was. No sooner had Roger asked whether the Council thought it a good idea than Isaac Stern shot it down. He said, "If we aren't able to decide what is needed in this country in the arts—and God knows a great deal is needed—than we should resign and let someone who knows serve. The President of the United States chose us to advise him, we shouldn't put that job on others' shoulders." With this eloquence Roger was left with a blank agenda.

A deadly silence fell over the meeting. Finally, Albert Bush-Brown asked if the Council couldn't do something about the poor design of federal buildings. Roger said he thought they might, but didn't know exactly what steps we could take. At this moment, I said I had prepared a paper on that subject if the Council would care to look at it. Roger looked relieved and asked that the paper be distributed. I nodded to the secretaries and staff and they passed out copies of a paper marked Number five. Without his knowledge, I had written and had reproduced nearly twenty papers that the Council could consider within their authority under the law. The Council discussed the problem and proposed that one-half of one percent of construction costs of all new federal buildings be spent on fine arts decoration.

Then, one of the other members asked if there might be medals for outstanding artists given by the President. Again, I said I had a prepared paper on the subject. The Council recommended such medals. At this point, Roger turned to me and asked if I had any other papers prepared. We spent the rest of the afternoon going over the remaining material I had hoped would be needed.

That night Roger had the Council for dinner at his Georgetown home. Besides the Council members and their wives, the following government officials attended: Senate Majority Leader Mike Mansfield, Senator Pell, Agriculture Secretary Orville Freeman, Interior Secretary Stewart Udall, Labor Secretary Willard Wirtz, Under Secretary George Ball and Assistant Secretary of State Harry McPherson, Jr.

Also present were USIA Director Carl Rowan, White House Assistant Douglas Cater, Senator Pell's aide Livingston Biddle, and Abe Fortas and their wives.

At the end of the first day the following recommendations were enacted, but not released to the press: 1. extensive revision of the copyright law; 2. mandatory fine arts decoration of all future federal construction; 3. assistance for public radio and television programming in the arts; 4. additional activities in the arts in the national parks; 5. availability of federal surplus property to arts organizations; 6. the recognition of museums and cultural centers as equals to schools and libraries as cultural assets through legislation; 7. that Congress ratify the Florence Agreement dealing with the importation of cultural and educational items; 8. that programs for artists' housing be funded; 9. and that the federal government commit itself to encouraging the highest quality of design for every item under government jurisdiction. All but two of the recommendations were from the unauthorized discussion papers I had prepared.

The sub-group meetings at the Smithsonian the next day brought forth additional recommendations: that the federal government support international art exhibitions such as the Venice Biennale; that training programs for professional arts managers be somehow established; that a national theatre be established at popular prices; that the FHA finance theatres in shopping centers; and that an American Film Institute be established.

Everyone was aware that these recommendations were pie-in-the-sky and had little or no chance of ever becoming reality, but they wanted to act as the President had suggested, to tell him and the Congress what they saw as vital needs in the arts that the federal government could assist. If the National Endowment for the Arts legislation had not passed, most of the suggestions would have moldered in some archives, but as it happened almost all of the ideas became reality during the first five years of the Endowment.

Nevertheless, a note of optimism was creeping into our attitude for the first time, a solid belief that our hopes would turn into reality. We no longer gave each other office pep talks as if to convince ourselves that we weren't just shadow boxing. All the "ifs" now turned into "whens," because hearings were being held in both the House and Senate.

My assignment during this period was to continue my travels around the country trying to stir up grassroots support for what was now a definite program of assistance for the arts. Though the state arts councils provisions were not included in the original Administration bill, I was convinced they would be added before enactment, if Senator Javits had breath in his body and Roger kept moving toward believing the states were a powerful ally. I kept telling cultural leaders in the states to write to Javits and support his intent, and to send copies to Roger and me. When I was back in D.C. I was making frequent trips to the Hill to listen to hearings on our bill and note the possible amendments that seemed to be wafting in the wind. Also, Roger was becoming more and more dependent on me for technical and financial details of government operations. My speech writing days were far behind me and my administrative days loomed ahead.

Agnes de Mille, Stanley Young, Elizabeth Ashley, Gregory Peck, Leonard Bernstein, Roger Stevens and other members of the National Council on the Arts.

George and David

Of the twenty-six original members of the National Council on the Arts I developed a special relationship with only two, George Stevens and David Smith. Somehow it just happened.

These two men met for the first time at that April, 1965, meeting of the National Council on the Arts. The last day of the three day meeting was to end with a reception at the Museum of African Art, at that time on Capitol Hill. Although transportation had been arranged David and George had accepted my invitation to ride in my car. We drove down Independence Avenue while the two men chatted as people do who are first introduced.

It was a lovely April afternoon and many of the Hill residents were somewhere else enjoying the appearance of spring after a gloomy winter. I was fortunate and found a parking space around the corner from the two townhouses that comprised the museum at that time.

As I opened my door, one of the artists in the back seat asked the other a question. I don't remember the substance of it, but it was fascinating enough for me to stop in mid-stride and settle back into my seat; one hand still holding the door handle.

Then, these two artists, known to each other by reputation, found themselves in a more intimate conversation. In some way, they found a bond of understanding and they began to talk about themselves in an astoundingly open manner. For the next forty-five minutes or more, I listened, turning my head from one to the other as if watching two tennis champions play. They told each other about their lives, their art, their moral stance on art, and their hopes for the future. David Smith was to die on another sunny afternoon in August of that year in a stupid auto accident and George was to die ten years later in Hollywood, unemployed, lonely, and disappointed in the industry to which he had devoted his life and art.

During those years that I worked with the National Council on the Arts and many important people in Washington, I listened and partook of many entrancing discussions and conversations, but none equaled the candidness of the dialogue of that day. I don't know why it impressed me; perhaps it was only the first time I listened to two respected artists sharing intimately with each other. Maybe the same exchange couldn't have happened with any other two artists. It still amazes me that these two men were able to completely open up to each other on first acquaintance, and that I was able to listen.

For instance, when David asked George about his family background.

George: I was a kid in show business. My father was an actor who went to California when the movies started to undercut vaudeville. He didn't work much when I was a kid, so I didn't have much. I think that's why I identify with the underdog in my work. And you?

David: I grew up in Greencastle, Indiana. I, too think about the underdog in my work. I'd rather have an expert welder admire my work than get a good review from Hilton Kramer. Much rather. Anyway, I was a welder in the defense plants during the war. I was already an artist, but I fell in love with steel.

George: When did you really know you were an artist?

David: When the WPA paid me $26 a week to be an artist and paint. I said if the government says I'm an artist, then I'm an artist. The WPA supervisor used to come around once a month and I'd get out all my paintings—I was a painter then—and display them around my studio. When the WPA man arrived I'd say to him that he could have one-third of the paintings because he only paid me for eight hours a day, but I was an artist twenty-four hours every day. When did you know you were an artist?

George: I wasn't so confident so early. I ground second camera for Mack Sennett, and as I got better they used to send me out to shoot second unit scenes. When I had an assignment, I'd go to the film library and get out all the examples of all the scenes like the one I was assigned to shoot and I'd look at them so I could learn what to do. I did that for a long time; watched hundreds of chase scenes, love scenes in the desert, fight scenes—both comedy and adventure stuff—mostly outdoor scenes. I liked the outdoors, and that's mostly what they gave me. Well, one day I went to the library and instead of taking out all the whatever scenes by someone else, on an impulse I said, "Give me all the scenes I've shot in the past." I sat and watched all my past work and sometime during that long night I realized I was an artist. I had something of my own to say that was unique.

Later, the subject was their philosophy of art and George told a story about his adolescence. He was graduating from high school and the traditional senior prom loomed in the future. He had a date and a rented tuxedo, but what he didn't have was black shoes. No money was available to buy a pair, so he put black polish on his brown shoes. At the prom, of course, the black polish began to wear off and though probably no one noticed or cared, he was terribly embarrassed. He said that was what he tried to do with his work; relate to the people who don't have black shoes for the prom and try to fix it, and only make it worse.

As he told the story it unfolded like a scene from a George Stevens' film such as *Alice Adams* or *Woman of the Year*.

Then David told a similar story of embarrassment in his youth and both agreed they projected their poor, unsophisticated young selves into their work whenever possible.

At one point, George asked David about his craftsmanship. "If you know every time how a piece is going to turn out, that's a craft. If a piece keeps changing in concept as you work, and you never know how it will look when it's finished, then it's art."

George said that was also true of his films.

And that was what I remember of the conversation under the sunny twilight of April, 1965. During the following months, David Smith called me quite often just to talk. Somehow I had been included in the intimacy he and George had built; I hadn't participated, but it was there. David would talk and I would listen; most of the time he would begin the conversation exactly where he had broken off the previous call. He never talked about his work—he was too mature an artist to indulge himself that way—and he never asked about the Council or my work. Instead, he talked about his personal life. Maybe it was as Camus pointed out: it is easier for men to talk to a stranger than someone who knows them and cares deeply. He would talk about his marriages, particularly his most recent wife. He would break off a conversation with a terse "have to go now," and then call again perhaps ten days later and begin with "I was telling you about my ex-wife and, Chuck, let me tell you. . . ."

I don't remember much about these conversations, except that they were surprising both in frequency and content. I do remember one impressive call in which I asked him what he was doing at that moment. He said, "I'm sitting on my back porch having a drink and looking over my life's work. There aren't many men who can say that at the end of every day." I had read that when he finished a piece he simply took it to one of the two meadows on his large property—one behind the house and one between the entrance gate and the house—and would dig a hole, fill it with concrete, and anchor the piece there. I knew he was right; not many people, and not even many artists could make that statement.

I don't remember who called to tell me David Smith had been killed in an auto accident on his way home from teaching a class somewhere. I got the news on Monday, the accident occurred on Sunday and the funeral was going to be held on Tuesday. I realized David wouldn't call anymore, that I had lost a friend, it didn't immediately occur to me that we had lost one of the century's greatest sculptors.

I was alone in the office at the time. Roger was in Europe or in transit to Europe; at least somewhere unreachable. It occurred to me President Johnson might want to acknowledge David's death because he was an appointee of the President and a great artist. I called Douglas Cater in the White House and told him my reasons, and he agreed. When a call came from the White House confirming the President's interest, it was suggested that someone from the National Council on the Arts should represent the Administration at the funeral. I knew Stanley Young was an old friend, they were both from Greencastle, Indiana. Also, he lived in New York and could easily fly to Bolton's Landing upstate with me for the funeral. Obviously, the White House didn't believe my presence alone would lend the appropriate stature.

I picked up the President's letter that night and caught the first Eastern Shuttle in the morning. I had arranged for Stanley to meet me at LaGuardia where we caught a Mohawk flight for Glens Falls. Someone picked us up and drove us to Bolton's Landing. State police had cordoned off the property to protect the famous meadows. Our party was allowed through the gates.

At the house we found a number of David's closest friends. Helen Frankenthaler served as a kind of hostess. Ken Noland and his wife were there, a man from the Marlboro Gallery, and several others, about a dozen in all. Stanley and I were warmly welcomed, offered drinks which we accepted in lieu of breakfast, and then we were more or less ignored as the inner circle of the artist elite remembered David around the beautiful, huge table in front of the window overlooking David's meadow of sculpture. We chatted pleasantly until quite suddenly Stanley became overcome with emotion and went out into the garden. I hadn't known he felt so strongly about David's death. I followed him.

The small, unkempt, little vegetable garden was a few steps beyond the patio. I remembered David had mentioned in one of the phone calls that he had begun the garden to occupy his daughter when she visited during the summer. We stood a long time looking at the sloping meadow toward a row of pine trees bordering Lake George. I saw those strong, thrusting, impossibly balanced shapes David had created and realized the man's value as an artist. Some of the abstract shapes seemed to capture an unexpressed loneliness, some a strong statement of defiance, still others an almost bursting sense of joy. One could almost see the creator's mind develop and mature as one's eye traveled from sculpture to sculpture—always steel, always welded, always arresting—but evolving from piece to piece.

I looked at the ground to rest my eyes from that magnificent sight. A small patch of asparagus was growing there. A strange compulsion visited me and without conscious thought I found myself down on the ground cutting the stalks with my pen knife as asparagus is supposed to be harvested. I said to Stanley, "You have to do this regularly or the stalks grow into seed and you won't have them anymore. I had an asparagus patch once. I know that." Stanley nodded vaguely.

Then I had a handful of asparagus stalks and I felt embarrassed about it. I went into the house and handed them over to one of the women. Instead of taking them casually and putting them in the refrigerator, she accepted them with a strange look and an almost ritualistic gesture; her hands held high, palms outstretched, as one would accept a holy object. She turned and moved slowly to the table where everyone was sitting in silence, and placed the stalks in the center of the table made from a slice of an enormous tree, beautifully polished and unseamed. No one spoke. They all stared at the asparagus. Then, one by one, they removed their drinking glasses from the table as if they were defiling an altar.

I was confused and still embarrassed, and feeling like a complete outsider who shouldn't be peeking into this ceremony. I didn't understand what I had innocently generated. I turned to Stanley and asked if he understood.

"You dumb sonofabitch," He said, "you summed up the whole thing about David's death. You know, cut down in the midst of life, the phallic symbol, the necessary pruning of nature in order for another to take his place, the finality of severing a living thing."

I said I hadn't intended to do all that. I was just cutting the asparagus as I remembered it had to be done. As I said this I realized for the first time that while cutting the asparagus I had this strange feeling of being outside myself. It was the kind of action I never would take ordinarily. I still don't understand why I did it.

The funeral was held outside at a bandstand at the edge of Lake George. The whole town closed down in honor of David, except for his favorite bars where a wake was held after the funeral. Stanley gave a moving reading to President Johnson's rather formal letter.

At the next meeting of the National Council on the Arts, I told George Stevens about the funeral, including the asparagus incident. He understood it all completely. For quite some time, David's death and that extraordinary conversation in my car on the spring afternoon was a bond between us. George would say in that accent of his which sounded like he was reared in Philadelphia, "What a terrible loss to the Council it was when we lost David." Or I would say to him, "That project the Council rejected this afternoon, I bet David would have fought for it."

I of course had become a great admirer of George Stevens' films. I confess I had never noticed the director's name on the screen before I was involved with the National Council, except for Hitchcock. After I knew George I made a point of seeing every Stevens film whether in a theatre or on television. I realized he was remarkable in his ability to sustain a comic scene almost endlessly and keep it funny. He was also unique at knowing when to let the camera watch and not add tricky angles and approaches. He would let the camera sit still and keep running and let the actors carry the scene. (He told me he learned all that from directing Laurel and Hardy).

At one Council meeting we were chatting and I asked him how television had changed feature filmmaking. I didn't know then he was really telling me why he wasn't working very much.

He said, "The young directors cut their teeth in television. They learned to tell a whole story in a one-minute commercial, or throw several plots into a 30-minute sitcom. We used to have to tell an audience a fact several times. Audiences have learned to understand what's going on faster because of television.

"In the old days, in order to show a busy executive, we had to show a limousine pulling up to a curb in front of a big office building. The doorman says good morning with respect; the cigar stand man, the elevator boy, and several people in his office all say good morning with respect. Then, we had to show his secretary following him into his big office with a sheaf of papers for him to sign and tell him of a bunch of telephone calls. That was a busy man. Today, television shows a telephone with several buttons blinking, an ashtray full of butts, and a man's hand tapping his fingers nervously. That's a busy man, and they have 30-seconds left to sell you a headache remedy."

On another occasion I asked George about his directing for *The Greatest Story Ever Told*. In the Sermon on the Mount Scene I had noticed two interesting concepts. One was that he had only a sparse crowd in attendance and that gave the impression Jesus wasn't exactly the Billy Graham of his day. In the same scene, the camera drew back to reveal the strata of rock in the surrounding mountains showing the billions of years that had passed on earth, giving the impression that this event wasn't one of the greatest events of history. I asked George if these were conscious artistic decisions. He looked straight ahead; "Something like that, but I didn't plan it ahead that way." David Smith had said, "If you don't know how it's going to come out, it's art."

George Stevens was to make only one more film after *The Greatest Story Ever Told*. It was with an actress who starred in two of his most successful and artistic films, Elizabeth Taylor. He said she liked to work with him because he treated her like a professional and not like a spoiled movie star. In fact, he said he would appeal to her nurturing instincts and persuade her to spoil him. At any rate, the film was a failure and only saw limited distribution because of a number of factors which everyone involved knew and therefore predicted failure before it was even filmed.

Columbia Pictures had options on the services of Elizabeth Taylor, Warren Beatty, and George, and owned a script by Frank Gilroy called *The Only Game in Town*. Warren Beatty was too young to play opposite Elizabeth Taylor, she was too old to play a chorus girl, Columbia ordered this Las Vegas story to be filmed in Paris, and the script was predictable. Also, somehow Frank Sinatra wanted to do the film with Mia Farrow.

(At a Council meeting at Tarrytown, the switchboard operator rushed breathlessly into the room during a meeting. She announced that Frank Sinatra was on the phone for Mr. Stevens!!! Roger dismissed her with a casual wave of his hand saying, "I don't know Frank Sinatra." Then, George Stevens admitted it must be for him and left the meeting for a few minutes.)

Fortunately, when the Taylor-Beatty film was released few people saw it, and this film coupled with the failure of *The Greatest Story Ever Told* meant that George would never make another film.

I left the Council when Nixon was elected, so I didn't see George until I moved to Los Angeles in 1969. We had lunch several times. He told me then he probably wouldn't work again. He said, "I generally shoot 13 frames for every one I use. No one wants to pay for that kind of work these days. It's always been a money business."

The occasion I will remember for the rest of my life was a dinner we had in Montreal at the last Council meeting I was to attend as an insider. George told me two stories he said changed his life.

During World War II he was assigned by Eisenhower to film everything possible about the war. He filmed many battles from a combat stance, but it was entering the concentration camps that changed his life. He was there with the first liberating troops and shot most of the film one sees in documentaries on the Holocaust. The corpses he saw outside the camp, covered with pure white snow, were only the beginning of the ultimate horror he was to witness inside. As he unfolded the scenes for me, his detail made all the pictures return to my mind. I wept.

"To see those people," he said, "so degraded you could hardly recognize them as belonging to the human race. Face after face reflected such fear of us because we wore uniforms and uniforms meant degradation and death. They saw a brutal enemy in us. They couldn't believe at first it was over, the terror and death had ended with these new uniforms. They cowered, but somehow managed to find a spark of dignity in their humiliation as we tried to explain they were saved.

"And when it dawned on them that it was, in fact, over, the joy was restrained even then by the years of terror. Finally, joy broke through and we saw smiles—timid ones—and they wanted to embrace us. I felt utter revulsion as these shells of human beings hugged me and kissed my hands, because I knew at that moment I was capable of torture and of being tortured and I knew that I didn't want to be touched by these filthy people. Such guilt, I felt, could not be borne.

"After the war, all the studios wanted me to make a war picture because I was the only director who had seen combat. I couldn't do it. I couldn't do it precisely because I had seen combat and I had seen the concentration camps. I could only make peace pictures from then on. But then I read *The Diary of Anne Frank*. I took the book to 20th Century Fox and said I had found my war picture."

It was an extremely moving moment and as George told of the events, his feelings, the changes in his life that the experience wrought, all of this told with an underplaying style that had enormous emotion thinly veiled behind it. I had tears in my eyes. He, too, was tearful as he launched into another wrenching story.

With the approval of the studio he was now committed to the Anne Frank project. Otto Frank had survived the war and was now living someplace in Europe. George managed to contact him and convince him to meet and go to the house where the family had hidden from the Nazis for three years. Otto Frank had never been back to that house, but agreed in the interest of authenticity.

George said when they met it was obvious Otto Frank had prepared himself carefully for the painful experience. So painful was the anticipation that he had armed himself with an arsenal of pleasant thoughts to combat each devastating thought. For instance, he would say:

"This is the removable bookcase that separated us from the outside world. See, it moves on hinges. (Pause, then quickly) "After we're finished here we'll go to a wonderful bakery I know of, where they have delicious pastry."

Or he'd say; "This is where little Anne slept. After we leave here we'll take a barge ride on the canal; it's so pleasant."

As George described the detail of this man visiting the house where his family had hidden, and then had been taken and killed, I felt I grew more and more empathic with the two of them. I found myself filled with hate and pity. Then George described how they climbed the steep and narrow steps to the topmost garret where Anne went to write her thoughts. Suddenly, a large bird flew out through a broken window. The noise and sight frightened both of them. Otto Frank hadn't prepared a pleasant thought for such a surprise. He broke down. He shuddered and stopped. It was like the departure of Anne's spirit through that broken window, a flight to immortality perhaps, a sudden flutter of innocence and the disappearance for the last time of a child who would not grow to womanhood.

Two grown men sat at a dinner table in Montreal with tears on their cheeks.

The last time I saw George Stevens I would rather not remember. It was the tenth anniversary of the National Endowment for the Arts. The Kennedy Center was the place of the commemorating party. Most of the former members were there. President Ford made a speech. George saw me as I saw him. He threw his arms around me and hugged me hard. He was drunk. He hadn't worked in several years.

Not long after that night, he died.

▶━━━━━━━━━━━━━━━━━━━━━━━━━━━━

At Last
Summer and Fall of 1965

President Johnson was very public relations conscious and watched for possible incidents that could result in a bad press. One of the areas he decided might be trouble was the number of White House employees; he didn't want to be accused of having more than his predecessor. Consequently, workers of my stature were only issued 30-day White House passes. I would forget to go through the procedure for having my pass re-validated. So on some days reporting for work would sound like this:

(Mark entering, Guard at desk at entrance of Executive Office Building)

Guard: Good morning Mr. Mark. How's your son's cold?

Mark: Good morning Frank. Chris's cold is much better.

Guard: That's good. Are your in-laws still visiting you?

Mark: I'm afraid so. They're coming down tomorrow to have lunch. They want to tell their friends they ate at the White House. I tried to tell them the cafeteria isn't that big a deal.

Guard: My wife's relatives are the same way. Is your wife coming, too?

Mark: I don't know yet. I'll clear them later.

Guard: (Checking pass) I'm sorry, Mr. Mark, I can't let you in today. Your pass has expired.

Mark: I'm sorry. I'll get it renewed this afternoon.

Guard: But you can't come in, so you can't get it renewed.

Mark: Is my secretary in yet?

Guard: Yeah.

Mark: Call her and ask her to clear me.

Guard: Oh sure. Good idea.

He would call Luna, or anyone in our office, who would say I worked there, and then it would be all right to come to work. I would have my pass re-validated on my lunch hour.

The country was beginning to take notice of us. Letters were pouring in from every area asking for assistance of substantial amounts. Mostly, this was due to the print media publishing inaccurate articles about the National Council. The subject of the arts and government was so new to most periodicals that current law and potential law were one and the same to them. The majority was negative publicity interpreted as the periodicals wanted to believe. Between trips to various places to talk to cultural leaders I was swamped with correspondence.

Some letters were polite and tentative, but others were hostile and demanding. One letter stated the author had always felt conducting an orchestra was his secret talent and, though he had no musical training or known talent, he was certain if the government would provide him with a symphony orchestra, he could earn a living at it and make some people happy. I advised him that no orchestras were looking for an untrained conductor and that he should work in a music store and learn to read music. Because no humanities agency existed, the White House referred that mail to me, too. One letter writer wanted a grant to form a new religion; he had noticed theology listed among the humanistic disciplines to be assisted. I replied that the proposed National Endowment for the Humanities was serving only professional humanists. Would he please submit a list of religions he had founded in the past.

Meanwhile, the Congressional committees were hearing from everyone in the arts from Lillian Gish to Quincy Mumford, the Librarian of Congress. On June 10, 1965, an amended bill to establish a National Foundation on the Arts and Humanities passed the Senate by voice vote. No one from our office was present to witness the historic moment.

June 24 was the next historic date. The National Council on the Arts was meeting in Tarrytown, New York, when word came that the House Committee on Education and Labor, Adam Clayton Powell, Chairman, had passed our bill forward to the Committee on Rules. The future looked bright.

At this meeting the Council noted with sadness the death of David Smith before moving on to business.

The good news about the House and Senate gave the members a bullish feeling and they moved on to some aggressive resolutions.

A three-point mission statement was hammered out indicating we would only support and encourage our most talented artists in all fields, provide postgraduate training for them through the formation of new performing organizations, and use the artists and the organizations to increase the standards in the respective fields and to educate and increase appreciation among the public.

This time a four day meeting had been scheduled. We had decided to meet in Tarrytown at a private conference center largely used by corporations when seclusion and secrecy were required. We had many subjects to tackle this time and we wanted the members away from the press and too many receptions. After the first day of plenary session, the Council met in sub-groups. I was given the group that included Gregory Peck, Agnes de Mille, Stanley Young, and Richard Rogers. My task was to convince them to endorse a project Roger and Kathy Bloom had developed. The plan was to use Title III funds from the Elementary and Secondary Education Act to buy tickets to theatrical productions of regional theatres. The U.S. Office of Education would provide $300,000 a year for subsidized tickets, and we would provide $60,000 per year for pre-opening production costs. We, of course, would have to identify the theatres, or create them when they didn't exist. All this was dependent on our bill passing.

A word about the Elementary and Secondary Education Act (ESEA). It was one of the most far-reaching pieces of education legislation ever passed and could have been the beginning of an educational reform which is still urgently needed. It was the first time the federal government provided direct assistance to education both public and private. One provision of the Act, Title III, was specifically designed to foster "exemplary and innovative" studies and projects at the local level. The arts were a major part of this provision.

A later session of the Congress rescinded much of the innovative provisions and gave the administration of ninety percent of the programs to the state departments of education. Of course the arts received a much lower priority.

Most of my sub-group understood and endorsed the project after one explanation by me. I had some difficulty convincing Gregory Peck of the merit of it. (Later, he become so enamored of the idea he personally gave the money for a Los Angeles outpost; the Inner City Cultural Center). Richard Rogers, however, found the project befuddling. He kept asking questions about the budget and saying he didn't understand. Finally, it dawned on me that he was trying to estimate the profit involved in it. When I explained our investment was a subsidy, lost forever, not recoverable, he looked stricken. He said, "You mean the nut never gets paid off?" Later, I saw him talking animatedly with Roger, and I got the impression Roger was explaining it all to him again. Richard Rogers left the next day and only attended one other time, a ceremonial meeting in Washington. I don't know whether projects that were unprofitable bothered him, or whether he just didn't like us.

The anticipated quick vote in the House didn't materialize. The Committee on Rules was still in the hands of Judge Smith and he openly stated he resented the fact that this session of Congress had adopted a rule stating any legislation recommended by a committee could be forced from the Rules Committee after 21 days by the House as a whole. Further, he ignored our legislation and refused to let it out of committee. Finally, the leadership of the House decided to invoke the 21-day Rule and force six bills out from under Judge Smith, ours included. It was September 13, 1965.

The Minority Leader at the time was Gerald Ford of Michigan. He, and other conservatives, didn't want any bills to come out of committee because they didn't want any more federal programs. Their strategy was to defeat the advocates of the 21-Day Rule by parliamentary delay.

Roger and I entered the gallery of the House at about 11:30 and the session began at noon. When one of the conservatives insisted the previous day's Congressional Record be read—routinely the Record reading is waived—we realized we were in for a long day. Congressmen left the floor in herds as the Clerk droned on. After the chamber was nearly empty, another conservative insisted on a quorum call. It was the first of what became a record for the House, 22 quorum calls in one day. In those days, the Clerk read each name and waited for a response, a process which took 30 minutes to complete. The result was that more than 11 hours that day could have been absorbed by quorum calls, if the Speaker hadn't aborted several by calling for a voice vote. The session went on and on without approaching the vital issue of the 21-Day Rule. Congressmen came and went from the floor with the alacrity of teen age boys who only visit home to wolf meals and then leave for the sports fields.

By eleven o'clock that night the opposition collapsed and the House began voting to bring the bills out from Judge Smith's committee. It was decided among the liberal leadership that due to the obstreperous delay, only three bills would be forced out in that session. Our bill was fourth on the list. Larry O'Brien called the President at that late hour to verify the decision. President Johnson endorsed the three bills to be called up, but he insisted that the fourth bill was of vital importance and "must" be included if the House had to stay in session all night.

Had not President Johnson insisted our bill be included in the call up procedure, it is unlikely we would have had the arts program that year. As I remember the sixth bill on the list died in the Committee on Rules. So in a real sense, President Johnson is personally, directly, and historically responsible for the federal arts and humanities programs.

Another event we knew nothing about at the time was happening off the floor of the House. Adam Clayton Powell suffered the long day of quorum calls until the cocktail hour. Then he instructed his executive assistant, Chuck Stone, to go to the office and make a jug of martinis and park Powell's limousine at the Members' entrance to the Capitol. From then on, whenever a quorum call was delaying the proceedings, Powell would gather a group of his friends and they would head for the limousine. Congressmen knew precisely when their name came up on the roll call, so they could leave either before or after their names were called and have an intermission. As evening turned into night, there was a noticeable rise in the animation of certain Representatives after each quorum call.

Finally, the debate was resolved in our favor and the bills were called for the House "to work its will." It was now September 14. Speaker McCormack asked Powell how long he was going to allow the opposition, a routine question. Powell said, "We have suffered here today and tonight long enough. I will yield to the opposition as much time as I intend to take to pass these important bills. I yield the opposition 30 seconds."

McCormack: Will the gentleman from New York tell the Chair how many minutes he intends to yield to the opposition?

Powell: I told the Chair—30 seconds.

McCormack: I will ask one more time.

Powell: I will tell you one more time; 30 seconds is all I need to pass these bills. They can have the same amount of time to try to defeat them.

McCormack: The Chair awards one hour to the opposition.

Powell: It's your House, but they're my bills.

All this sort of dialogue is usually stricken from the proceedings the next morning by aides to protect reputations. More's the pity.

With the bill forced from the Committee on Rules, it still took some time for the House to work its will. The House recessed at one in the morning. One day later the bill reached the floor for debate on its merits and a vote of yea or nay. This opportunity shook the clowns from their safe niches and they had their moment in the sun. Rep. Gross (R)IA) was the chosen spokesman, and Rep. Hall (R)MO) fed him the jokes.

Gross introduced an amendment that read, "after the word 'dance' insert the following: including but not limited to the irregular jactitations and/or rhythmic contraction and coordinated relaxation of the serrati obliques, and abdominis recti group of muscles—accompanied by rotatory undulations, tilts, and turns timed and attuned to the titillating and blended tones of synchronous woodwinds." Debated as the "belly dance amendment," it was defeated. Rep. Gross then introduced another amendment, this time to include squash, pinochle and poker in the arts section. This was also defeated.

The only amendment to pass designated the Department of Recreation as the official state arts agency for the District of Columbia. (This misjudgement was not corrected for several years).

A motion to recommit was then introduced. This is a motion to send a bill back to committee to be buried, and it allows for "the sense of the House" vote without committing anyone to a vote on the actual passage of a bill. Through this method a member can change his mind and for various reasons vote for or against a bill according to the results of this motion. The motion to recommit was defeated by a vote of 251 to 128. This assured passage, so a voice vote was taken and the bill passed. No member of the House was actually recorded as voting for or against the establishment of a federal program for the arts and humanities, indicating that few were secure in the appropriateness of such a program. The next day the Senate concurred, also by a voice vote.

At one point during the debate on the belly dancing amendment Rep. Frank Thompson, who was leading the debate for our side, pointed out to Rep. Gross who introduced the amendment, "The outstanding surprise of the day is that a gentleman from a farm state (Gross R)IA) (says he) does not know the difference between a belly dancer and a bale of hay."

Rep. Gross answered: "Mr. Chairman, I hope that the gentleman this time will not try to put words in my mouth. The gentleman from Iowa has some vague idea of the difference between a bale of hay and a belly dancer."

Rep. Thompson replied: "I shall correct myself and admit that the gentleman from Iowa does have a vague idea."

This dialogue was left in the *Record.*

The House vote took place on September 15 and the Senate on September 16.

For the first time in the history of the country, the federal government was committed to a program of direct support of the arts and humanities. It was the beginning of what was to evolve into the largest single source of assistance for the arts in the nation, and also a symbolic seal of approval for any artist or arts institution. Several weeks later at a dinner at the Players Club in New York honoring the National Council on the Arts, Agnes de Mille summed up the true meaning of that Congressional action.

"For years there were dancers sweating in underheated studios, in front of cracked mirrors, wearing ragged tights and worn out shoes, giving their lives to an art they believed important—and no one cared. Well, those dancers are still there in underheated studios, before cracked mirrors, in their ragged tights and shoes, but now they *know* their government cares and they *know* dance is important."

And a vote of confidence on the part of the government was about all it amounted to at the time. Their government had acted favorably toward the arts for the first time, but the money was miniscule, the staff barely existed at the moment, the policies were largely unformed, and the ignorance of those in charge was enormous. The complicated structure of the National Foundation on the Arts and Humanities existed on paper and that was historical, but the reality of a program was still only a thought far from fruition.

The signing ceremony was set for September 29, 1965. Unfortunately, I had scheduled a luncheon appointment in Kansas City on that day to talk about the Laboratory Theatre Project, the joint venture of the Office of Education and us. At first, I decided Kansas City was more important than a mere ceremony, but then I came to believe I deserved the satisfaction of being present for the climactic day; I had been a small part of it and wanted to be there. As it turned out by shrewd planning and the blessing of time zones I was able to be in Kansas City in time for dessert.

I was given the privilege by the White House of inviting a number of guests to the signing ceremony. Among those on my list were Helen Thompson of the American Symphony Orchestra League (ASOL) and Nancy Hanks, president of the Associated Council of the Arts (ACA). Both had personally opposed the legislation.

Nancy Hanks and the board of ACA had refused to endorse the legislation because it was their opinion the Endowment Chairman had too much power. They feared czarist tactics on the part of the Chairman, though they were careful to say Roger was in no way suspected of such abuse. However, it was possible. As a founding board member of ACA I was hugely disappointed and tried to persuade the board to at least not oppose the bill, but even that plea failed. Nancy and several board members came to Washington and lobbied against the bill.

Helen Thompson, had the passive title of Executive Secretary with the American Symphony Orchestra League, but in reality she ruled the organization with a tight fist.

A rumor persisted that if Goldwater had been swept into office in 1964 instead of Johnson, she would have been appointed Chairman of the National Council on the Arts. At any rate, Helen has alienated many congressmen and the White House by testifying against the Administration bill and invoking the names of influential Republican business and industrial leaders who were symphony board members. This was a peace offering on my part.

Helen was bumped from the invitation list, but Nancy's connection with the Rockefeller Brothers Fund kept her in good graces. Later, I sent Helen a commemorative pen from the President and a peacemaking letter.

In the Rose Garden that bright, clear September morning 250 notables in the arts witnessed the signing and President Johnson's speech. The text had been hastily written to replace a speech Roger had rejected. President Johnson said in part:

"Art is a nation's most precious heritage. For it is in our works of art that we reveal to ourselves, and to others, the inner vision which guides us as a nation. And where there is no vision, the people perish."

"We in America have not always been kind to the artists and the scholars who are the creators and the keepers of our vision. Somehow the scientists always seem to get the penthouse, while the arts and the humanities get the basement."

President Johnson went on to make specific suggestions for the future; his favorite kind of speech. Among other commandments to the Arts Endowment were:

"We will create an American Film Instititute, bringing together leading artists of the film industry, outstanding educators, and young men and women to pursue the 20th century art form as their life's work."

He also called for a number of other programs which became a reality in a short while; an arts in education program, commissions to writers and composers, support for symphony orchestras. He also called for national theatre, opera, and ballet companies, none of which came to pass in the first 25 years.

But the stage was set for federal aid to the arts and humanities. All that was lacking was a script to follow, actors to act, and money in the box office of the agency. The next question was how to proceed toward an appropriation? Was it possible that $5 million would be available to us?

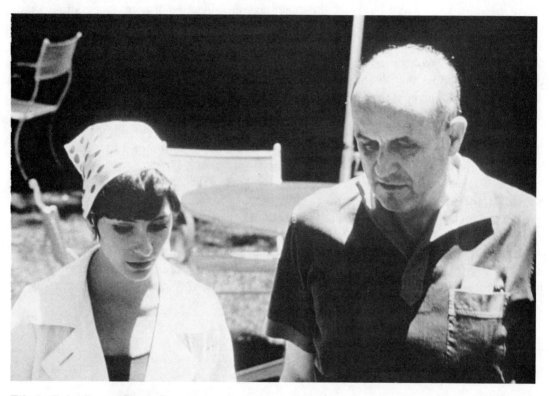

Elizabeth Ashley and Roger Stevens.

Carrying Ignorance Uphill
Fall of 1965

Where do we go from here? The complicated nature of the agency was enough to confuse one and engender panic, and the task of translating any law into funds and people, and learning how to proceed from a Council resolution to a U.S. Government negotiable check was even more staggering. One would think that a 200 year-old government would have established an agency to assist in the establishment of new agencies. In fact, there was such a service, but the unanimous advice was not to approach that agency until we knew exactly what we wanted. "They'll ruin it," was the dominant chant.

The day after the signing ceremony Roger said to me, "Find out how you get an appropriation and how we can hire some people to get started with this thing."

The buck starts here. I had absolutely no idea how to proceed. Fortunately, Roger went to New York for several days and didn't witness my thrashing around like a fish on a line, trying frantically to determine what step was first. Then, someone from the Bureau of the Budget called to say we had been assigned to the Appropriations Subcommittee on the Interior and Related Agencies.

"Why weren't we assigned to Education, or something related?" I wondered. We didn't have anything to do with the Department of Interior.

It was later explained to me that committee assignments are determined by the Speaker on the basis of workload. The U.S. Commission on Fine Arts and the Smithsonian were already assigned to the same appropriations subcommittee.

When I got the news I realized I had at least the hope of a starting place. My handy dandy *Congressional Directory* gave me the name of the committee clerk. I called him and threw myself into a prayerful posture and begged mercy.

This clerk informed me, "A supplemental appropriations bill is being marked up in both Houses."

"Right. What is a supplemental appropriations bill?"

He explained we could only get our first appropriation by going before the supplemental appropriations subcommittees because the regular cycle of appropriations had already passed for the current year.

"Oh," I said as if I understood, "how do we do that?"

He informed me of the procedure. His committee held both regular and supplemental hearings on agencies under their jurisdiction, as did all other subcommittees of the House, but in the Senate a special supplemental appropriations subcommittee dealt with requests for funds outside the regular cycle of appropriations. Further, the procedure was to begin the process with his committee.

"Oh, how do we do that?"

He suggested I come and see him as soon as possible. We arranged an appointment.

The clerk reminded me of my shop teacher in high school, Mr. Tomkiewitcz. He was short for crouching behind pillars of the law, had a neck made muscular from shaking his head negatively, wore spectacles for searching for fat in budgets, narrow eyes for scrutinizing programs, and blunt hands for pounding the table and demanding forthright answers.

As soon as we exchanged pleasantries, he made a little speech.

"I have here some questions such as you are likely to be asked by the Chairman when you appear before the committee. You may make any notes you care to make and comment on the questions. I don't want you to try to answer the questions now. Just listen and make notes. You will come to the hearing with an opening statement about why you need the funds at this time and then the Chairman will ask the questions."

He then proceeded to ask a series of questions. Every few seconds he would look up and stare at the blank pad he had placed in front of me. Finally, he said again that I could take notes if I wanted to. I said politely that I seldom found it necessary to take notes. He read more questions and then said more forcefully these were the questions *it was most likely the Chairman would be asking Mr. Stevens.*

Suddenly, it dawned on me. These were the precise questions we would be asked and he was giving me an opportunity to write them down so I could prepare answers for my Chairman.

"Ohhh," I said, "can we start again, please?"

He did. I wrote feverishly.

I went back to Roger and told him that the clerk had given me all the questions we would be asked. He wouldn't believe me at first. He kept saying they wouldn't do that. Finally, he believed me and I wrote the answers and the opening statement.

Roger was mellowing. When I first came to work with him he wouldn't approve the writing of my own name without studying it closely. Now, after the 21 drafts of the National Council statement and the secret papers I had prepared that fed him material at the first Council meeting, he would tend to approve my writing more quickly. Still, my goal was to stop him from reaching for his "correcting" pen as soon as I laid a piece of prose on his desk.

When all the questions had been answered to his satisfaction, I suggested we have a rehearsal. I had heard from people in positions similar to mine that they always held rehearsals with their bosses. I played the committee chairman and Roger answered the questions. I had them all written out in the sequence in which the clerk had read them to me. When I could think of a logical follow-up question I would ask it. Roger was amazing in his ability to answer a question and yet not answer it. At one point I asked a follow-up question that stumped him. He merely smiled, and with a twinkle in his eye, said: "Mr. Mark really knows this area better than I do; I'd like him to answer that question." Through all the years of testifying before Congressional committees, he always threw the questions he couldn't answer to me. I usually went down in flames because I didn't know the answer either.

In those days the House held closed-door hearings. The Chairman, Rep. Denton (D)IN) sat across the table from Roger, the clerk was opposite me at Roger's left. Two Republican Congressmen and three Democrats occupied other chairs.

I was nervous but everything went well until Chairman Denton inadvertently skipped a question and Roger didn't. The answer was completely irrelevant but Denton didn't notice and Roger was so intent on reading the recorded answers that he didn't realize his error. The clerk and I noticed and exchanged puzzled looks. Then, the Chairman read the next question and Roger read the previous answer. Three or four times they exchanged wrong answers to right questions; neither of them listening to the other's words. I tried to point to the right answer on Roger's paper, but he brushed me aside. When the clerk leaned over and whispered in the Chairman's ear, Chairman Denton looked embarrassed and the proper sequence was restored. This speaks to the relative power of a clerk versus an aide to an agency head. Looking back, it was funny, but I didn't know at the time that the clerk and I would have a chance to fix the record the next morning. At that moment I thought the nonsense answers were fixed in history.

The mixed up sequence went something like this:

"Mr. Stevens, what specifically do you intend to do for individual artists?"

"We intend to keep explaining that there is nothing to it. It's all a myth."

"I see. Now, when do you intend to begin this program?"

"As little as possible."

"Do you intend to have programs in all the arts as provided by the legislation?"

"No. We intend to be selective."

The next morning the clerk explained to me that we could make any changes we wanted in the testimony as long as we both agreed the change would make a better record. Quickly we agreed to move the answers to the right questions.

Meanwhile, I learned every agency is assigned a certain number of staff positions of various grade levels according to the amount of funds they are expected to administer. This is an arbitrary number and can be appealed. Fine; to whom? To the Civil Service Commission. Ok, who there? I was literally collaring passengers on the bus in the morning and asking them what I should do next. I asked friends, neighbors, other offices in the Executive Office Building, even the Secret Service agents who sat outside

69

Vice President Humphrey's office across the hall from ours. I struck on the idea of consulting with the National Science Foundation about procedure; they had a similar function and were only about ten years old. By coincidence, I learned that the original director of the NSF was still in Washington and had an office in the Academy of Science building. When I told Roger about it, he wanted to go along with me to see what he could learn about heading an agency.

The former director turned out to be a little old man sitting in an office that looked like nobody worked there. He seemed terribly lonely and extremely grateful to have someone ask his advice. We stayed a long time and both of us learned some important principles. He told Roger never to announce a grant himself, but always have the National Council announce awards. He told me to fight for super-grades, as many as possible; that this was the best time to do it. (There were at this time only 2,000 jobs ranked GS16, GS17, and GS18, called super-grades. These are the top executives just below official Presidential appointees.) We had been allotted two such positions, obviously one for the deputy chairmen of the Arts Endowment and the Humanities Endowment.

At that time I was still the unseen consultant to the U.S. Commission on Fine Arts and Liv Biddle was a full-time volunteer. Diana Prior-Palmer and Frank Crowther were being paid out of Roger's salary and pocket or were on temporary clerical assignment from some other agency. I obviously wanted to be the Deputy Chairman of the Arts Endowment, but one Saturday morning when I was reporting my minimal progress on organizing the agency, Roger broke the news that it wasn't to be. The Deputy job had been reserved by Senator Pell for Livingston Biddle. Roger was very kind about it and said he would do all he could to get me at least a super-grade rank. Although I was disappointed, I was still grateful to be part of this history making time and for having a significant place in the agency.

Of course this news gave me added incentive to fight for more super-grades. Eventually, I won three positions; a GS18 for the deputy, a GS17 which our legal counsel demanded, and a GS16 which became mine because Roger said, "It's yours."

About mid-September we got word the Appropriations Subcommittee had voted us $2.5 million for the last six months of our fiscal year instead of the full $5 million authorized in the legislation which President Johnson had requested. Roger tried to use his influence with the members of the full House Appropriations Committee which had to ratify the subcommittee's recommendation, but with no results. A full committee seldom reverses a subcommittee of its own.

I dashed into the room where the full committee met and grabbed the report telling us we had $2.5 million for support of the arts for the last six months of the year. Though this was September we couldn't possibly receive the actual allotment before November and couldn't process a grant to anyone before January. The committee had set our agenda for the months ahead.

I took the report to Rep. Frank Thompson's office, our mentor and advisor. His staff advised taking the reduced funds and not appealing to the Senate. They called the

Congressman off the floor and he agreed. I called Senator Pell's office and got the same opinion. Then I called Roger in New York and told him everyone advised us not to appeal to the Senate for full funding. He told me to notify the Senate clerk that we would not appeal. The fatal mistake for which I paid dearly was that I did not ask the White House about the appeal; after all, the President requested $5 million and this was the disposition of his request. I didn't know much at the time about the sibling rivalry that exists between the Executive Branch and the Legislative Branch, but I was to learn.

Several days later, President Johnson had his gall bladder removed at Bethesda Naval Hospital. In the recovery room he was reviewing routine legislative materials with his staff and focused on the supplementary appropriations bill that had just passed the House. Our tiny appropriation was only a small paragraph in that bill. The President asked what had been done. The Staff didn't know. The President said dammit find out. The staff called Roger Stevens. He told them we had accepted. The President said, I was told, "Tell Roger Stevens that damnit I don't ask for money I don't need and that the least he can do is to fight and fight vigorously."

At that moment, I was collapsed at home with some kind of virus. I had been working extremely long hours under stress and fatigue had finally caught up with me.

About four o'clock that afternoon the phone rang. It was Roger.

"I hear you're sick."

"Yeah."

"How sick are you?"

"Some kind of bug hit me."

"Do you have a temperature?"

"Yeah."

"How high is it?"

"Last time I took it it was 103 degrees."

"That's not high enough. You better get down here. We've got a lot of work to do."

It was a wrenching time for Roger Stevens. He had let his ability to handle a situation get away and had depended on someone else to do a job. He had always prided himself on never having to ask a secretary for a telephone number, or never asking a business associate for a fact. I think he believed he was only valuable and appreciated by other people when he did favors for them or gave of himself. He expected nothing in return because he didn't believe he deserved much. Whatever he wanted he got through his own efforts and now he wanted to do as the President demanded and he didn't know how. He had given away too much responsibility to me and couldn't get on top of the situation quickly enough to save it.

I pulled myself out of bed and drove to the office through the rush hour traffic coming at me from downtown. Roger had told me what the President had said about fighting vigorously.

He asked, "How do we appeal to the Senate?"

"I don't know."

"Can you find out?"

"I can try."

First, I called my contact at the Bureau of the Budget, Emerson Elliot, with whom I had worked in preparing the statistical material for the House hearing. He informed me in rather cold and unendearing terms that I was asking for advice concerning the Legislative Branch and he was of the Executive Branch. No help there. Now where? I tried a couple of other contacts that I had developed, but they were either out of town or out of the office. I wanted some information before I called the clerk of the Senate Committee, so I wouldn't be as ignorant as I was at my first meeting with the House clerk. Finally, I had to give up and call him.

He told me the appeal had to be on file with Senator Pastore's Committee by eight o'clock the following morning and the hearing was that day. Great news. I had had two weeks to prepare for the House and I was in good health. It was then late on Friday. My fever must have increased three points and I could feel panic creeping up my spine.

"Look," I said to the clerk, "I don't know what I'm doing. I don't know how to appeal. I have a high fever, the President ordered us to appeal, my boss is on my back to do it, and I haven't the faintest idea where to start. You are not on my side I realize, but if you won't help me we will be dead before we're born. Can you help me?"

He said, "I really shouldn't do this, but call Mr. Dunn at this number in the Department of Interior and tell him your story as you just told me. He has the best record of appeal in the government."

I thanked him gratefully and did as he suggested. Mr. Dunn agreed to help me and told me to bring all the materials I had on hand from the House hearing, the hearing report, and anything I thought relevant to his office immediately. I did. The man held his entire staff overtime just to help me. With scissors and glue he pasted together the right language and procedure for the Senate clerk and had his secretary type it for me. When he asked me a question I would struggle to overcome my feverish stupor to give a semi-intelligent answer and then lapse back into a partial coma. At about eight that evening he handed me my materials all neatly packed up with the number of copies of the appeal needed to fulfill the requirements and told me we were finished. I thanked him for several minutes and his staff for several more. I felt a hundred pounds lighter and on the road to recovery. Then he spoke the saddest words I had ever heard. He said it was all finished, except for the argument. I thought we could use the same opening statement of need as in the House. He said that wasn't allowed; I had to have completely new arguments.

He explained the House and Senate are jealous of each other. If I used the same arguments in the Senate, and they gave us more money, it would look as if the House didn't understand our needs and the Senate, in its wisdom, did. The next time we appeared before the House subcommittee they would remember that we went over their heads.

I don't believe I ever received worse news in my life. I had used every possible argument in the House hearings and couldn't possibly think of new ones for the Senate.

Instead, I composed a letter of resignation as I walked back to our building at the pace of an errant schoolboy on his way to the principal's office.

I asked Roger to try to think of some new arguments while I delivered the "boiler plate" material for the appeal to the Capitol. He was hanging around wanting to feel involved in the situation, like an expectant father outside the maternity ward; I fully expected him to start boiling water any minute. I think he felt totally helpless for one of the few times in his life, and I think our whole relationship changed during that awful night. When I returned from the Hill he had a carry-out dinner waiting for me, something he ordinarily wouldn't have thought of. He kept asking me how I was feeling and if he could help. I was in no physical or emotional condition to be diplomatic, so I finally asked him to please go home because he was distracting me.

I wrote the testimony until nearly midnight before literally collapsing on my type-writer. Then I went home for a few hours sleep and some self-administered medical treatment. I had based the new arguments on the hue and cry that was prevalent about the fear of government control of the arts. Some of the commentary was highly critical of certain arts institutions and national arts service organizations and therefore required going off the record at the hearing; a technique we had learned and used for short inter-vals during the House hearings. I was shortly to learn that the House and Senate played by different rules.

Throughout this period from the time the bill passed until the Humanities Council and staff was appointed, I had the task of preparing all the material for the Humanities Endowment. Roger refused to have anything to do with the Humanities side of things and I, too, was only interested in our side, but the law had married the two endowments in many ways. Appropriations was one way; the law said we were each to be ap-propriated an equal amount. I had to write testimony for the Humanities and invent programs to be established by them as well.

For the House hearings I invented some programs and took some from the elaborate report of the Commission on the Humanities. I am happy to say the Humanities Endow-ment, when it was established, never adopted any of the programs I invented. The twinness of the two endowments was later ignored by the Congress, and then abandoned.

On the Saturday morning we were to appeal, I decided I couldn't handle the hu-manities in addition to the arts in my weakened condition. I called Frederick H. Burkhardt, the President of the American Council of Learned Societies, and told him he had to catch the next Eastern Shuttle to Washington to testify before the committee. He hesitated and was obviously disturbed at the prospect. I said if he wasn't here we would simply tell the President the humanities refused to appear after being invited; that is, when he asks why the humanities didn't get an appropriation. He agreed to race for the shuttle. The White House prestige strikes again.

Senator Pastore was in one of his feistier moods that morning. My fever and flu were worse and I was barely able to follow what anyone was saying, including my own words. At one point the Senator looked over at me and mistook my pained expression for criticism. He said, "Young man, I can see that you don't approve of what is going on. Well, let me tell you it's a way of life around here and you either get used to it, or you leave. Do I make myself clear?'' At that point he threw a pencil, hitting me on the shoulder. My response was the only one appropriate for a young and confused bureaucrat. ''Yessir,'' I said.

When Roger leaned forward and ask that we go off the record to explain our need for the full $5 million the President had requested, Senator Pastore informed him these were not closed door hearings and some members of the press were present. I looked around for the first time and recognized several reporters, one from the Washington Post who always wrote about all our public statements. Senator Pastore said we could submit a confidential report for the committee's eyes only, if we would care to do so. Roger first gave me a withering look for putting him in this embarrassing position, and then the expression was tempered with sympathy as he realized who was going to write the confidential report. We were told we had twenty-four hours to submit the report.

Before we had gone to the hearing that morning, Roger and I had met at the office to look over the proposed testimony and have it typed in final form. He had ordered a White House limousine to take us to the Hill for the hearing. Then, most unusual for him, he told the driver to wait. The purpose, he said, was to take me home after the hearing because I looked so drained.

In the light of developments, as we left the Senate Office Building, he said, ''I'm afraid you can't go home quite yet, you've got a lot of work to do at the office.''

In addition to the report, the committee asked for verification or amplification of certain facts, so Fred Burkhardt and I spent most of the afternoon working on the humanities side of the testimony. Then, I concentrated on the arts side, and started writing the report after a quick meal from a carry-out. I was determined to finish before I collapsed.

I asked Roger if he could come to the office about nine that night and managed to contact a secretary who agreed to come in at ten. By nine I had almost finished with a detailed report that caused Roger to say for the first time—but definitely not the last time—''Don't let anyone tell you that you can't write fiction.'' He approved the report with only superficial changes, which was unusual. He probably felt guilty for causing my illness to be fatal. By eleven the report was typed, and I delivered it to the Hill and was in bed by midnight.

I had had only about four hours sleep since I was rousted from my sick bed Friday afternoon. My body was aching in every joint, I was still high feverish, and just plain exhausted from the work and stress with no sleep. I had just fallen asleep when the phone woke me up. A voice with a heavy accent said;

''Misser Mock, yes?''

''Yeaaa.''

''Your brudder-in-low, Ben, sick. His apartment, he say cum. Bleeding.''

I admit my first reaction was to gauge how long a man can bleed before it's serious. I desperately did not want to get out of that bed and leave sleep behind and drive downtown again.

My sister's husband had been out of work for a long time because he wanted to leave advertising and work in civil rights. There was not much need for an advertising expert on dairy and meat products in the civil rights movement of the 60s. I had managed a successful contact for him in the Office of Education's program on desegregation and he was living part of the time in D.C. and part with his family in Philadelphia.

I mumbled to the man on the phone to tell Ben I was on my way and hung up. I started to fall asleep again and then shocked myself awake with the guilty knowledge that a man, a relative no less, was bleeding to death in a dreary hallway while I was safe in bed.

By the time I arrived at the apartment house downtown, my telephone contact informed me that an ambulance had taken Ben away.

"Where?"

"Hospital."

"Which one?"

"Don know."

For the next hour or so I drove to hospitals in the greater Washington area trying to find Ben. On about the fifth try I found him at the Hospital Center in Northeast. He was fine by this time. His bleeding ulcer had stopped and he had some sort of tranquilizer in him. He apologized for involving me. "Just get in the car and shut up." At my house I pointed to a door. "In there is a bed. Sleep in it. Do not wake me under any circumstances."

I slept most of that Sunday.

It was all for nothing, the Senate didn't give us any more than the House. However, the President must have thought we fought vigorously because we never heard otherwise. As stated earlier, this incident was a kind of dividing point in the relationship of Roger Stevens and myself. After that crisis, I think he rather enjoyed the luxury of depending on someone for at least one of his major projects; at least he kept increasing my responsibility without increasing my authority.

I felt a large debt of gratitude to Mr. Dunn for giving me the essential help in my desperate state. I suggested to Roger we extend some gesture of thanks to him and he suggested we give the man the use of the box at the National Symphony that he bought every year. With gleaming enthusiasm I called the man and invited his family to use Roger's box the next week. He responded with absolutely no enthusiasm at all. A day later he called to say that a greater show of gratitude would be not to compel him to sit through a concert. I thanked him for his honesty.

My phantom employment with the U.S. Commission on Fine Arts had been terminated near the end of October. The whole ordeal of the Senate appeal had been done as a volunteer. On November 1, the Bureau of the Budget called to tell us they had $700,000 for "salaries and expenses" for the two endowments; what did I want to do about that? I put myself on the payroll as the first administrative act of the Arts Endowment. I was still employed as a consultant. I told Liv Biddle he could start drawing a salary and work full time as a consultant. White House influence had struck again and obtained the temporary transfer of an administrative officer from the Office of Education, a Mr. Schmidtlein by name. He was to stay only until we received our appropriation. I prevailed on him to stay long enough to complete the paperwork for all of us on the job, making us at least temporary employees.

By then I had learned a little about how to organize a federal agency. With the job slots I had gotten approved by the Civil Service Commission I suggested to Roger that certain jobs would be duplicated in the two endowments. Having one person serve the two endowments by performing the same job for both made sense to me and allowed for more program positions in each endowment. Legal Counsel, Administrative officer, Grants Officer, grant processors, etc. could all be shared positions. Roger agreed and I organized the staff with about 15 slots for each endowment and 12 shared staff positions. Then I began petitioning the Civil Service Commission for specific positions.

Strangely, the application forms to be used to create positions required the signature of a legal counsel and the administrative officer of the applying agency. Since we were applying for those positions, it was impossible for the legal counsel and administrative officer to sign the applications. So I assumed both positions and signed. All kinds of other documents required the signature of someone who didn't exist at the time, so I signed innumerable forms by assuming various fictitious positions, more than 500 times. Months later the Government Accounting Office, or Government Services Administration, or somebody, charged me with these crimes and insisted on a hearing. When I tried to ignore their phone calls, they appeared in my office with a court reporter and briefcases stuffed with the evidence. Their intention was to take verbatim testimony from me on each document. When I began answering every question by pleading expediency, it was obvious that such tedious questioning was fruitless. After a boring twenty minutes of repetition they gave up and said they would rule on the "crimes" and report to their superiors and mine. In the end, it was decided all the documents had to be re-drawn and signed by the proper official even though that person wasn't in the position at the time. It took two efficient secretaries two full days to redraft the forms and have them signed.

One of my contacts at the National Science Foundation was the Assistant Legal Counsel, Charles Ruttenberg. Roger and I were both impressed with his ability to interpret the law as we wanted it interpreted, a rare person in Washington, where almost all lawyers start conversations by shaking their heads. We wanted Chuck to be our Legal Counsel. I called his boss to see if his deputy would be interested in the top legal job with us. He said definitely not. Several days later I phoned Chuck on another matter and mentioned our disappointment that he wasn't interested in joining us. He said he was extremely interested and had been hoping we would ask him. Obviously, his boss didn't want to lose him. We got him two weeks later.

▶ ────────────────────────────────

The Black Chapter
Fall of 1965

Two incidents occurred about this time, one that I regret because it brought pain to one person, the other almost caused our agency unnecessary trouble.

After the appropriation was approved and staff was possible, our problem was space. At the time, we were bombarded with correspondence that required replies. We had two secretaries who were paid by some other agency, but I was falling further and further behind in answering all the mail. After the appropriation hearings the mail increased even more.

With the $700,000 and the heady feeling of the newly rich, I began hiring people.

One of the first persons I hired was June Arey. I had known June in Winston-Salem as a volunteer. She had just survived a bizarre divorce and was anxious to leave Winston-Salem. She had a general arts background and could answer all those letters I was neglecting.

Schmidtlein was still with us as administrative officer on loan. Altogether, six of us were crowded into the file room of the temporary offices of the Kennedy Center along with the copying machine and the coffee dispenser.

Also, Roger had mentioned to a Catholic theatre organization he would try to make room for their offices in the Kennedy Center when it was built. It was part of his tactic for mustering support for the project wherever he could find it. The nuns in charge of the association misunderstood, or he was too vague, and they appeared one morning with habits and household at the temporary offices. There was simply no space available, except the supply closet. Instead of explaining the mistake, Roger told the Kennedy Center staff to clear the closet and welcome the nuns. Until we moved out the nuns sat just inside the suite entrance at their little desks guarding their precious files in the supply closet behind them. People coming to the office for the first time to do business with the Kennedy Center were often startled to see nuns in their habit guarding the front door. Also, the supplies from the closet were now stored on shelves in our so called office.

Clearly something had to be done about space.

Then, the agency benefited because of my Machiavellian behavior. Twenty-five years later I still am uncomfortable thinking about it. It was the only time I can remember that I took advantage of someone in my entire career.

The White House administrative officer who gave us the bad news about Roger's need to draw a salary, James Sasser, had jumped to an identical position with President Johnson's Civil Rights Council. This agency was established by an Executive Order. The Civil Rights Commission legislation then passed, and automatically dissolved the Council. Sasser was without a job. When an agency ceases to exist the administrative officer remains responsible for the physical assets of that agency; in this case Sasser was in charge of disposing of the suite of offices. Since he was out of a job and had all this furniture and furnishings at his disposal, he wanted to trade the property for the position of administrative officer at our brand new agency. His Machiavellian motives were perhaps as unsavory as mine turned out to be.

The offices Sasser had to dispose of occupied an entire floor of a fairly new building one block from the White House. All the rugs, draperies, desks, chairs, and ashtrays were in place. I wanted the free space and furnishings, but I didn't want Sasser.

After two days of contemplating the situation I approached Roger. I told him I thought I had a scheme for getting the space we needed at no cost, but I would be doing something unethical. Roger said he didn't want to hear about it; it was entirely my decision, but free space was highly desirable.

A few more background details are necessary. The Humanities Endowment now had money for organization, so they became extant for the first time. Barnaby Keeney, president of Brown University in Sen. Pell's home state of Rhode Island, had been the Chairman of the Commission on the Humanities, and was scheduled to be the Endowment Chairman as well. However, he needed six more months at Brown in order to qualify for a pension, so the retired director of the Guggenheim Foundation, Henry Allan Moe, began serving as Acting Chairman until Keeney was to take over in June of 1966.

My scheme involved passing the buck to Henry Allan Moe. I would tell Sasser that because we hired the legal counsel, who was to serve both Endowments, without consulting the humanities people, they insisted they have the final word on the other key joint position, the administrative officer. I told the whole story to Moe and asked him to decide through interview whether he wanted Sasser or not. I subtly hinted that he probably wouldn't like the man. Then, I persuaded Sasser to sign over all the property before the interview. Moe thought Sasser lacked authenticity and rejected him. We were then in possession of a whole floor of completely furnished offices at no cost. We moved the following week.

In a sense I did pay for those offices. I have had a bad conscience ever since about tricking James Sasser.

The other black incident was more mysterious and could have resulted in a serious situation.

The Council had met the previous June 24, 1965, at Tarrytown. With the good news from Congress that the passage of our bill was a likely occurance, the mood of the members was joyful. A practice of inviting various artists and experts in particular fields was established with this meeting and W. McNeil Lowry, Vice President of the Ford Foundation and director of the Foundation's arts and humanities program, was invited to talk to the Council after dinner.

The cocktail hour was rather prolonged that first evening, and Phil Hanes had provided the wine with dinner. Agnes DeMille was angry that Mac Lowry had not given the American Ballet Theatre, her company home, monetary attention as he had all the Balanchine clone companies. She felt that Lowry would rather throw money at a third-rate Balanchine spin-off company than give a dime to ABT. To guard against expressing her anger during his visit, she deliberately chose George Stevens on whom to vent her frustration during the long cocktail hour. This was an innocent mistake.

George Stevens, as we have seen, was fundamentally changed by his experiences with the death camps during World War II. Somehow, he connected the Holocaust with the anti-semitic stance of Henry Ford in the 1920s. As Agnes continued to fill his ear with a recitation of the unfairness of the Ford Foundation during dinner, he found himself growing uncontrollably angry over Henry Ford's anti-semitic pronouncements.

As Mac Lowry was speaking after dinner about the Ford Foundation's program in the arts, George Stevens suddenly rose and began berating Lowry for anti-semitism, anti-ABT, and anti-union crimes.

The Council was stunned. The silence was so electric one could almost feel a physical shock. No one broke the silence for what seemed minutes. George said he wasn't going to stay in the same room with Lowry.

Jim Sweeney, who was sitting opposite George, reached across the table and took George's hands. He kept saying he loved him and at the same time pulled him down into his seat. Still, no one recovered from the shock. Then Stanley Young began speaking pure gibberish. He spoke no intelligible words for about a minute, but he broke through to others and there was a general hubbub. Roger gently apologized for the interruption and asked Mac Lowry to continue, which he did.

Five minutes later, George was on his feet again, now red-faced and yelling his attack. He said it was an insult to submit these people to such an insensitive display and he was leaving right then to send a telegram of resignation to President Johnson. (Calling a press conference was implied in his remarks.) He then threw down his napkin and stamped from the room.

Again, a stunned silence. Everyone studied their plate. Feet were shuffled, heads turned, vacant stares prevailed. Mac Lowry stood impassively, as if he were standing in a doorway waiting for a summer storm to pass. Again, Stanley Young came to the rescue. In a calm voice he quietly asked Lowry if he would outline some of the pitfalls the Council should avoid, based on the Ford Foundation experience. "In other words," he said, "what mistakes has the Ford Foundation made that we should be aware of and could therefore avoid."

Lowry looked insulted and said, "The Ford Foundation has made no mistakes."

At that, everyone felt like joining George. Lowry had missed his chance to abandon arrogance and become human. Everyone knew of at least one mistake he had made in their particular field, not admitting it alienated those present when conciliation was desperately needed.

Quickly, Roger interrupted to declare an adjournment. Lowry stayed only a little while after dinner.

Roger dashed after George Stevens and somehow persuaded him not to send the telegram and not to resign.

Had Lowry responded to George's attack a serious situation could have transpired. Had George sent the telegram and called the press conference, the whole federal arts program could have been jeopardized because some people believed artists incapable of suppressing their egos and cooperating. Those opposing government support would have used such an incident as evidence of the impossibility of the concept. We were lucky in the result and the lesson learned.

One other event which was not black for us, but certainly was for another White House Assistant to the President is worth mentioning.

On June 14, 1965, the first White House Festival of the Arts in the history of the country was held. It was also the last.

The Princeton University historian, Eric Goldman, was brought into the Johnson White House to add a note of intellectualism independently of the inherited Kennedy Harvard crowd. Once in residence, Goldman was given little or nothing to do. His assistant, Barbaralee Diamondstein, would call me occasionally for lunch and try to assess our activities, but nothing was heard from their office. Their office was in the East end of the White House which meant "the social side" rather than the business end.

Somehow Goldman and Diamondstein fixed on our area as the area in which they would like to become active and obtained permission to organize a White House Arts Festival. No one asked Roger for advice or asked him to help. It was easy to see that Goldman wanted to have influence in the arts and didn't want to share with Roger and/or the National Council on the Arts.

Invitations were sent out and the news spread across the arts community of the nation. I began to receive phone calls from people I knew from all parts of the country. "How can I get an invitation?" was the question they all asked. I was happy to say I thought it was a huge mistake not to have invited whoever was calling, I would tell them this was a social event and not part of our more serious activities. Then, I would give them Goldman's phone number.

Goldman was getting quite a few refusals, but didn't understand that many of these artists were opposed to President Johnson's Viet Nam policies and didn't want to link their names with his. About three weeks before the event, poet Robert Lowell sent a letter to President Johnson and sent copies to all the important newspapers. The letter essentially said thank you for the invitation, that he agreed with most of the President's domestic programs, but couldn't in good conscience accept the foreign policy, and therefore no thanks to the Festival.

The letter got more coverage than it deserved and set off a multitude of refusals. A week before the Festival, Bess Abel, Mrs. Johnson's social secretary, called Roger and asked him to do what he could to save the festival from becoming a disaster. Roger began calling on friends and Council members to come and support the President with their bodies, even if their minds questioned certain policies.

I began calling artist and patron friends who had begged to come and told them they now could attend because we were now in a life saving role.

In the end, 300 people attended what is best described as a twisted experience. Some of the guests behaved horribly. Dwight MacDonald circulated a petition against the war in Viet Nam, but only persuaded four or five people to sign it. Others, like John Hersey, made little anti-war remarks before they performed, but nothing major ever developed. A kind of pall clung to the occasion. Had the festival been planned well and given some form it could have been an excellent boost to our cause.

As a result, Goldman and Diamondstein were given less to do and left after a long period of extremely modest activity, never again in the arts. He later wrote a book about his venture into the world of governance. Diamondstein moved to New York, and became an arts consultant. Roger's help in partially rescuing the festival was appreciated by the White House.

Gregory Peck and Philip Hanes.

▶ ────────────────────────

Cutting Our First Tooth
Still the Fall of 1965

At the November meeting, the Council could at last replace good intentions with actual action, the leap from dreams to dollars. The first grant ever made to a performing organization went to the American Ballet Theatre in the amount of $100,000. A policy was established stating that box office receipts would qualify as matching funds under the requirements of the law. Additional grants were awarded to the Venice Biennale ($32,480), a feasibility study for an American Film Institute ($91,019), small grants to composers (up to $2,000), grants to choreographers for new works (seven grants totalled $92,500).

Several other projects were launched though they resulted in no specific action. Low-cost studio/living quarters for visual artists was discussed at several meetings before action was taken in 1968-1970. An intention of expanding art museum collections to outlying areas was endorsed, but not acted on through any specific project. Over the next five years the Council awarded grants for various museum expansion projects. A proposal to provide sculpture in public places was tabled for further study and approved at a later meeting.

Two projects that were not successful were also brought forth at this meeting; one was launched the other merely proposed. Rene d'Harnoncourt suggested a national competition among visual artists, with the selected artists to be paid a monthly rental fee while their works were in a touring exhibition. Study was undertaken for this project, but the objection of the museum directors was so strong the project was abandoned. The directors believed such an arrangement would set a precedent, driving operating costs up and forcing museums to stop using works by living artists because of rental fees.

The other project that received mixed opinions from the Council members was a new plays project. The intent was to discover ten outstanding new plays. The myth of the undiscovered genius is always widely prevalent and this was an attempt to learn of any truth in the myth. A jury of distinguished theatre experts was assembled as final judges, and the solicitation of new plays was widely broadcast through various channels.

Preliminary readers eliminated the obviously poor plays before the jury of agents, directors, producers, and playwrights studied the better scripts.

Only five plays were found worthy of development and possible production. All five were eventually produced, but only two were judged to be significant discoveries. "Does a Tiger Wear a Necktie?" was produced by Brandeis University and later had a run On-Broadway. The other play had a significant history.

"The Great White Hope" by Howard Sackler had its world premiere at the Arena Stage in D.C. Sackler first appeared at the theatre with an incomplete play. Working with the director, Ed Sherin, and the leading actors, James Earl Jones and Jane Alexander, the play was completed and opened on time. Broadway producers came to Washington to see this carefully selected new play and it was optioned for a New York production with the original cast and director. Consequently, the play was responsible for enhancing the careers of those principles after years of modest success in the regional theatre movement. The play won the Pulitzer Prize in 1969, and became a successful film.

Roger was concerned that Arena Stage was largely responsible for Sackler's eventual success and the fact that he never thanked the theatre monetarily for its essential help. Sackler was invited to Roger's office and asked to make a tax deductible contribution to Arena Stage. Roger pointed out that Sackler's taxes would be enormous because of the $1 million income that year. Sackler refused to part with a penny.

His subsequent plays have not been successful.

Another significant action at the November, 1965, meeting was the adoption of a policy of not funding building or remodeling projects in the arts. It was thought, rightfully, that funds were too limited and building projects too large in scope for the Council to handle with such meager appropriations. The subject of establishing panels of additional experts to advise the Council on issues was discussed and the decision was to form such panels as deemed necessary "to advise the Council with respect to projects, policies, or special studies as may be undertaken by the Council from time to time."

Other projects and programs were either launched at this meeting or feasibility studies begun. (For a complete listing of all activities between 1965 and 1970 see Appendix.)

Staffing was now the major activity. Livingston Biddle, Charles Ruttenberg, and I were given Presidential appointments because President Johnson decided he wanted to approve all super-grade appointments, a practice that was sustained for only a few weeks for some reason. Vol. 1, Number 23 of Presidential Documents for January 3, 1966, reads "December 27, 1965—The President announced today the appointment of Livingston L. Biddle, Jr. as Deputy Chairman, and Charles C. Mark as Director of State and Community Operations of the National Endowment for the Arts". This was followed by a short biography of each of us. Ruttenberg's appointment was announced in another number.

Actually, Liv and I were called and told to report to the White House at specific times; he in the morning and me in the afternoon. I thought I was going to be examined

84

by the President to see if I was worthy. I was nervous and Liv didn't help much. He came back from the White House and refused to tell me about his interview, except to tell me it was terrifying.

When my turn came I walked over to the West entrance as instructed, caught the stoney stares of the press corps as I was ushered into the Fish Room, the room where we had met for the first Council meeting. I sat alone in the large room for several minutes and then the door opened. It wasn't the President, it was a kindly looking aide named Jake Jacobson. He said the President regretted not meeting me, but he was tied up. We chatted for a few minutes. He said he had a daughter who wanted to be a ballet dancer and asked my advice. He wanted her to go to college first, but she said that would delay her career. I suggested Butler University, which had a ballet major and an academic program combined. He thanked me. I was back in the office in thirty minutes. I told Liv I saw the President, paying him back for the insensitive prank he pulled on me.

Diana Prior-Palmer was given the job of Government Liaison, her last assignment. Frank Crowther was made Assistant to the Chairman and continued as speech writer. June Arey was given the title of Director, Office of Program Evaluation and was in charge of fielding the unsolicited requests for grants that flooded into the office. Liv Biddle recommended Eleanor Pollock for Public Affairs Director, and Sureva Seligson as Director of Research, coming to us from the Democratic National Committee.

Henry Geldzahler was a prominent Pop art figure in New York who later became associate curator of American Art and Architecture at the Metropolitan Museum of Art. He became the consultant on the visual arts, later to be moved into the directorship. Ruth Mayleas had worked closely with Stanley Young at the American National Theatre and Academy; he recommended her for Theatre and Dance Program Director. Paul Spreiregen became the Director of Architecture and Design, recommended by the architects on the Council. David Stewart was hired as Director of Education and Public Media because he had had experience in teaching and in educational broadcasting.

The Music Programs were directed by Fannie Taylor. Isaac Stern had taken the responsibility of finding the music director. He called me one day to say he was recommending two people he was certain I had never heard of. One was Donald Steinfirst, a music critic in Pittsburgh and the other was Fannie. I knew them both having worked with Steinfirst on an early Council project and I had known Fannie years before at the University of Wisconsin when I was a student and where she headed the town-and-gown theatre programs. I had heard that Donald Steinfirst was not in good health. We hired Fannie Taylor.

The Director of Creative Writing was Carolyn Kizer, a poet of reputation, author of several poetry books and champion of the small literary magazine. She went on to win the Pulitzer Prize for Poetry in later years.

Altogether, it was an extremely reputable and talented staff to serve an even more talented Council.

We chose the shared staff people and secretarial assistants from a pool of eligible Civil Service applicants, except for a young actress, Anna Steele, who was hired to be secretary in the Research Department. The Administrative Director, Robert Cox, and I were given the task of orientation of the new staff, and Roger left me to informally supervise everyone. I was flattered to be given the responsibility, but I also had the job of organizing the states for the development of state arts councils.

During this process of establishing the agency, fighting for personnel with Civil Service, learning how to install procedures for who was to do what, locating space, acquiring furniture and actually putting people on the federal payroll, I would often meet people in the government who said, "It is so unusual for one person to actually have responsibility for establishing a federal agency from scratch."

I would smile and immediately offer to share the glory with them if they would care to help me. No one accepted my offer.

It was the most frustrating time of my life. Whenever I believed I had finally completed one facet of the organization jigsaw puzzle, someone would remind me that I still had to complete this form in quadruple copies, or clear something with this bureau, or apply for this clearance. When it was all finished and I saw the offices busily peopled and actively helping the arts in the space that I had acquired through deception, I felt satisfaction. I remember sitting in my office late one evening after my Presidential appointment had been announced to the press which ignored it completely, and thinking about the long road that had led from unemployment in St. Louis and a vague conversation with Roger Stevens to this point. It had been a journey worth undertaking. I felt myself extremely lucky to have traveled it with only light carry-on baggage and the secure piloting of Roger Stevens.

Now, a new chapter was about to begin, one I had been anxious to undertake. I think it is accurate to say I was the most enthusiastic advocate for the state art councils provision of the legislation. Liv Biddle and the program directors, all seemed grateful I was willing to attack the "state problem," as they saw it. Sen. Javits had been able to push through that part of the bill, thinking only of New York.

I saw the situation as a simple matter of politics. Roger also saw that the future of the arts had to rest with a mass movement anchored in a broad political sea. Our federal program had no constituents, if the states weren't organized. Roger liked the idea of having the states organized as one voice for advocacy, but he had little faith in the vision of the state legislatures. I had worked as a lobbyist with the Wisconsin legislature on my first job out of graduate school, but I really didn't understand the job I was taking on.

One more word about our staff. We had staff meetings whenever Roger felt the activities were outpacing his amazing ability to remember everything said, proposed, activated, or secured. On a moments notice he would ask me to spread the word and the directors would gather around a table in Roger's large corner office.

Carolyn Kizer, who was extremely bright and attractive, was also extremely sensitive. She invariably arrived with her voluminous papers and a box of tissues. If the meeting took a turn toward criticism, or if she felt strongly about a proposed program that wasn't immediately appreciated by Roger, or if I scolded her for some bureaucratic omission she would burst into tears and sop up tissues faster than newspapers running from a modern press.

Ruth Mayleas always sat at the far end of the table with body language that spoke volumes; she would defend to the death her decisions and opinions. She also smoked Galois cigarettes while she defended that which hadn't been attacked.

Fannie Taylor always managed to manipulate Roger with feminine charm and a deprecating matter. She also had a sly, subtle sense of humor that Roger liked and she seemed more organized than anyone else.

Frank Crowther would sit on one of the visitor's chairs away from the table and offer interruptions which were ignored.

June Arey, after she became the Dance Program Director, would argue with Roger at staff meetings. Everyone else had sensed Roger would not admit shortcomings in front of other people, but June never learned that. I told her directly it was self-defeating but she persisted.

Sometimes I would suggest a staff meeting because Henry Geldzahler had come down from New York to do some business. Henry thought he was only in charge of decisions and that someone else would implement them. At staff meetings Henry would always ask about the reason the grant letters to visual arts grantees hadn't been sent, or why the checks hadn't been sent to grantees. I would tell him he hadn't done the work so nothing had been done. He would say he wasn't a bureaucrat and wouldn't do it. I would say his grantees wouldn't get letters or checks until he did do it. Eventually, he would do it reluctantly with a furious attitude.

Roger resented the fact Liv Biddle had been forced on him by Sen. Pell. Consequently, he didn't give Liv the usual duties of a Deputy Chairman. Instead, Liv was given light housekeeping duties and special projects of a long-term, low priority nature.

David Stewart and Paul Spreiregen didn't want to be at staff meetings. They wanted to work on their programs and reinforce their careers.

And so, a typical staff meeting would begin quietly with Roger listening to reports on the activities of the directors, shift to a discussion of things accomplished, and the tension would begin to rise. Ruth Mayleas would blow acrid smoke and dismiss my request to visit a theatre in Arkansas, Fannie Taylor would defend the provinces, June Arey would insist Roger change his mind about something, Carolyn Kizer would start plucking tissues like picking strawberries, Frank Crowther would offer a gratuitous comment, and Liv would try to calm everyone by announcing we were getting a second copying machine. Then, Roger would adjourn the meeting and tell everyone to get back to work.

Occasionally, Roger would become annoyed with cacophony and tell the assembled staff they were only window dressing in his scheme of things. He would tell them he could run the agency alone with only me to handle the details and Chuck Ruttenberg to keep us legal. I don't think he really meant it, but the attitude of the directors would suddenly change and they would become submissive. Usually after one of these meetings the directors would come to my office and verify something Roger said that they didn't quite understand because of his soft, slurring voice.

The Union of the States
Winter of 1965–66

The original Administration bill did not have a provision for state arts councils. Subsequent testimony from witnesses and the political skills of Sen. Javits moved the Congress to include state aid in the final version. When the bill became law it said in part that the governor of each state could designate a body to be the official organization to receive funds under this program. The general opinion was that the governors would establish a state arts council by designation and then pressure their favorite concrete contractors to supply the necessary funds to match the federal money, dollar for dollar. In their collective wisdom the Congress allowed one year from the passage of the bill for the implementation of the state provisions.

Roger was more interested in the other sections of the law and began his long thought of plans for theatre, dance and music. He couldn't get interested in an arts project that was once removed from the act of creation. I wanted to see if the legislatures could be persuaded to vote an arts council funded by state revenues. I thought that if one or two states did it, others would copy. When I reminded Roger of the state funding provision and my eagerness to start on it he said, "You do it. Run it as a separate agency. I'll get involved only if you ask me."

I saw the states as essential to selling government aid to the arts without interference. Also, with the example of New York state appropriating $500,000, I believed even a modest $100,000 in each state would be more help to the arts than we were with the federal appropriation of $2.5 million. I had seen a grassroots interest and considerable political acumen while traveling the country. I believed the political leadership of the states could be educated to see the benefits the arts brought to local communities as the most important aspect of the quality of life. (Quality of life was a popular political phrase at the time.) I also believed the legislators could be convinced the arts were a positive service to the middle-class voters. I could hear myself saying to stubborn legislators, "You help the poor, the downtrodden, minorities and underprivileged, not to mention the disabled, the blind and the halt, but what are you doing for the middle-class-hard-working-American-family-oriented-taxpayer?"

With this assignment and these thoughts I began a 200,000 mile journey to all the states and territories in pursuit of the establishment of state agencies that serve the arts.

Congress in its wisdom doesn't indicate how to pursue a goal that it establishes. Quite a gap exists between "There shall be" and "There it is." The first step seemed to be to inform the governors of the possibilities of the new federal program in the arts. I asked Roger if President Johnson would like to write a letter to all the governors and invite them to send two representatives to a meeting. He thought the President would like to boast a little about what he had accomplished for the states.

I contacted the American Council on the Arts (ACA) to see if they wished to co-sponsor the meeting with the Endowment. They did. Then, I drafted a letter for the President's signature calling a meeting in Chicago in January, 1966. President Johnson approved the draft. Meanwhile, I sent a copy to Nancy Hanks, who was then the president of ACA. She called immediately and suggested the President say a few more kind words about ACA in the letter. She thought one paragraph out of five should be in praise of the co-sponsorship of ACA. I thought not. I told her the letter had already been approved and I thought the President said what he wanted to say. She said she understood I wrote the letter. I confessed I did, but said I wouldn't send it back to the President.

The response was encouraging. Every state and three territories sent representatives to Chicago during the coldest January of recent memory. Roger and I noticed immediately that ACA was emblazoned all over the hotel while the Endowment was hardly mentioned anywhere. Was Nancy Hanks still miffed that the President didn't say a few kind words? We remained patiently quiet.

We had let ACA produce the agenda as well as the arrangements with the hotel. The first session of the conference was all ACA; its importance, its value to councils of all types, and its pledge for the future. Roger was sitting next to me on the dais and became concerned that ACA was taking the meeting away from us. I reminded him of one of the slogans of the Schlitz Brewery, "Never interrupt a competitor while he's making a mistake."

I said, "These people are here to learn how to get federal money for the arts. That's all they care about right now."

When our turn finally came around, the whole meeting enlivened. Questions began to flow from the previously inanimate group; skeptical questions about the old bugaboo of government control of the arts, about the reasonableness of taking tax revenues for culture, and whether the matching money from the states had to be from the public trough. There were questions about the propriety of government arts support, but I noticed no one rose to say they wouldn't ask for the money.

The questions about government control had become so frequent from my first days in the program that I had long ago developed standard answers. I would ask if anyone could name a Republican opera, or a Democratic symphony. Then I would say that after one year in Washington I had noticed the government couldn't control the government; that it was a huge monolith that oozed its way along like a giant snail, leaving a residue of paper and red tape behind. I would ask them how they would go about controlling the arts if they were the President, or a Senator, or a Supreme Court Justice. Mostly I would point out that only countries with an ideological government attempted to control the arts. The only ideology Americans accepted was freedom of speech, and that couldn't be reconciled with control of the arts.

One of the events planned by ACA for the meeting was a Chicago Symphony concert. It was frighteningly cold that night. After the concert the one hundred delegates stood outside on the sidewalk looking for cabs to take them back to the hotel. None were available. Several of us started hunting cabs in the surrounding streets. When we would find one, we'd take it back to Orchestra Hall and fill it with elegant ladies and gentlemen in evening clothes. After some time we had retrieved almost everyone and had the last group in a cab, except for one man. He was the delegate from Hawaii, Masaru Yokouchi. When he didn't move into the cab, I jumped out and grabbed him. It was then I realized he was wearing only a tropical weight tuxedo and no overcoat in weather that easily touched 15 below zero.

After he sat in the front seat with me for a while he asked if it was bad for his nose and ears to hurt. I told him when they stop hurting it's a bad sign. I asked him why he didn't get in the cab when I called and he said he couldn't move until I pulled at his sleeve. He said he once experienced forty degree weather when he was a Boy Scout and his troop hiked up Mauna Kea for an overnight hike. In Chicago he would have frozen to death rather than be impolite.

I asked the cab driver why he wasn't at the hall when there was a concert. He said concert goers didn't tip generously so cabbies avoided the location. When we arrived at the hotel I was much aware of his remark, so I generously tipped him. He looked at me with incredulous eyes and then at the tip in his hand and said, "F---ing music lover."

The major arrangement to come from that meeting was my promise to come and assist, consult, speak, and/or confer with any state at any time about a state arts council, or its business. Consequently, I was hardly off the plane back in D.C. when the requests began to come in and I was off on an odyssey that made Ulysses' wanderings seem like a day trip to Disneyland. On one trip, Roger and I were swimming at Waikiki beach in the morning, then I flew to Seattle, crossing three time zones, then up to Fairbanks, Alaska, recrossing the same three time zones, and finally drying my swimming suit over a hot wood stove at midnight. I still don't know what time it really was in my head.

In addition to the sales talk I had honed during my years with the Winston-Salem Arts Council and the Arts and Education Council of St. Louis, I had to exaggerate frequently. I told governors and assembly speakers that the governor of an adjacent state was forming an arts council and that they needed one or their state would look primitive. If they agreed to try legislation, I would go back to that adjacent state tell the same story, but with more credence.

In North Carolina I had an appointment with Governor Sanford for a Saturday morning. When I arrived at his office I was greeted by two of his young aides who told me the governor wasn't available, but they would represent him. We settled down in an outer office and the questioning began. They were cautious, because North Carolina already had a state museum, a state symphony orchestra, and more outdoor dramas than a quart of mosquito repellent could soothe. Every few minutes one of the phones would ring and the aides would answer. Immediately after these calls, new questions would be asked. Finally, I realized that Gov. Sanford was in his office with the door open and could hear our discussion. He was probably working on other matters, but kept an ear open. When he had a question he would phone it in. Eventually, North Carolina formed their arts council.

Arizona was a different problem. I had written the guidelines for the states' applications in a marathon session at my dining room table; more than 30 pages were required to satisfy various legal restrictions implanted in the law for various illogical reasons. While I was out of Washington somewhere, my secretary contacted me to tell me Arizona's chairman, Lewis Ruskin, said he would not submit a budget with his application, and that he had recorded Roger Stevens on tape at a party in Arizona saying he wasn't required to. The law specifically said the states, or any grantee, had to submit a budget for the proposed project(s) and conform to that budget. Roger was clearly wrong and in no way could I simply ignore the situation. The states were beginning to talk to each other as they all tried to muddle through that first year. If Arizona was excused, it could set off a general rebellion.

Still, I couldn't say my boss was wrong in public. I told my secretary I would call her back while I tried to think of a way out. I called her back and dictated a letter to Mr. Ruskin in which I said Roger was essentially right. A budget was required only if there was to be a partnership arrangement, and of course such a partnership was mutually desirable, wasn't it? As a businessman he wouldn't go into business with a partner unless there was full disclosure, would he? Well, we will disclose all our plans and assets, if he will do the same. It was then I changed the name of the whole program to the Federal-State Partnership Program. It still functions under that name, and it's all because of Mr. Ruskin and his tape recorder.

In Connecticut, Anthony Keller, the first executive director, said the funds were so small that he was just going to have a competition and select twenty artists and give them each $5,000. I had to persuade him that his plan was not wise politics. Competitions always develop a few friends among the winners and a lot of critics among the losers. Spreading the funds around the state to organizations was a much wiser course. Roger Stevens had told the National Council on the Arts that his job was to find projects of highest quality, greatest need, and most politically sensible. Though quality and need were by far the most important, the needs of the arts were so great that we should be able to find sufficient projects that were also politically sensible. Connecticut agreed.

I went to Denver and told a large audience I was happy to be here in St. Paul once again.

The District of Columbia is considered a state for purposes of this program. When the bill was about to be voted, a Republican Congressman proposed the D.C. Recreation

Department be the arts council instead of establishing a separate body. He made his suggestion the price of his vote. An amendment was hurriedly introduced and passed. For several years the D.C. Commission on the Arts limped along as a step-child of recreation with appropriations of only $25,000.

I got a call one day to come to Georgia to talk to the Budget Committee of the State Senate about the benefits of a state arts council. No one told me that the Budget Committee was the entire State Senate. I think the final score of the debate was slightly in favor of the Senate; I admit to being humbled by those professionals.

Guam didn't attend the Chicago meeting, but the island has a representative in Washington, Wan Pat, and he smelled the federal money. They qualified in the first year because of their man in Washington camping out in my office making certain their application was correct.

Not every state was a problem; some were pleasant experiences. I was invited to Hawaii to stir up grassroots interest in an arts council and allay fears of government interference. I was to make a series of speeches on the various islands. Just as I was preparing to leave, all the airlines except Pan Am went on strike. I went to Roger for advice. He asked the White House for help. The man in charge of transportation in the White House arranged for Pan Am to give me special clearance. When I arrived in Los Angeles a representative met me and escorted me to a room filled with people who appeared to be camping out. A long table was covered with airline tickets in organized order. The Pan Am man talked to his colleague behind the table and my ticket was placed near the beginning of the more than 400 already there. Everyone stared at me with expressions ranging from hostility to unabashed awe.

The man behind the table apologized in a loud voice for not putting my ticket at the very top, but he explained an Australian was taking his wife and eight children around the world as an anniversary gift and they simply had to have top priority. I generously said I understood. Then, in a much lower volume, he asked me what I did in the White House. I told him I negotiated. He nodded as if he understood. I was on the same plane with the Australians returning home.

When Alfred Preis, executive director of The State Foundation on Culture and the Arts of Hawaii, said a few speeches he actually meant 17 speeches in five days and none of them in the same place. We checked in and out of hotels like thieves in the night as we moved around the islands. Fred Preis had organized the tour with utter efficiency, but still it often meant rising at dawn, driving to an airport, and then driving several more miles to attend a breakfast club of Japanese or Chinese businessmen. Invariably, I was served sushi to eat and chop sticks to eat it with. After I mastered the taste and digital skill the local people seemed to view me less cautiously.

Once, Fred told me after a later dinner meeting that he had a charter plane meeting us at an air strip close by. This was on Kauai. The plane couldn't land on time because the airstrip was covered with smoke from the burning of the adjacent sugar cane fields. When we were airborne and I was belted into the co-pilot's seat of the twin-engined Beachcraft, I asked the pilot why commercial planes didn't fly from commercial fields at night. He told me it was much too dangerous because of the prevailing cloud cover and the surrounding mountains. The logical question followed. "Why are we up here?" He said he knew where all the mountains were and then by way of illustration made three vague gestures each accompanied by a shrug of the shoulders, supposedly pointing out the hazardous mountains. I looked at Fred and he was wearing a thoroughly terrorized smile. In the end, the pilot proved he was a practical joker.

After forty-five minutes he looked at his watch, shook it vigorously, held it to his ear, and said it seemed about time to dive through the clouds to land. With these words he did exactly that. We broke into clear air at about 4,000 feet and we were exactly lined up with the main runway of the Honolulu airport. The pilot knew what he was doing.

After my 17 speeches in five days the airline strike was still strong. Thousands of tourists were stranded in Hawaii. Mostly, these were working young people who had saved a year for a two week vacation in paradise. They had run out of money. The hotels wouldn't let them stay. The state declared an emergency and opened the school buildings as emergency shelters as they would in a typhoon. Still, the airports had hundreds living there. I checked into the Hilton Hawaiian Village and waited on the beach for the strike to end. I needed the rest.

After a week of rest I was anxious to get back to work. The White House couldn't help me coming home even though Roger told them he needed me for important work. Pan Am was hopeless because of the enormous number of people they were flying out daily. BOAC, the British airlines was flying and advertising for passengers. I went to see them with my handy book of TRs, the government's Travel Request coupons that will buy transportation to anywhere.

My offer to buy a ticket for London with a government TR was met with extreme caution. I was asked to see the manager. The manager said he had never been offered a TR by our government and besides, he doubted I really wanted to fly to London. I told him I was offering a perfectly valid TR and he should accept it as an Anglo-American good will gesture. He said that I should understand I would actually have to fly to London, that leaving the plane in New York was illegal. I said I understood, though I had every intention of leaving the plane in New York and instructing our Administrative Officer not to pay for the New York to London portion of the ticket.

I was given a middle seat between an old gentleman who wore a sign around his neck that read, "I speak only Mandarin. Please help me," and a young Japanese girl who was joining her sister in New York. She laughed at my left handed chop stick technique and I laughed at her clumsiness with a knife and fork on the long flight. (She could leave the flight in New York because she boarded in a foreign port. It was illegal for BOAC to fly passengers from one American place to another.)

On the long plane trip I thought about Fred Preis' interesting life. He and his wife were Viennese. When Hitler annexed Austria they decided to flee the country. Fred was a student of Hawaiian culture, perhaps the only one in Austria, so the decision was made to reach Hawaii. After some hardships they arrived just in time for Pearl Harbor, and Fred was immediately put in a camp for alien enemies because Austria was an ally of Hitler's. Eventually he was released and after the war won the contest to design the Pearl Harbor Memorial.

When we touched down in New York I left the plane, told the U.S. Customs I hadn't left the country and demanded they give me my luggage. They did and I took a train to D.C.

Idaho gave me another pleasant memorable experience. One day I received a call from Idaho Sen. Church's office requesting I make a speech and attend a conference in Boise. I regretfully said I was already booked for two events in California that were practically back to back at almost that same time. Half an hour later I received a call from Sen. Church himself subtly telling me he would greatly appreciate my changing my mind and making the requested speech. Again, I explained the situation, but he asked for dates and details. Then he asked if I would come to Boise, if he could arrange transportation that would allow me to be back in Los Angeles for my second speech there. I said I would be happy to come to Boise if I could get back on time. An hour later I was told a Lear jet would be at my disposal for the two days.

The first speech was at Lake Arrowhead at an arts in education meeting. A student was assigned for the drive to the private plane facility at the L.A. airport. He couldn't find it. I was no help. We were both getting nervous when it suddenly occurred to me that for once in my life I didn't have to rush for a plane; the plane would patiently wait for me until I arrived. The student immediately drove slower and we found the correct location in a matter of minutes.

I was the only passenger. The co-pilot fussed over me, making martinis for me, serving hot canapes, arranging for a desk to magically appear out of the wall. We landed in Boise in less than an hour. I made my evening speech, stayed through the morning sessions, flew back in the afternoon and spoke in Los Angeles the following night.

While I was on one of my extended trips, Gregory Peck came to Washington to work on American Film Institute business. He asked Roger if he could have a place to work and secretarial help. Roger took him to my office.

My secretary, Rosa Dare Keats from Danville, Virginia, was one of the most efficient people imaginable. She had mastered all the secretarial skills, she was arithmetically accurate, and she knew how to protect me from unwanted intrusions. She was fiercely loyal to her immediate boss and singleminded in her crusade to improve her working conditions. She was also a strict fundamentalist Baptist.

On this particular morning she saw Roger Stevens, who had never talked directly to her, and Gregory Peck, whom she had only glimpsed when he walked through the office several times. Roger said, "Rosa, If you're not too busy today, would you mind working for Greg? He has some phone calls and some letters to write."

When I returned from my trip, the first thing I saw as I entered the office was a vase with two dozen long-stemmed roses sitting on Rosa's desk. She handed me the card without a word. It read, "Roses for Rosa, who was so much help to me. Best, Greg."

After that, whenever Greg Peck came to town, he would call Rosa and she would go to his suite at the Watergate of Madison Hotel and take dictation. On her vacation that year she flew to Los Angeles where Greg and Vernique Peck entertained her in conservative Hollywood style.

I believe Rosa felt suffering my workaholic habits and slipshod administration was worthwhile for the privilege of knowing "her Greg."

For me, in every sense these were the best of times, these were the worst of times. I saw little of my children for two years. They almost called me Uncle Daddy. I was eating badly, sleeping fitfully, attending too many late night receptions and intimate parties. My life was airports and hotel rooms, it didn't matter where.

Why? I wanted to prove something. I wanted to achieve something. I believed in the strength of the arts outside of the major centers; in the amateur theatre of my young life, in the craft classes I remembered being taught in the public schools by the WPA while growing up, and the music and WPA orchestras and bands brought to us in the WPA-built band shells in the parks and through school concerts. These were the influences that turned me to the arts, and I believed this was where the arts had to go to find the ultimate audience and the next generation of artists. I believed the key to building that audience and nurturing those artists was in the geography of the nation, in every state and community. I still believe it.

During those two years, nearly half the states took legislative action to establish state agencies to serve the arts. Was it the lure of $50,000 of federal money that caused it? Hardly. Was it because a pesky federal official badgered them into it? Ridiculous. I believe it was because President Johnson and the Congress knew that it was the right program at the right time. The nation was ready to start thinking about the arts and doing something about them. By and large, the arts institutions had governing boards composed of local conservatives. Private funds to meet annual deficits were drying up as the noblesse oblige generation was leaving for the great concert in the sky. The trustees of symphony orchestras didn't want federal subsidy, but they thought they could swallow state help which was more controllable. These ruling trustees had children who were better educated in the arts and they were producing children as they reached maturity. These sons and daughters of the ruling classes on the local level wanted more for their children than three opera productions a year and five symphonic concerts. They pushed for a state program of greater opportunities in the arts.

But not Iowa. I tried two or three times to generate some enthusiasm among the cultural and political leaders of the state and failed. The attitude was of the "let them what use it, pay for it" variety. With a governor who refused to appoint an arts council, I had no place to turn. However, I thought I would make one last try.

In the Des Moines airport I coincidentally met an old acquaintance from the University of Wisconsin. He told me he had just completed a survey for the Iowa legislature that dealt with the residence of recent graduates of the state universities. He said that a high percentage of college graduates from the Iowa schools left the state within four years of graduation. The implications were that Iowa taxpayers were spending $50,000 to educate Iowans so they could work productively in other states.

When I met with the governor that afternoon, he was negative as usual, I mentioned the survey and its implications. He actually jerked when I mentioned it. He wanted to know how I knew about it. I merely said I had my sources. He said the survey had been suppressed because it could severely damage support for the state universities.

I suggested that perhaps one of the reasons for leaving Iowa was the fact that students were exposed to high quality art while in college and then sent back to their small towns of the state where no art was prominent. They missed it and went to find it elsewhere. The governor asked if a state arts council could be part of a university. I assured him that he, as governor, could designate any state agency he chose to be the arts council, according to the law, and for many years Iowa was the only state that had its arts council attached to a university because that governor said so.

Wisconsin had the opposite problem. On a visit to my native state to investigate a project in small community arts development that I liked particularly, I was summoned to the Chancellor's office. Bob Gard, my old friend and the author of the small community project, said I wasn't obliged to respond to the summons, but he was obliged to deliver it. I went.

The Chancellor had stripped the computer of all data referring to my years on campus and began by telling me all he knew about me. He reminded me that I had had an athletic scholarship and the university had been instrumental in providing a scholarship in graduate school. He said he was proud of me for the acting awards and the playwriting award I won, and then we got down to the reason for the visit.

Could I somehow influence the governor of Wisconsin to recognize the University of Wisconsin as the official state arts council? I said no. Why? Because the governor is to determine the body he wants to be the council, according to the law; I only administer the law. But didn't I have some influence? Not that kind.

We talked through and around the subject for perhaps twenty minutes before it was clear I wasn't going to help them. As a result the university opposed all other plans for a state arts council and it took years before Wisconsin managed to build a strong public force for the arts.

The heart of the matter was that people interested in the arts in their state saw the enactment of the Endowment legislation as an important breakthrough, and were willing to fight for the participation of their state. The only real threat to riding the crest of public opinion to a successful conclusion came the week before the famous meeting in frigid Chicago.

California was one of the four functioning state councils in business before the Endowment act was passed. Therefore, California's actions were watched carefully by the other states as friend and foe considered plunging into this heretofore unexplored quagmire. The Chicago meeting of governors' representatives was to take place January

26–29, 1966. On Friday, the 21st, I received a call from Martin Dibner, the executive director of the California Arts Council. He told me the political rivalry in the Democratic Party between the governor, Pat Brown, Sr., and Jess Unruh, had caused the State Comptroller, Hale Champion, to mess up the arts council's plan for making grants. Consequently, Ralph Bellamy, Chairman of the Council, had called a press conference for Tuesday, the 25th, to blast the whole idea of state subsidy for the arts, and resign. What could I do to straighten this out?

First of all, I thanked him for waiting until late on a Friday afternoon to involve me in this mess. Then I said I didn't know if I could do anything, but I would sure as hell try. The whole state council movement could be killed by a nationally respected artist like Ralph Bellamy making headlines damning the whole idea the day before all the states were to meet. I faced the problem squarely by running to Roger for help.

He suggested I talk to President Johnson's man in the White House who was in charge of relations with the states. I had to try three times before I got through to him. I explained the situation briefly. "So you see, California will be sailing upstream with much publicity while all the other states are moving downstream. They could kill the President's hopes for a state arts council program."

The concluding sentence got the man's attention. (I can't remember his name; I think it was Wilson.) He asked me to repeat all I had said with more detail. When I finished, he asked me to come to his office in the White House at 7:30 that evening.

I worked at my desk until it was time for the appointment. I went over the situation once more and answered some questions about the history of the California Arts Council and the fact that Jess Unruh had fathered the council. When I finished, the man took a piece of paper and wrote a name and a phone number on it and handed it to me. He said to call that number in the morning and explain the situation to the man as I had to him. I reminded him that the next day was Saturday. He said the man would be there. Who is he? He's Pat Brown's man in Washington. Oh.

I had a burning question to ask this man based on my experience. In one of the states I was shown a list of the legislators and a dollar amount next to each name. I was told a state arts council could be bought by buying the votes of these lawmakers. So, I asked the President's man in charge of state relations whether many state legislatures could be bought.

"All but two."

I asked if he would tell me which states were pristine. He refused. I left his office depressed.

I called the California representative on Saturday morning and repeated my story one more time. When I got to the California going upstream while the rest of the states were going downstream I had to repeat everything again. The man said he would contact me with good news very shortly. I spent an uncomfortable weekend, but he called Monday morning to say Ralph Bellamy had called off the press conference because Hale Champion had released the arts council funds and plans could proceed. The arts sometimes need to get involved with politics.

By the end of 1966, when it came time for the states to apply for federal grants, out of the 55 eligible states and territories, 45 had been organized during that year. Eight states had some viable form of council functioning before 1966. Two territories were to organize later. The Northern Marianas were included in the law later bringing the eligible total to 56.

The 45 state arts councils that sprang into being were the result of a number of factors. The availability of federal funds for the purpose of supporting the arts was an important factor in some of the less populous states where $50,000 is an amount to pursue. The active lobbying by the cultural leadership in some states was the factor that carried the day. Often the cultural leaders were important contributors to political campaigns without asking much in return. Another aspect, as mentioned before, was that the climate was right, the populace was beginning to turn to the arts for a meaning to their lives, not in large numbers, but a significant portion of the population. Last of all, I was out there pushing, cajoling, stretching the truth, and persuading the political leaders, and strategizing with the cultural forces in every state.

The first year of grant eligibility was the 1966–67 fiscal year. Thirteen states and territories applied for up to $50,000 on a matching basis for carrying out programs and projects in the arts. They were California, Connecticut, D.C., Kentucky, Michigan, Missouri, New Jersey, New York, Puerto Rico, Rhode Island, Virginia, Washington, and West Virginia.

Thirteen states and territories applied for nonmatching study grants of $25,000. They were Guam, Indiana, Iowa, Maine, Mississippi, Montana, Nevada, North Dakota, Oregon, South Carolina, South Dakota, Tennessee, and Virgin Islands.

Twenty-eight states applied for some combination of study and program grants. They were Alabama, Alaska, Arizona, Arkansas, Colorado, Delaware, Florida, Georgia, Hawaii, Idaho, Illinois, Kansas, Louisiana, Maryland, Massachusetts, Minnesota, Nebraska, New Hampshire, New Mexico, North Carolina, Ohio, Oklahoma, Pennsylvania, Texas, Utah, Vermont, Wisconsin, and Wyoming.

States applying for the program grants were functioning as state arts councils and had developed their procedures. Those applying for study grants, which didn't require matching state funds, were gearing up for a full program next year. Those applying for the combination study-program grant intended to have a functioning council before the year was over.

By the end of that year, I had spoken at 40 governor's conferences on the arts, traveled to almost all the states at least twice, and spent unending hours in phone consultations.

In fiscal year 1966–67 state legislatures voted appropriations of $2,664,640 for the arts. Of that amount more than $1 million was appropriated to two state councils, New York and Virginia. The Virginia funds were used to operate the entire Virginia Museum of Fine Arts which included a Museum Chapter Program in a dozen or so cities of the state. Twenty-three states received some appropriation, 12 states received $10,000 or less, while only five states received more than $100,000.

By the following year, 37 states received some appropriation, eight received $10,000 or less, and seven received more than $100,000.

After twenty years of the program the state legislatures were appropriating $218,805,104, and only American Samoa and the Northern Marianas received less than $100,000. Undoubtedly, the appearance of funds from the state treasuries is the most important new resource for support of our cultural life in the twentieth century. No one knows what the condition of the arts would be if the states hadn't begun their assistance, but we do know that the arts are healthy in most places because of this support.

Other Considerations
Still the Winter of 1965–66

Just because I was flying all over the country trying to influence the states, that didn't mean I was free of other responsibilities at the old home office. By February, 1966, most of the professional staff was located in a series of offices aligned along one side of the building located at 18th and G Streets, N.W. My office was originally almost as large as Roger's corner suite and was next to his, but as more staff was hired my large room was carved up to create two additional spaces.

On February 11 and 12, 1966, the National Council on the Arts held its fourth meeting. Three new Council members were sworn in; Herman Kenin, President of the American Federation of Musicians, Harper Lee, author of *To Kill a Mocking Bird*, and painter Richard Diebenkorn. Herman Kenin officially filled the vacancy created by the death of sculptor David Smith, who had died in the fall of 1965. However, the Democratic controlled Congress was concerned that none of the artists' union representatives had been appointed to the original Council. To alleviate the situation Rep. Thompson introduced an amendment to the Act that expanded the Council by two members; hopefully to appoint union representation. President Johnson got the message but appointed Kenin to the Smith vacancy, showing his independence of Congressional wishes for the new "union" seat. Then he appointed Lee and Diebenkorn to the new seats. Sibling rivalry again.

Roger spoke to the Council about the events of December 20th. It was on that day that the Endowment actually passed the first federal grant award to an arts institution. All the Council were invited to attend the season opening performance of the American Ballet Theatre at the New York State Theatre at Lincoln Center. Most of the members from the area were able to attend. I was on the West Coast but managed to book a flight straight to New York in time for the performance. Afterwards, Lucia Chase invited the Council and several others to her apartment for a party.

Vice President Humphrey had been scheduled to come and present the first grant award to Lucia Chase, but he was representing the President at the funeral of Jawaharlal Nehru and no one knew if he would be back in time to do the honors.

All the men were in black tie except two; one of them was me. Having just arrived from Los Angeles I hadn't time to change. The other man kept smiling and gesturing that we were dressed inappropriately. Finally, he came over and introduced himself. He was Aaron Copland.

The apartment was filled to capacity and throbbing with animation. I happened to be in a doorway and suddenly realized Vice President Humphrey had arrived and was wedged in beside me; neither of us able to move and no one noticing he was there. I introduced myself and asked if he had had a good trip back from India. In his usual lively manner he proceeded to tell me about the trip. He said he had stopped on the way to his airplane to visit Indira Gandhi. He said that he was positive, from all she said, that she would never be Prime Minister.

Then, the guests began to be aware that the Vice President had indeed arrived and a way was cleared to Lucia Chase's side for the presentation of the check for $100,000.

The New York Herald Tribune reported: "The Treasury of the United States has saved a national treasure. Not directly, perhaps, but the taxpayers, through the government's recently established National Council on the Arts, saved the American Ballet Theatre from extinction."

It was a two minute ceremony that marked the beginning of what came to be the largest source of needed funds for the arts. From the $2.5 million for the first six months of active programming, the Arts Endowment has grown to an annual appropriation in excess of $170 million. More importantly, the heart of the program is in the requirement that federal money be matched dollar for dollar from some other source. This stipulation has generated more than seven dollars of state and private contributions for every dollar of federal money.

Another event on this weekend gave me more insight into the persona of Roger Stevens. I had mentioned some weeks before that though I had been in theatre, been in the arts for a number of years, I had never been to an opening night on Broadway. Roger said "Oh, really" and went on with the conversation which wasn't about my underprivileged upbringing.

Some weeks later when we were both in New York for the historic presentation, I was at a dinner party at a friend's house on the Eastside. Roger was rehearsing for an appearance in a memorial television program for Adlai Stevenson, who had recently died. Surprisingly, my host told me Roger wanted to speak to me on the phone.

He delayed the television rehearsal to call me because he suddenly realized he had a play opening that night and I had never been to an opening. He had arranged for tickets for my wife and me, and spent another five minutes telling me not to try to catch a cab, but to take a particular subway, where to get on, and where to get off the train. The play was "Generation," with Henry Fonda.

Often Roger would suddenly do something intensely personal for me when it was least expected. I was always astounded by the number of highly stressful events in which he would be involved without appearing to be under any stress at all. That weekend's calendar for him had the American Ballet Theatre opening and grant awarding party, the opening of a Broadway play he produced, and a network television appearance; any one of those events would have brought a nervous state to most men, and three would have brought ulcers.

Returning to the chronology of the unfolding history of the National Endowment for the Arts, we have the meeting of February 11 and 12, 1966. This was the meeting with two new members. We met in the Indian Treaty Room of the Executive Office Building. When we booked the room we didn't realize the acoustics were terrible and that one could hardly understand what was being said. I offered that this room was the origin of the Indian proverb about the white man speaking with forked tongue. Everyone laughed, but it didn't make the meeting any more pleasant.

One of the important decisions at this meeting was the approval of the Stanford Research Institute as the agency to study the feasibility of an American Film Institute, a project that Elizabeth Ashley, Gregory Peck, William Pereira, and George Stevens had recommended.

The $100,000 awarded to American Ballet Theatre was an emergency grant. Another $250,000 was pledged by the Council at this meeting, provided ABT could first raise an equal amount from private sources. Other dance companies were given support at this meeting; that is, actual grants were voted. Looking back, it is amazing that such little grants could satisfy the choreographers in those days. Martha Graham and her company received $40,000 and that enabled her to create a new work and $141,000 was enough to take the company on a national tour. Alvin Ailey requested and received $20,000 to sustain his company for 12 weeks and create a new work. Merce Cunningham asked only $4,910.

Also approved was a grant to the Washington State Arts Commission for a summer residency for the Joffrey Ballet Company. Bob Joffrey and I had appeared before the Junior Chamber of Commerce of Tacoma and won their support. The Joffrey Ballet, as a result of this initial grant, had three successful summer residencies in the Northwest and established a climate that led to the establishment of the Northwest Ballet as a professional company.

The Council voted to assist the American Conservatory Theatre of San Francisco (ACT). ACT began life in Pittsburgh, where it did not find fertile ground. It was saved from dissolution by the Professional Theatre Program at the University of Michigan on a temporary basis and finally found a home in San Francisco. With the Council providing a grant and Roger assisting in raising the matching private funds ACT seemed to be on solid ground at last.

Another important program set in motion at this meeting was the Artists-in-the-Schools Program. It began as Carolyn Kizer's idea for a grant to the Academy of Poets to send young poets into the classrooms to read and discuss poetry with students. The first step of this program was to initiate meetings with senior poets and classroom teachers discussing with them how to impart the vitality of language to their students. The program began in the school systems of New York, Detroit, and Pittsburgh and was later expanded to Minnesota, Illinois, California, and several Southwestern states. The project met with what was described by David Dempsey in the *Saturday Review* as "staggering success." This success was the foundation for what was begun in 1969 as the Artist-in-the-Schools Program that encompassed all the arts and continues until the present in all the states.

At this meeting the members of the Council concerned themselves with how the small appropriation could aid the work of the originating artist. Several members made the point that universities desire artists-in-residence, but once on campus the academic load imposed on them precluded enough free time to do their creative work. A plan was proposed whereby artists-in-residence were made artists-out-of-residence; that is, leaving the campus on a sabbatical leave for a semester so they could work without teaching. Fifty grants were allocated at an average of $7,500 each for a total of $375,000. At that time the amount was nearly the average salary for a semester.

Isaac Stern and Leonard Bernstein pointed out that composers are often given small grants by orchestras to compose a work, but seldom, if ever, do they receive the funds to have the score copied. Preparing all the parts for all the players can cost more than the amount of the commission. Therefore, the Council voted $100,000 for copying grants for completed works to prepare them for performance.

(This resulted in nearly 67 grants averaging $1,500, reflecting the poor economic condition of those who did copying work. Incidentally, one of the grants was awarded to a composer living in North Dakota. Federal policy dictates always calling the Congressman from a district where a federal grant is awarded and allowing him/her to make the first public announcement. In this case, the Congressman was called and the staff person apologized that the grant was only $250. However, the Congressman was delighted and said that was the first federal money to come to his district in several years.)

In literature, a scheme to purchase and distribute books of decided merit which had not captured a popular readership was discussed, and funds were earmarked for this project, but it was never established because it became too complicated and involved too many objections from the publishing world.

However, young talent in literature and in the other creative arts was rewarded in another project. The Association of Deans of Colleges of Fine Arts was asked to name the most respected schools teaching writing, music, and the visual arts. Then, these schools would be asked to select the outstanding graduating students in these fields for a graduation project of their invention. Each student was awarded $1,000 to carry out the project. Usually the desire of the student was to travel to a museum, a city, or an institution which would enrich their background. Architectural graduates were later included in the program.

The plan for an invitational visual arts exhibition for which the artist participants would be paid a rental fee was again discussed and enthusiastically supported, especially by new member Dick Diebenkorn. The plan was dropped soon after this meeting. The other visual arts project tentatively voted was for regional exhibitions co-sponsored by various museums throughout the country. This was also dropped as a program. Art museums thought they couldn't raise the funds to match the grants for either project and didn't even want to try. Later, individual art museums were awarded grants for various touring exhibitions.

Funds were also voted for a Festival of the American Indian, and for the Venice Biennale. (These first Council meetings were transcribed verbatim by a court reporter. I wrote the minutes of the meetings from the transcription. This transcription kept referring to the "Vienna Follies" which I finally realized meant the Venice Biennale.)

The final business was the appointment of committees to investigate specific programs. Mssrs. d'Haroncourt, Sweeney, Wittman, and Bush-Brown concerned themselves with the ill-fated project for a regional exhibition with rental fees. Misses Ashley and De Mille and Mssrs. Peck, Young, and Smith took on the plans for the regional theatres. Harper Lee, Ralph Ellison, and Paul Engle were to study the problems of literature.

The historic announcement at the end of the meeting was that the Martin Foundation had made an unrestricted gift of $100,000 ($20,000 annually for five years) to the Treasury Fund. This was the provision in the law that allowed private money sources to contribute to the National Endowment for the Arts and have such gifts automatically doubled from an appropriation. This provision of the Act became known as the Treasury Fund. In this first year $2 million was made available, but only $34,000 was actually matched. It was important, however, because this idea new to the Congress was actually proven feasible when the Martin Foundation made the grant.

In those ancient days the federal fiscal year ran from July 1 to June 30. Therefore, hearings on the next fiscal year's budget were held in the early spring. March 1, 1966, was the date set for the House hearing, followed ten days later by the Senate. My job again was to prepare the testimony. This time around I had the input of a complete staff who could give me their plans and proposals.

In a sense, this period was one of transition. Up until that point, proposals for future projects, programs, studies and so forth came from either Roger, myself, or members of the Council. When a staff was assembled, the specific proposals began coming from the directors of the various programs with the advice of the Council members on general issues and then modified, expanded, or honed by Roger, myself, or other staff members. Developed proposals were then put into writing by the staff directors, given to me for final editing and shaping, then approved by Roger, and presented to the Council for final approval. Before each Council meeting, complete descriptions of each proposal or application, both those recommended for approval and disapproval, were mailed to the Council members. After the Council approval, projects were then implemented by the staff and regular reports made to Roger and to the Council when they met.

This time the hearing before the House Committee went smoothly. The program directors were all brought along to the hearing and were arrayed in a row behind Roger, Liv Biddle, and me, ready to supply details about their proposed programs.

This was the first year for the states to be eligible for funding, so I was more in the forefront as well as Roger's back-up. I indicated that all the states had now organized state arts councils and would apply for grants either for programming, study, or a combination of both. The committee seemed pleased with this report and individual members asked about the status of the councils in their states. I reported that the governors of all the states had sent two representatives to the Chicago meeting. However, the members of an appropriations subcommittee are extremely experienced in listening to the claims of Executive Branch officials and they examined me closely on the question of actual amounts needed to fund the applications anticipated. Since I had said all states would be applying for either programming funds ($50,000) or study money ($25,000) the committee wanted to know how many of each. I responded by saying most states hadn't decided whether to apply for the study grant or the programming money.

Then I was asked whether all the territories included in the law would be applying. I had to answer truthfully and say American Samoa hadn't been in contact with me at all.

The questioning and the subsequent action taken resulted in an appropriation of $2 million instead of the $2.75 million requested by the President. In fact, the Committee was right. The total expended in that 1966–67 fiscal year was $1,987,853. The committee seemed to know the needs of the states better than the President or us.

The Senate hearings were a different situation. Sen. Hayden was the Chairman of the Subcommittee on Appropriations for the Department of Interior and Related Agencies. He was the first ever Senator from Arizona and was then more than ninety years old.

The hearing began with the clerk escorting the ancient Senator to his seat. He could barely walk and seemed so fragile one feared he would break apart any second, but he took his seat and was in command. The questions, as with the House hearings, had been pre-established. Sen. Hayden looked down at the carefully prepared list of questions and read the first one in a shaky and aspirate voice. Immediately after finishing the question his head dropped forward and his eyes closed while Roger answered. He went through this process of waking up to speak and sleeping through answers two or three times.

Then it was my turn. He asked a couple of questions about the state program and then slept. Then, he asked a question I wasn't prepared for and which I didn't want to answer directly. I began to slip around the answer, thinking he would never notice my ploy. To my surprise his head popped to attention and he said, "Answer the question. Answer the question, sir."

After about two more questions to Roger, he whispered in the clerk's ear and was gently taken from the room.

Sen. McGee (D>WY), as vice-chairman, took over. He asked a couple of questions and then asked if we had the answers written out. We said yes and he said no good cause was served by wasting everyone's time with this ritual. He suggested we submit the written answers for the record so that all of us could get on with our work.

In the end, the full committees of both Houses agreed to appropriate $4 million for the next year's programming, the $2 million for the state councils, and $1,965,692 for the Treasury Fund; a total of $7,965,692 to be spent in support of the arts. In addition, we were given $1,019,500 for salaries and expenses.

One gets so many mixed messages about our elected officials. We read of the corruption and dirty deals and then we see the professional demeanor of the members on television during the scandalous affairs. My own experience with both branches of the federal establishment, and with the civil servants, was always excellent and pleasant. I have nothing but respect and admiration for the hard work and intelligence of these people. On occasion, a Congressman would try to use his position to gain an advantage for a constituent, but by reminding him of the clause in our law forbidding interference by anyone in the programs of the National Endowments he would back off. I usually felt the Congressman was merely showing his constituent that he tried to be of assistance. Almost without exception, the officials I dealt with were honest and helpful, thoroughly professional and extremely capable of doing the work they were supposed to do.

One Congressman on the House Appropriations Subcommittee always voted against us. Nevertheless, he would ask Roger to supply him with tickets for Broadway shows and cultural events in Washington. When he spied us in the gallery of the House he would smile and wave and was completely friendly, but then would consistently vote against us on appropriations or any other legislative matter. We simply felt he was reflecting the wishes of his district's voters, and though Roger tried several times to change his mind, he continued to hold a negative attitude.

In general, members of both Houses who were opposed to federal support for the arts in the beginning were converted as our agency matured. The state arts council movement influenced a great many of them as they saw their state legislatures back home vote increasing funds for the arts on the state level. Politicians in Washington carefully watch the political climate back home, particularly House members because of bi-yearly election campaigns, and when they see state politicians embrace an issue they are not far behind.

For the most part, the career civil servants were as intelligent and helpful as the legal language and procedure allowed them to be. While I was frantically searching for the keys to organizing our agency I asked for help from dozens of officials who had no real reason to take the time and energy to answer my questions and be helpful. I was given complete cooperation every time.

During the five years that my federal career spanned, I did encounter some people whom I came to call "survivalists." They were federal employees, state executives, and one or two people on our staff at various levels of responsibility. They were the kind of people who acted only in their own interests. Someone described the type with an analogy that best depicts the attitude. The analogy referred to a particular state arts council executive.

"If he were a bomber pilot during World War II, and he realized his damaged plane was about to run out of gas, he would bail out without telling the crew. Then, when he was asked what happened he'd say, 'Everything was all right when I left.' He would imply some crew member did something to cause the crash."

However, these people were the exception and not the rule.

The members of the National Council on the Arts with whom I worked were also dedicated, sincere volunteers of the highest order.

When I first met with these awesome people, I was completely overwhelmed. To see so many famous faces from the different art disciplines in one room is rare indeed. What can I contribute to their understanding of the arts? Do I dare to even try? At first, no. To sit in the room and listen to the exalted level of discussion was a privilege and a memorable experience in itself. It didn't matter which of the arts we were discussing, every member had an insightful, intelligent, and philosophical point of view to contribute. I have not experienced such a high level of discussion anywhere before or since those days.

The first glimmer of confidence in myself came at that first meeting when the secret papers I had prepared became the focus of the meeting. I had a niche of my own from which I could contribute. I knew more about our legislation and its possible interpretation than any of the members.

The next breakthrough for me came with this fourth meeting of the Council in February of 1966. I was responsible for the preparation of all the material presented to the Council members for their consideration. The program directors hadn't been on their jobs long enough for them to present and defend their own programs. So, as each agenda item was brought into discussion, the questions on details were directed to me. Is their an adequate budget for this project? What is the background of this organization? How long have they been in business? I was a fact factory now on not only government procedure, but also on the substance of our projects. With each meeting, however, the program directors found confidence growing and soon they were defending and detailing their programs to the impressive group. I always had a copy of each proposal and was free to express an opinion about the merits or practicality of it if the director failed in some way. Some directors tended to oversell a project, others didn't offer enough information.

I was to play an even more confident role with the council members later, beginning with the next Council meeting, but that's another chapter.

To and Fro: Keeping up with the Past, the Present, and the Future Creates Bureaucracy
More of 1966 Activities and the Spring of 1967

With a staff of nearly twenty people, actual federal funds under our control, projects underway, in the planning stages, and in the future, life began to be complicated at 1800 G Street, N.W.

With actual grants being issued for various projects, I had to learn a new concept. The term was "obligated funds." In government, appropriated funds that have been set aside for some purpose are said to be obligated. The check may not be drawn on the appropriation for several months or years, or in the full amount, but the full amount is tied up by the Treasury, unless it is "de-obligated." Someone has to keep a running account of funds allocated to various programs, obligated, and funds disbursed. Since I was already saddled with writing the budget, I was also responsible for knowing where all the money was at any given time. This also meant watching over future projects to see that we had enough money to fund them.

These sorts of daily routines naturally led to another bureaucratic ritual called "The Progress Report." We needed two kinds; one on the progress of approved projects and one on the financial status.

In 1966, the list of projects and funds obligated was easily managed, but as we entered 1967 it became increasingly difficult. At the moment, we had the American Film Institute Study happily underway, the teaching artists had been selected for the sabbaticals, the students for graduation awards were being selected.

The scheme to buy up books of merit and distribute them to libraries was abandoned after investigation due to high costs and complications of distribution.

The simple grants for technical assistance to established organizations had all been completed.

The Laboratory Theatre Project cosponsored by the U.S. Office of Education was progressing. The Office of Education had committed its share of funds, so the only obstacle remaining was finding the three theatres to serve as the homes for the project.

One day a woman appeared in my office unannounced. Her name was Lucile Blum, President of the Louisiana Music Society, or some such organization. She had been one of the delegates to the Chicago meeting on state arts councils, and was in the process of organizing Louisiana into a state council. We had talked on many occasions. She struck me as the kind of person who enjoyed having power. She seemed to have a need to check every detail before and after each transaction.

She wasted no time. "Chuck, what's this I hear about you giving Shakespeare Theatres away."

"Well, that's not quite right, Lucile. We have a project with the Office of Education to provide funds to theatres that will perform classic plays for high school students. We're trying to locate the theatres now."

"You don't have them yet? That's what I want to know."

"No, but we've been working on this for months now, and we're close to selecting the three theatres; one in the East, one in the West, and one in the South."

"But you haven't got them yet."

"Almost."

"How can I get the Southern one?"

"It's too late, Lucile. The cities we've been working with have worked for months to line up everything."

"Just tell me what I have to do to get one."

"Well, for instance, you would have to have a well equipped theatre full time. I mean all day every day."

Lucile Blum opened her commodious hand bag and took out a stub of a pencil and a penny notebook. She pursed her lips as she wrote and spoke; "Get thee-A-ter."

"That's comparatively easy compared to convincing your Superintendent of Schools and School Board to commit about $300,000 of Title III money from the Elementary and Secondary Education Act to this project each year for the next three years."

She wrote: "Get School Board."

"Then, you have to find an artistic director who wants to do this project, a business manager, designers, back stage crew, and all the people necessary to run a theatre."

"Oh, you'll help me do that, won't you, if I get the rest lined up?"

I laughed. "Yes, Lucile, if you can do the rest in about three weeks, I'll help you get the people to run the theatre. But I warn you its an impossible task. It would take months to arrange all that."

A week later she called to say the School Board had agreed to participate. "Now, don't go giving those theatres away to anyone else, 'cause I want one."

At the end of the next week she called again to say she had leased a legitimate theatre in downtown New Orleans.

I was astounded. So certain was I that Lucile couldn't do it that I hadn't considered the possibility. We had about committed ourselves to Fort Worth as the Southern location, and now we would have to alienate one or the other. A call from Fort Worth solved the problem. They asked if the theatre was required to have a union stage crew and union actors. We were required by our legislation to fund projects that respected union agreements, so the answer was yes. Fort Worth withdrew and New Orleans got a regional theatre company.

I asked Roger's help with the staffing I had promised. He called Stuart Vaughn, who had just left the Seattle Repertory Theatre. Vaughn was delighted, knew exactly the people he wanted, and began working immediately.

The other choices were an organization we founded in Los Angeles, The Inner City Cultural Center, which was personally backed by Gregory Peck, and the Trinity Square Repertory Theatre in Providence, Rhode Island. Both of these flourished and grew to serve their communities, but the New Orleans venture collapsed after a few years for lack of a strong community base.

Altogether, we had managed to put nearly $2 million of our $2.5 million into the disbursed or obligated column between February and May, 1966.

The following year was also the time of the first funding of the states. I had reported to the Congress that all of the states and four of the special jurisdictions, like D.C. and Puerto Rico, would apply for some form of aid. Only South Carolina elected to keep me from telling the absolute truth. I called and asked why they weren't going to apply, and the governor's office said their arts council wouldn't be ready to receive funds for a long time. I told them I had reported to the Congress that all states would apply, and that applying didn't commit them to anything and I would appreciate it if they at least asked for the $25,000 grant to study their cultural needs. South Carolina applied, which was fortunate, because their council moved faster than anticipated and they needed the funds to study their cultural needs.

The states applied for various amounts depending on the attitude of each state legislature. Roger said jokingly my 30 pages of bureaucratic guidelines would scare off most of the states, but it didn't.

Indiana was one of the states that reluctantly embraced the federal arts program. The chairman there was the publisher of a newspaper and influential with the governor. He saw to it that his longtime friend, Hertha Duemling, was appointed executive director. My impression was that the Chairman wanted to find an occupation for his ancient mistress and he seized the occasion of the state arts movement as the opportunity. The woman was completely unqualified and not mentally alert. I never knew their respective ages, but my impression was that he was tottering along well past seventy and she was probably near seventy.

All the state applications had been submitted, reviewed and ready for the Council to approve at the May meeting, except Indiana. I called the appointed executive director. She said she was just completing her application. I wanted her request so I could complete my financial report. She wasn't certain yet. When could I expect it? Soon. How soon? Any day. Why the delay? Because it's special.

Eventually it arrived. It was a red folder decorated with Valentine paper lace around the edges. Each page had a little simple drawing done in pastel pencil. One page of financial items had an angel drawn on the two upper corners, the page outlining a proposed study had little busy bees in the margin. The state of Indiana was requesting from the federal government the sum of $16,581 to conduct a study of the state's cultural resources and develop a plan for their support. With paper lace and childish drawings, they were requesting support.

Since the appropriations for the states was less than the requested amount and the states applied for funds ranging from Guam's $15,376 to those states requesting the full $50,000 in matching funds, we had a problem of equity. In the end, we decided to give the states applying for the $25,000 the full amount, and states asking for the $50,000 to be matched by state legislatures received $37,053. If a state applied for less, the amount they requested was the amount they received.

Roger was frustrated by the Treasury Fund. Here rested $2 million of federal funds that could not be used unless it was matched dollar for dollar by private funds. We had gotten a few small, private grants where Roger, or somebody friendly, had personal contacts, but most of the money was there and unused. Roger reasoned that donors were reluctant to give primarily because they had no control over the use of the money; it would be a gift to the government for the bureaucrats to use as they saw fit. If, however, we could tell the prospective donors exactly what project their gifts would support, and that their gift would automatically be doubled, the contributions might be more forthcoming. Was it legal to tell prospects the use of their money in advance? Chuck Ruttenberg, our Legal Counsel with leanings toward liberal interpretations of our law, took it under advisement. His conclusion was that it was perfectly legal for the Council to establish a number of priority uses for the Treasury Fund should money become available from that source.

In other words, the Council could say that there is a need for support for X, but we don't have money to support X. However, if we did have money we would first of all support X. After all, the Council was charged by the Congress to identify the needs of the arts in the country.

With this opinion in hand, Roger informed the Council at the May, 1966, meeting. It was decided that educational television would be the first use of available Treasury Fund money and funding the American Film Institute would be the second.

Another legal question was the problem of conflict of interest. Many of the members were involved with major cultural institutions. As already seen, Agnes De Mille was one of the pillars of the American Ballet Theatre. Roger and Anthony Bliss were on the board of the Met Opera. Oliver Smith was a board member of American Ballet Theatre. Phil Hanes was on several boards. Some organizations similar to the Arts Endowment bar their trustees from receiving grants. Roger and the Council thought such a policy would keep people from accepting the President's invitation to serve as Council members. Conversely, if members of the Council were allowed to apply for grants and lobby for passage among the members, that would be unjust.

Roger, and Chuck Ruttenberg discussed the problem at length before resolving it to their satisfaction, and then it was put into legalese. Four simple rules were laid down: 1. No Council member could submit an application; 2. no Council member should receive any remuneration from any grant made to an organization with which the member is associated; 3. if a member has any participation in a Council grant project, that involvement is to be clearly spelled out in the application; 4. members will leave the room when such projects are discussed.

The May meeting of the Council was also the occasion for welcoming a new member. David Brinkley had resigned because he felt he could not participate fully in the work. He was on call for assignments from NBC and could not be available for Council projects or meetings. He said his body and soul belonged to NBC. In his place President Johnson appointed our 1962 Nobel Laureate John Steinbeck. He, like all the appointees at this time, participated in the deliberations immediately, expressing himself in his characteristic guttural speech, forging insights of value.

At the gatherings after the formal meetings, John Steinbeck, Harper Lee, and Ralph Ellison, the three writers, huddled together and drank vodka. Steinnbeck had a difficult speech defect after he drank for awhile. Ralph Ellison had a serious stutter. Harper, called Nell, was the only one of the three who was understandable after some time.

One conversation with Steinbeck was memorable. I happened to mention I thought his novel *In Dubious Battle* was his best work, but I couldn't remember the title at the time. He couldn't remember the title either. However, he said he thought it was one of his best books, too, but the critics didn't like it. At the time of publication, he said, most critics were either leaning toward fascism or communism and the rightist critics called it communistic, and the leftists called it fascistic. Consequently, the book never enjoyed a large sale.

Then, suddenly, he began reciting stanzas from Milton's "Paradise Lost" for the purpose of finding the lost title. When he found Milton's words "in dubious battle" he smiled and said, "that's it." He couldn't remember the title of his own novel, but he could remember whole chunks of "Paradise Lost."

Steinbeck was a friend of Charlie Chaplin's when Chaplin lived in Los Angeles. He told me one time that Chaplin was easily influenced by H. G. Wells, who was also living nearby. It was H. G. Wells who talked Chaplin into embracing the Communist position on a second front during World War Two, the statements that caused Chaplin to be harassed by the Congressional committees and contributed greatly to the reasons he left and went back to Europe. Steinbeck said he could always tell when Chaplin had had dinner with Wells the night before because of the new ideas he would spout.

But this was the meeting at which I was, for the first time, describing and defending a program wholly my own. When the grants to the states came up on the agenda, suddenly all eyes were focusing on me. The Council had spent little time discussing the state program and I had little understanding of their attitude toward it. I decided the best method by which to learn their attitude would be to suggest a motion of approval of all grants and listen to any discussion which might follow. Roger entertained a motion and one was made and seconded. No one objected and no one praised the program. I spoke of the 295 separated projects to be carried out in the states under these grants and found no curiosity among the members. I mentioned that our investment of $1.3 million in state arts projects would generate an additional $1.7 million in matching funds for a total of $3 million. Mild approval was expressed. Stanley Young called for the vote and my program was passed and established without a single objection or hurrah after about ten minutes of consideration. I never understood how $2 million in grants could generate so little excitement, or even interest.

Three grants reviewed for reapproval had long-term significance. One was a $5,000 grant to Ralph Black, who was at that time the Managing Director of the National Ballet based in Washington, D.C. At the time, there existed no national service organization serving dance. The grant was to cover the expense of a national conference of dance companies, both ballet and modern, with the hope a service organization would evolve. The conference was scheduled for a hotel in New York.

I arrived late at the hotel on the morning the conference was to begin. I left my bag at the hotel desk and went straight to the first plenary session. From the beginning there was struggle. Dancers are not known as team players outside the practice studio and offstage; they tend to be suspicious of each other and of all cooperative plans. After the first two hours I realized good reasons existed why orchestras, theatre and opera companies had their national associations and dance companies didn't.

As the day wore on and more people rose to object to the previous speaker who had objected to someone else. Rumors began to surface. One group had it on good authority that Ralph Black wanted a national association for dance so he could raid other companies to sign dancers for his company. Another group denied this, but insisted I was behind this meeting so the Endowment for the Arts could award a large grant to all dance companies. My denial was met with jeers and laughs. The third rumor was the co-chairman of the conference, Hy Fain, Executive Secretary of the Amalgamated Guild of Musical Artists (AGMA), the dancers' union, wanted an organization so he could unionize all dancers.

By afternoon, Ralph Black was becoming totally frustrated and angry. I suggested adjournment until the morning.

Out of a total attendance of perhaps 200, more than half were from New York. However, many of the managers and artistic directors present hadn't seen each other in a long time and the rooms that night were filled with parties. A number of New Yorkers were staying the night in the rooms of the out of towners.

I decided the only salvation of the objective was to lobby among the cooler and most respected heads. Leon Kalimos, manager of the San Francisco Ballet, and choreographer Alwin Nikolias were two I felt most capable of knocking sense into the paranoid.

With them and alone I went from room to room, party to party, denying rumors and stating that the Endowment's only interest was in having a dance umbrella organization comparable to orchestras and theatres. The process took all night.

In the morning the wiser heads took over the leadership and the Association of American Dance Companies was proposed and adopted. I heaved a sigh of relief, picked up my bag from the front desk, paid for the room I never occupied, and flew back to Washington.

(The Association of American Dance Companies had a number of good years after a shaky start and then was dissolved for lack of an active and cooperative membership.)

Another reapproved grant—that is, a grant that Roger tentatively approved, but required the advice of the Council—was a $50,000 grant to The Opera Company of Boston. The evidence was that it would have ceased to exist if the Endowment hadn't been able to meet this emergency.

The third grant was also an emergency. The American P.E.N. organization (representing poets, playwrights, essayists and novelists) had never been a strong organization when compared to its counterpart in other countries. However, new leadership had managed to interest some of our nation's most notable authors in participating and had offered to host the next international conference. The problem was money. P.E.N. had never managed a budget larger than $9,000, but the conference would require $200,000. The Ford Foundation had pledged $75,000, Rockefeller Brothers Fund another $25,000, the P.E.N. membership $12,000, and an additional number of smaller gifts had been raised. The needed difference was $40,000. The grant was recommended by the Council and it was a true turning point for the organization which has been strong ever since.

When another problem arose with the P.E.N. conference, Roger was able to help. Certain writers who wished to attend were denied visas by the State Department because they were alleged Communists. This had never been a problem in other Western countries, so it was bad foreign cultural relations for our country. In particular, this focused on a certain South American poet who frequently wrote anti-American works. Roger prevailed through his White House connections and all invitees were automatically allowed to attend.

Subsequently, that poet went back to South America and wrote so enthusiastically about what he had seen of this country that he was later expelled from the Communist Party.

It was about this time Roger returned from a quick trip to London with an astounding story. He had read in the London papers that American financier Joseph Hirshhorn was in England negotiating with Lord Perth for Great Britain's acquisition of his enormous collection of contemporary art. The proposal being discussed was for the construction of a separate museum in Hyde Park to house the collection, the estimated value of which was in excess of sixty million dollars.

Roger was able to contact Joe Hirshhorn and persuade him to postpone a decision until Roger could arrange for a definite proposal from the United States. Hirshhorn had said he had tried negotiating with both the U.S. and Canada and neither country wanted to meet his wishes. Roger asked if he had ever talked with President Johnson about his wishes. Hirshhorn said no. Roger said he would talk to the President about a meeting.

When he told me the story on the morning of his return he was concerned about whether he could interest the President in such a proposal considering the negative response Hirshhorn had gotten from other officials earlier. However, President Johnson was enthusiastic and in typical Johnsonian fashion made the situation more attractive by suggesting he and Lady Bird have an intimate dinner for the Hirshhorns in the White House.

A dinner was arranged. Roger and Christine were in attendance. After dinner President Johnson suggested he and Joe Hirshhorn go up to the family quarters for a little talk about what it would take for the Hirshhorn collection to reside in this country. Roger said he never would forget the sight of five foot four Hirshhorn and six foot four Johnson ascending the stairs with the President's arm around the tiny man's shoulders.

When they returned to the guests below the deal had been verbally negotiated: a museum named after Hirshhorn on the Mall in exchange for the outright gift of the collection to the Smithsonian. Congress voted the necessary legislation as agreed to that night at the dinner.

If Roger had not been in London, if Hirshhorn had not basically preferred America to another country, if Roger had not promised the President's interest, if President Johnson had not been interested after all, and if the President had rejected the proposal, we might all have to travel a long way to see that magnificent collection. Instead, it resides in a wonderfully airy and accessible museum by Gordon Bunshaft along side other great museums on the Mall in D.C.

(In 1970, an inquiry was launched in the Congress concerning the character of Joe Hirshhorn. Various charges were leveled but never substantiated, including accusations involving Hirshhorn's money dealings with Canada, his tax deductibility for the gift of his collection, and his general reputation. I had just launched the Arts Reporting Service at the time and having been privy to the original deal was intensely interested in why the hearings were being held at this time.

I started my own investigation and discovered a coalition of various forces trying to negate the original deal. I wrote a series of articles in ARS which were entered by S. Dillon Ripley, Secretary of the Smithsonian, into the record of the hearings. Somehow the Hirshhorns learned of the articles, invited me to Greenwich to see the collection at their house before it was moved to Washington, and spend an afternoon with them. We became friends.)

Fertilizing the Grassroot
And Untold Tales of 1966

Growing up on the Southside of Milwaukee didn't provide much of an education about the history of Wisconsin and the Wisconsin Idea of the La Follettes. However, with the GI Bill under my arm and a bus ticket to the University of Wisconsin, I learned about the long tradition of using the state university to serve all the people of the state. The LaFollette slogan was "The boundaries of the state are borders of the university."

The arts were part of that tradition. The University of Wisconsin had the first artist-in-residence, not to be on campus, but to be out and around the state teaching rural people the skills of the visual arts. John Stuart Curry was one of the first Wisconsin artists. When I attend the university Aaron Bohrod was in residence and out and about the state. Every winter the Student Union had the Rural Art Exhibition, works by farmers and small town dwellers created during the cold winters. The Pro Arte Quartet was also in residence along with a pianist to provide free concerts around the state.

Robert A. Gard was brought to the U. of Wisconsin from Cornell to found The Wisconsin Idea Theatre. By 1966, he had had 20 years experience with motivating and inspiring the small towns of the state to form amateur theatre groups and creative writing groups, and he had a dream. He wanted to promote the arts throughout the state through newspaper ads and meetings to find out what people in these towns wanted from the arts. Bob Gard was an old friend, so when the Endowment was established he called me and told me of his idea. It was when I went to see him about it that the Chancellor of the university sidetracked me into trying to influence the governor.

Bob Gard submitted a formal proposal in time for the May, 1966, meeting of the Council. Since I handled those proposals that involved more than one art form as well as the Federal-State Partnership Program, the proposal fell under my responsibility. I believed in Bob Gard's dream. I was convinced that the future growth and solid foundation for cultural progress had to be formed from the grassroots activities of the general populace. As long as arts activities were enjoyed, supported, and controlled by the current small minority of middle and upper class patrons, our cultural life would be a sometime thing. If we truly believe the arts were essential to the human spirit, could make our lives fuller and richer, then we were obligated to try to bring them to the people who had been ignored until now.

The presentation to the Council read in part:

> *"This sort of project is urgently needed in order to gain some perspective on the vast gray area known as "grassroots art." Many of the states receiving funds under Section 5.(h) of the Foundation Act are largely rural. No plans, systems, or perspectives exist at present to determine the value of programs proposed by these states. After a study, such as this one, has been largely completed, the Endowment can then encourage other states to make use of the techniques and successful projects developed as a means of providing more meaningful programs for their rural areas. Until such a study is completed, or at least well under way, and some conclusions reached, it is recommended that all amateur, or grassroots projects be denied, unless they are of a similar developmental nature."*

This presentation was written with these arguments for specific reasons. Most of the members of the Council at that time were greatly concerned about the arts institutions with which they were involved. In 1966 costs were rising rapidly and support for the arts in general was at a low ebb. Their focus was on the survival of national institutions such as American Ballet Theatre, Metropolitan Opera, and the resident theatres across the country. Though the Council as a whole had an astounding perspective on the overall cultural needs of the country, specific proposals that were not aimed at alleviating the crisis in major institutions tended to receive less enthusiasm.

It was true that many of the states were planning rural projects and in addition we were inundated with applications from small, semi-professional, and amateur organizations. Roger liked the proposal because I said we could deny all other grassroots projects for three years until this study and pilot project were completed. I stated in the presentation that the states could more effectively use their mandated grants, if the study gave them guidance.

Nevertheless, when "The Smaller Community and Rural Arts Project" came up for discussion the reaction was completely negative. Some of the Council members were amused that we should even propose to spend $58,000 a year for three years on such a project. Roger, realizing I was intensely interested in the project and that it would be rejected if a vote were taken, declared a recess for lunch.

Leonard Bernstein had not attended the morning session, but he arrived during the lunch break. Before the afternoon session he asked me to review the morning's business. When I told him the rural arts project had been tabled he told me that was one reason why he wanted to come to the meeting. I thought he was another negative vote, but he said he read the full proposal and he thought it important.

When the session resumed, Roger tried to ignore the project, but eventually he had to allow it to come to the floor. Bernstein listened to me debating with most of the

Council and then raised his hand to speak. After a dramatic pause he said, "This project has nothing to do with art, but it has everything to do with why we are sitting here." He then went on most eloquently to describe the need to break out of the elite image the arts now hold and to make the arts available to all our citizens wherever they reside. He talked about building audiences by introducing people to the complexities of the arts through hands-on experiences and the nurturing of latent talent, how artists are discovered in the most unlikely places. In short, this man who represented art in its highest form was an unexpected and effective ally of Bob Gard's concept of developing the inherent need for a creative outlet in all people.

When he finished the attitude of the Council had been reversed and the project was passed unanimously.

In the long run it became one of our more sustaining accomplishments. Roger became an advocate as he saw the outreach programs of the less populated states blossom and develop. The final report of the project resulted in a slim book, *The Arts and the Small Community,* that has been reprinted several times and is today the inspirational source for small community and rural programs throughout the country.

Council members Isaac Stern and Warner Lawson became interested in another grassroots project, a method of teaching music which was at that time comparatively unknown in this country. The system was developed by Zoltan Kodaly in Hungary. The claim was that one could stop any person on the street in Hungary under thirty years of age and ask them to sight read a piece of music and they could do it. Children were taught to read music accurately from pre-school onwards through their elementary education. Using a system of hand signals, children learned to recognize pitch and intervals on the scale.

The proposed project was an attempt to adapt the Kodaly method to American music, since one of the keys to its success was the fact the system used Hungarian folk music familiar to every child. Ten selected people, already trained in music education, were to be sent to Hungary to work with teachers of the Kodaly method. They would collectively adapt the system, and when they returned to this country they would train others.

The project passed and received a $50,000 commitment, eventually a total of $91,000 was invested in the project. Partly as a result, the Kodaly method of music instruction is now known and taught in quite a few private music schools.

This meeting discussed and tabled an elaborate program designed to help young musical artists become established in their careers and build audiences for them. The program proved to be too expensive for our budget and too elaborate in administration. Meanwhile, during a blizzard in Beloit, Wisconsin, an almost identical program was being berthed by accident.

At a scheduled Beloit Concert Series concert only about a dozen people braved the snow storm. The young baritone felt he had an obligation to perform, though it seemed bizarre for a man in white tie and tails to sing lieder to a dozen people in snow coats, galoshes and mufflers. After a number or two, the young man opened his tie, and began talking with the audience about his life as an artist and about music. Soon, he was sitting on the edge of the stage and the audience members had moved to a circle at the front of the auditorium. He talked and sang, they asked questions, and everyone went away feeling this was a different and well worthwhile experience.

From that accidental beginning, Affiliate Artists, Inc. grew. Young artists in music, dance, theatre, folklore, and so forth, are contracted to a community organization and present informal "informances" a la the Beloit experience. The Endowment invested $130,000 in Affiliate Artists during its earliest years. Part of those funds were Treasury Funds made possible by an $80,000 contribution from the Sears-Roebuck Foundation.

This was also the meeting when the first grants to the regional theatres were voted. The grants ranged from $6,000 to $125,000.

These were satisfying and memorable projects, but the real excitement and stress took place between Council meetings.

The cartoonists of America, both comic strip and political, desperately wanted to have a Museum of American Cartooning in Washington, preferably on the Mall next to the National Gallery of Art.

They had a loose association that was inspired to campaign for such a museum. They wrote to President Johnson requesting to meet with him and discuss their desires. The President agreed, but then discovered some important business that took priority—a technique often employed by Johnson—and he told the cartoonists the Vice President would take his place. As it turned out, Vice President Humphrey was sent to a funeral someplace and couldn't make the meeting either. The cartoonists were told they would meet with Roger Stevens, the President's Special Assistant for the Arts.

They were angry.

Roger didn't know they were angry. He took me along to the meeting which was held in a conference room in the Executive Office Building. They of course thought they would at least be meeting in the White House proper, so that was further reason for feeling they were slighted.

When we walked into the room we saw perhaps twenty well dressed men sitting around the large table in silence with looks of quite definite annoyance. At each place was a legal pad and freshly sharpened pencil provided by the White House. Introductions were made. Walt Kelly, Rube Goldberg, Milton Caniff, Hal Foster, and most of the prominent political cartoonists of the day were present.

Roger told those he recognized how much he had enjoyed their work over the years and apologized for the absence of the President and Vice President. No one smiled. He began talking about the Endowment and how little money we were given by the Congress, and how influential they could be in increasing that amount in years to come. They picked up on this line and said if they had a museum in Washington they could be very friendly, but if they were rejected they could be unfriendly in their work. I had remained silent. I noticed that though all these men made their living with paper and pen, none of them had made a move to doodle or draw on the pads that had been provided. They sat with their hands far from the tools before them.

The meeting was deteriorating rapidly. They were venting their anger and disappointment as Roger continued to try his best to break the icy atmosphere. When he had finished saying that the so called cultural explosion of this Administration was largely exaggerated and more talk than substance, I saw an opportunity to inject a bit of lightness into the discussion by trying one of my old lines from speeches I had made.

I said, "The cultural explosion has been more or less a shot heard 'round the room."

They all laughed. One of them said that was a good line. Another said so-and-so would probably use it next week. Humor and word play broke through and they suddenly became animated. One by one several of them picked up the pencils or drew pens from their pocket and we began to have a friendly conversation free of threats and threatening looks. When the meeting was over several presented Roger with signed caricatures they had sketched.

Roger promised to arrange a meeting with the Secretary of the Smithsonian, S. Dillon Ripley. This was done and they were offered a place in one of the Mall museums.

The other untold tale was much more serious and could have resulted in a profound setback for the arts had circumstances been slightly altered and had Lady Luck been away for the weekend.

One of the projects that had come from the fertile mind of Isaac Stern was a plan to establish what he called the Master Chamber Orchestra. The avowed primary purpose was to build orchestral leadership for all the orchestras in the country. The idea consisted of recruiting potential leaders from the major orchestras to play in the master chamber orchestra where all the players alternated taking musical responsibility. Players were to be restricted to a two year tenure and then returned to their regular orchestras, with the hope they would be better able to carry a leadership role. The secondary benefit was that this would be an excellent chamber orchestra which would tour and concertize in places usually away from the tour routes of the major orchestras. It was a good plan and much needed according to the music people who endorsed the project. Alexander Schneider was to be the music director.

However, the plan was not the reality. Sasha Schneider took an ad in the musicians' union newspaper recruiting musicians from the major orchestras and offering more salary and benefits than most musicians were receiving at the time. The orchestras saw this as seducing their best players. The promise of touring was seen as competition from a government sponsored orchestra. Since symphony orchestras had opposed the Endowment because they feared government interference, this project seemed to confirm their worst fears.

Orchestra managers and conductors paraded through our office like troops passing in review; each one stayed just long enough to damn the project and invoke the name of his Congressman. Yet, the project went forward; Schneider and Stern saying it will all quiet down. Besides, no one wanted to set a precedent of abandoning a project because of a little opposition.

With this background, chapter two of the chamber orchestra debacle can begin. I was in New York on one of my routine visits to the Ford Foundation. At the Foundation, the receptionist always offered the use of a telephone while waiting for one's appointment. I had no need to call my office, but it would fill the time, so I did. My secretary told me it was urgent I call Sy Rosen at the American Symphony Orchestra League (ASOL). Okay. I called. Sy said he couldn't talk then, but there was real trouble. He asked me to stay where I was and he would call back in a few minutes.

When he did he told me that Helen Thompson, the League's Executive Secretary, had written a letter to all board members of symphony orchestras, all conductors and managers, and assorted others, asking them to write President Johnson demanding that he stop the master chamber orchestra project. Further, that one representative chosen by the orchestras be immediately made a member of the National Council on the Arts, and that all future music projects be first approved by the ASOL. The letter had been reproduced and printed, and Sy's assignment for the day was to see that the letter got into the mail by close of business. Helen Thompson was leaving for New York momentarily to put her demands before Herman Kenin, Council member and International President of the American Federation of Musicians.

Ouch, was my first word. I realized many of the conservative trustees of orchestras opposed our programs and I also realized many prominent family names were among the trustees of orchestras. The White House staff would recognize many of those names as important people in their communities, the kind of people a President hoping for re-election doesn't want to alienate. And if Helen prevailed in her direct onslaught, the idea of a totally independent federal arts agency would be seriously damaged. We would be vulnerable to attack by every national arts association at every turn.

Sy obviously knew the trouble the letter could cause. He said Helen was so adamant that it would mean his job, if the letter did not go out. I said I would do my best to stop it.

Sy Rosen was not a neophyte. He was a trained symphonic musician, playing the double bass, who turned to management as more suiting his temperament. He had successfully managed the Buffalo Philharmonic and a few other smaller orchestras. He took the job at the ASOL at the urging of people he respected who more or less forced him on Helen. It was generally believed the ASOL needed to be more responsive to membership opinion and not so subservient to Helen and he was supposed to be in charge of orchestra relations. Helen kept undercutting him. He was tortured by the position and frustrated by Helen's management style.

I immediately tried to reach Roger, but he was out of the office and wasn't expected back until afternoon. I couldn't escape the appointments I had made in New York. I called Sy again to urge him to stall until Roger could be apprised of the situation and talk to Helen.

I kept calling Roger from his office in New York and finally reached him around five in the afternoon. I briefly explained the situation and listened to him explode. I told him he could hear the text of the letter from Sy and suggested he call Sy. I cautioned him not to explode at Sy because he was a hero for bringing the whole thing to our attention.

Liv Biddle later reported the phone conversation between Roger and Sy. Roger would listen for awhile, then explode, then remember Sy was on our side, and calm down, then explode again, and repeat the pattern.

Roger reached Helen Thompson at Herman Kenin's office in New York. He quietly explained to her that no one can dictate to the federal government and force their will on it. He said if she circulated that letter, President Johnson would insist that the chamber orchestra project continue and she and the league would be considered nonpersons for the rest of this Administration. However, if she withdrew the letter, the project was going to be dropped anyway because it had caused such a stir among the orchestras. She called Sy and told him to destroy the letter and at the same time fired him.

The project was dropped at the next meeting of the Council over Isaac Stern's strenuous objection.

Roger's speech addressing the necessity for opposing a Council member for the first time was emotionally charged. He spoke of the compatible relationship we all had, and the pain of making decisions which hurt well intended people. He compared his unpleasant present task to that of a submarine commander required to order the submarine to dive while knowing some crew members were on deck and would be lost at sea because of his action; an action necessary to save the ship and the majority of the crew. Then he said, "Isaac, I'm terribly sorry."

I didn't think he needed to apologize to Isaac because Isaac had allowed the project to get out of hand.

Sy Rosen went on to manage the Pittsburgh Symphony, the Philadelphia Orchestra, and Carnegie Hall. Helen Thompson was retired a few years later.

By this time Roger was feeling comfortable in his role as the most closely observed man in the country by the cultural community and the arts press. Up until now he had studiously avoided major pronouncements concerning the needs of the arts and trying to explain the arts world to the general public. The print media had been consistent in requesting him to express his deepest thoughts about the job ahead and his beliefs.

He had given a number of interviews and his speeches had been reported widely, but to date he avoided putting his thoughts and philosophy into print. However, after the Endowment actually was established and the Council had a substantial number of projects underway, it seemed time to tell the country what had been wrought and what might be expected. In the light of the criticism of the 1989–90 period, his deep concern for artistic quality seems all the more important.

Saturday Review was chosen as the vehicle and in the March 12, 1966 issue, Roger wrote a piece called, "The State of the Arts: a 1966 Balance Sheet." In it he expressed his observations about the performing arts and the domination of the East and West Coasts. He pointed out that only the major cities scattered throughout the country could really boast of a high-caliber cultural life. He said that this situation could be changed by private local efforts in combination with state and federal assistance. He praised the state program as one to stimulate local efforts; the beginning of a change of attitude on his part toward the federal-state partnership.

Roger kept expressing two truisms over and over until finally they became generally accepted in government and among the conservative patrons. He repeatedly pointed out that artists only agreed on their total inability to agree on anything concerning the merits of a work of art. The expect unanimity from artists and critics was folly. The second fact of artistic life was that people not in the arts found it difficult to understand the right of the artist to fail. Roger wrote that the public expects only great books to be written, only great plays to be produced and great music to be composed, only masterpieces should be painted, but it doesn't happen that way. At other times he used that argument with Congressional committees, pointing out that scientists were heros for failing in their experiments dozens of times before they succeeded, but artists were expected to sit down and create genius work spontaneously.

In the article, Roger implied that neither he nor anyone else could define the perfect relationship between federal, state, and private resources, that we are embarking on a new enterprise the results of which will not be known for some time.

The article was typical of Roger's personality and beliefs. He believed most strongly in his heart that the arts had made his life more interesting and richer, and was convinced every life could be so enhanced. His first and deepest love was for books and from literature came his deep commitment to theatre and all the other arts.

He was also a pragmatist. He believed federal programs could often help, but private, state local government resources and energies were absolutely essential to progress. The response of the states to the state program was beginning to influence his thinking and separating him from the general thinking of the Council. As I reported state legislature after legislature voting for a council and appropriating state funds for a program. Roger began to mention my program more and more with the Council members and the politicians. Congresspeople were also aware that people back home had embraced a program which none thought to be more than an added provision which might be embraced by the more urban, arts-oriented states like New York and California, but certainly not by their state.

At the heart of Roger's stewardship of the federal arts program was an unshakable demand for the highest standards of art as manifested in the most imaginative and specific terms. When that stewardship passed to other chairmen, no successor to date has possessed that profound instinctive understanding of all the arts. He could read the description of a project and immediately determine the aesthetic value, the long term impact, and the practicality of its execution. When Roger erred on rare occasions, it wasn't a misjudgment of the aesthetic component, it was a lack of understanding of the social or political ingredients.

(Conversely, Nancy Hanks, who became the Endowment's chairman in 1969, seldom erred on political or social ingredients, but made aesthetic and management errors whenever she imposed her judgement on an idea. Fortunately, she was perceptive enough to seldom indulge her artistic judgement. She was superb at lobbying and at handling public relations, whether it was the Congress, President Nixon, a cultural organization, or the general public, but her aesthetic judgement was in poverty.)

Another Day, Another Dollar
Fiscal Year—1967

On May 31, 1966, President Johnson signed the appropriations bill that gave us $4 million in general program funds, $2 million for the state program, and all the left over amount in the Treasury Fund from the previous year, or nearly $2 million for the fiscal year beginning July 1, 1966. All our funds, except the administration money was "no year money." In government terms that meant the funds from one year were automatically carried over into the next year; ordinarily government appropriations which are not spent within one year revert to the Treasury. This policy tends to encourage departments and agencies to spend their full appropriations so next year will bring an increase. The belief is that funds not spent means they are not needed and Congress will appropriate less money the next year.

Evidence of increased available funds and activity on the part of the Council can be seen in the size of workbooks sent to Council members in advance of each meeting. Since the Council was obliged to advise on every application for a grant, the books reflected more requests and more proposals. The book for the August meeting of the Council had nearly twice the number of pages as the book for the previous meeting.

The meeting was held in Washington in our own building. Word spread through the building that world famous artists would be roaming the halls. People who worked for other agencies and private firms lined the hallways outside the room where our meeting was in session. It disturbed me to see these people fawn on the movie stars when we broke for lunch and ignore the artists who had given the world more permanent gifts; John Steinbeck, Agnes De Mille, Richard Diebenkorn passed unnoticed.

Materials for this meeting indicate the Poets-in-the Schools project was more successful than imagined. In New York, the Academy of American Poets had requests from 200 additional schools to share in the "Poetry in the Classroom" pilot project. Several newspapers and leading magazines had praised the project. In the end, the expanded Artists-in-Schools program became one of the largest of all the Council's efforts.

A worthwhile program that flourished for a number of years and then faded was the American Playwrights Theatre Program (APT). Under this arrangement new plays were selected by a team of experts and sent to the 153 subscribing university, community, and resident professional theatres. If 25 or more theatres agreed to produce one of the selected plays, the playwright was given a $25,000 award, plus production royalties. "The Night Thoreau Spent in Jail" was one popular play produced under this program.

The International Theatre Institute Congress which had never met in our country before was awarded a grant. Perhaps one of the important accomplishments of the Endowment in early days was the establishment of a precedent supporting international arts conferences. Since those early grants, several have been held in this country and as a result the U.S. joined other nations in sharing international cultural concerns for the first time.

One of the stone walls the Council kept banging against was the unimportance that courses in the arts were given by colleges when high school graduates applied for admission. Standard admission tests ignored the arts and high school arts credits weren't counted toward admission. The Council sponsored studies and lobbied for changes, but to no avail. The universities claimed the high schools needed to give importance to the arts and then they would have to recognize such credits. The national high school associations claimed that if the colleges would recognize arts credits they would encourage students to follow their arts inclinations.

By the 1980s the tide of that battle had begun to turn. College entrance examinations began to recognize arts credits in many places and several states legislated minimal mandatory arts credits for high school graduation. The change was brought about by effective influence from the state arts councils and the militant pursuit of such goals by the art educators throughout the country.

One of the arts institutions looked upon today as effective in building audiences and giving young singers and musicians an opportunity to advance their careers had its genesis at this meeting. The San Francisco Opera director, Kurt Herbert Adler, proposed the establishment of "a small, flexible opera ensemble for performing both condensed and full length versions of operas for an ever-widening circle of schools, neighborhood, and community organizations . . . and in smaller 'grass roots' areas where opera on a large scale is not feasible." The request was for $211,000 an amount to be matched by private funds by San Francisco Opera. From this successful first step grew the Western Opera Theatre which has played to audiences throughout the country and inspired other opera companies to establish similar small, outreach companies.

A later incident involving Western Opera Theatre (WOT) illustrated the attitude that was dominant in some parts of the country at that time. WOT was booked to play a high school in Orange County, California. The business manager called me to say the booking had been cancelled by the school superintendent because the company was operating in part on federal funds and he wouldn't have federally supported "socialist" organizations appearing in any of his schools. When the music supervisor protested and said the money was available in the budget for such outside attractions to enrich the students' experience, the superintendent substituted a patriotic song singing contest among all the schools, culminating in a festival of patriotic songs at one of the schools.

I called the superintendent and tried to explain our participation was minimal, that the San Francisco Opera was supported by several millions of free enterprise, all-American dollars and that the hard-working-American taxpayer had voted through their representatives to help out struggling, inventive arts enterprises. He wouldn't budge. Then I reminded him that transporting students to his patriotic song festival would require the students traveling over highways subsidized largely by federal funds. How could he allow that? He hung up.

One of the projects underway was an annual literary anthology of the best writing found in the small magazines of the country. The plans were elaborate to insure fairness and comprehensive coverage of the vast field. Editors of the leading literary magazines were invited to submit the work of three authors published by them in the previous year. A distinguished panel would select the pieces to appear in the anthology. Each author would receive $1,000 and the editors who originally published the work would receive $500. Seven leading publishers agreed to publish each anthology on an annual rotating basis.

Although the anthologies received a warm reception from the nation's literary critics and proved popular with readers, the program never reached all seven of the willing publishers. In 1970 the anthology became a cause celebre in Congress because of a poem published in *Anthology/2*. The poem was one word "lighght" which some Congressmen thought meaningless and that $1,000 was an exorbitant price to pay for one word. The "lighght" debate expanded to examining other works in *Anthology/2* where some explicit sexual writing was found and then these Congressmen saw a chance to investigate the whole Endowment. Nancy Hanks, who had succeeded Roger as Chairman with the Nixon election in 1968, promised to stop producing literary anthologies, if the Congress would stop investigating. It was the first example of political interference by the legislature that resulted in a victory for the politicians.

Comparing the political battles of those days with the war that raged in 1990 seems like comparing grapefruit to a grape. The Roger Stevens approach was to remind the political foes of the provision in the legislation prohibiting any federal official from interfering with the artistic decisions of the endowment. Nancy Hanks approach consisted of immediate surrender. She would apologize and promise never to do it again, if Congress would call off the dogs.

The Association of American Dance Companies, the Council was told, was now a reality; the first national service organization for dance. Officers had been elected, projects outlined, and a timetable approved. The Council voted $25,000 to start the group on its way.

The Council had also approved the formation of the Coordinating Council of Literary Magazines, another cultural group greatly in need of a national service organization. CCLM was used for a number of years to make small grants to large and small magazines for special projects.

Again at the August, 1966 meeting, a project referred to as the Drawing Project was supported with an estimated $150,000. As described to the Council the concept was to commission 100 contemporary artists to create original drawings and to select 50 existing drawings from museum collections for mass distribution to high schools, art centers, and other educational facilities. A panel of curators would select the artists and extant drawings and also write a text to accompany each set. The project was presented and approved, reported on, but it was never carried out. No reason was ever given, nor was it officially rescinded. A similar project in which painters would create prints—lithograph, silk screen, etchings, etc.—which would be reproduced and sold at $5 per print to nonprofit educational and arts institutions was also approved but never carried out.

At the back of the presentation book for this meeting was a section on future projects for the Council to consider. One of the projects briefly outlined approached the subject of touring for dance companies. "Recommended for further investigation was a program whereby professional dance companies would tour and not only give formal performances but in each place visited give lecture demonstrations as well. The New York State Council on the Arts has set a pattern for this which might be followed." From this beginning came the Dance Touring Program which has been credited by many dance critics and arts managers as one of the major reasons the audience for dance grew from one million to eleven million during the decade from 1970 to 1980.

The most important and difficult project having its genesis with this meeting was the artists housing project. The J. M. Kaplan Fund of New York was awarded $100,000 by the Council to be matched by Kaplan funds to develop plans for an artists' housing project. To quote from the minutes of the August, 1966, meeting of the National Council on the Arts: "The artists' housing is a program of housing on a co-op or rental basis to artists for the purpose of living and working in a single unit . . . . $100,000."

What seemed like a simple, straightforward project turned out to be the most complicated and frustrating enterprise we attempted when it got underway.

The sixth meeting ended with a farewell salute to those members who were leaving because of expired terms: Agnes De Mille, who was always in the forefront of every discussion and on the side of the originating artist; Eleanor Lambert, from the Council of Fashion Designers, who seldom spoke, remaining aloof from the other members; Elizabeth Ashley, the tough minded actress with the quick tongue, who never hesitated to express herself; Ralph Ellison, the novelist with the most penetrating mind I've ever known, who added a larger dimension to every discussion; Fr. Gilbert Hartke, the dedicated theatre teacher who knew everyone in the country and kept their names alive; Gregory Peck, sincere, serious, tough minded, who chewed ideas thrice before digesting them; Otto Wittmann, the museum professional who knew not to try his intellect in other areas of art; and Stanley Young, an embracing bear of a man who added wit and broad knowledge to many discussions and always had the right warm word. Roger urged the departing members not to abandon the Council but to keep attending meetings. Almost all attended future meetings. Camaraderie had been built in those 18 months.

Settling Down and Unsettling Events
Into the Second Year—1967

On September 29, 1966, the National Foundation on the Arts and Humanities celebrated its first anniversary with a White House press conference attended by President Johnson. Prior to the conference President Johnson met privately with Roger and Barnaby Keeney, who was now installed as the Chairman of the Humanities Endowment. Keeney took detailed materials relating to the programs in the humanities which he presented to the President. The President seemed only mildly interested. Roger presented him with a book of press clippings on our programs in the one year of our existence. President Johnson grew animated and spent considerable time browsing through them and reading the favorable press. Roger told me later the President praised both endowments for the excellent accomplishments, but commented that acceptance by the press and the public was especially gratifying.

The academic approach to a political opportunity was typical of Keeney and the Humanities Endowment. Their office was filled with scholars of note but few of the world-wise. The quotation most often used by both endowments to explain the difference between the two was this: "If you study it, write about it, think about it, or criticize it, you're a humanist. If you actually do it, you're an artist." Also, Barnaby Keeney was constantly underestimating Roger simply because Roger didn't hold a PhD. They would sit down to negotiate some issue and Roger would defeat Barnaby before he had anotated his first footnote.

A few days after the anniversary date, *Chicago Tribune* Music Editor Tom Willis wrote:

"In the arts and in the field of education, President Johnson has made far-reaching, idealistic federal commitments without precedent. The arts in particular have received a series of shots in the arm which . . . are among the most creative fiscal allotments ever made. Taken in sum, they suggest a distinctively American plan for government aid to the arts which may overturn a good many notions and bromides. . . The remarkable fact is that the National Council on the Arts so far has been a muscular, fast-moving, and unorthodox arm of government which plants its punches where they likely will count most and wastes neither energy nor money . . . the council has created more excitement and less controversy than anyone had a right to expect."

The month before both Roger and I had been invited to attend the Second Annual Conference of the Rocky Mountain States Governors. Usually we didn't attend the same meetings because of a duplication of effort, but this was an important opportunity to get our messages across to seven states traditionally more concerned about conservation than culture. From the opening address by the host governor of Utah to the closing summary, the phrase heard most often in the public and private utterances was "the quality of life." We had come armed with our sales pitch about the joys and value of a cultural life and the responsibility of the states to support it, but we found no need to do anything but agree with the governors. They wanted us there to see how much we could contribute to the quality of life, not whether it was a good addition to their cooperative program.

Consequently, a division of the organization formed at that meeting—The Rocky Mountain Federation—was established to deal with arts and humanities programs and the Council awarded several grants for development projects over the next few years. From this beginning, the concept of regional states consortia developed that blanketed the country in later years.

Just before the first anniversary of the Endowment I went to Hawaii for the Governor's Conference on the Arts, one of forty I attended that year. Roger was invited to speak so we arranged to meet in San Francisco and take the same flight and do some work enroute. After the plane left San Francisco I made my way up to Roger in the first class section to begin work. The flight attendant informed us that wasn't allowed. Roger could go back to tourist class, but I couldn't go forward and upward. No vacant seats were available in tourist class. As we were in the process of trying to find someone to take Roger's seat in first class so he could sit with me in the peasant section, the pilot announced we were returning to San Francisco. He gave the usual excuse that a gauge was malfunctioning.

When we arrived on the ground we were greeted by one of United Airlines most smiling public relations women. She apologized in depth for the equipment failing us and said she knew we wanted to work; would we like a private office until the plane was repaired? We would. We were both confused about this sudden personal attention until we passed a newsstand and saw a full page photo on the front page of a tabloid of Roger and Mrs. Johnson. The headline read "First Lady Crosses Picket Line." Roger had escorted her to the San Francisco Opera the night before and they had to cross a picket line established by the striking musicians. The alert United Airlines PR women realized that the first-class passenger complaining on that flight was a VIP, hence the VIP treatment.

The work we needed so desperately to accomplish was for Roger to sign a number of letters prepared in his absence. We took care of this business in a few minutes and then read the magazines in the office belonging to some airport official until the flight was ready to resume. One of the letters was to President Marcos of the Philippines thanking him for a box of cigars. When we left the office I placed that letter on top. I handed the stack to the PR woman and asked her to drop them in a mail box. She glanced at the top letter and stuttered that she couldn't help but notice the addressee. Roger gave her a stern look and said she wasn't to mention it to anyone; it was confidential.

When we went to the gate to re-board, the woman handed us two new tickets and asked for our old ones back. These were both first class tickets side by side. She said she knew we had more work to do and we could just go on board now ahead of the other passengers. When the other passengers came on board we were already sipping Mai Tais.

On the five hour flight we managed to sip two or three of those smooth rum concoctions. The movie in flight starred Frank Sinatra. Roger kept asking who that was, but he seemed to know all the bit players who appeared. A bartender would have half a dozen lines and Roger would remember he once played a small part in a play he had produced ten years ago.

I enjoyed these long flights with Roger. He would be relaxed and expansive and tell stories of real estate deals and plays he produced. He would also talk shop and think of new schemes to try.

When we arrived in Honolulu Fred Preis, the executive director of the Hawaii Council and Masaru (Pundi) Yokouchi, the Chairman, were there to greet us with the usual leis and music. However, the hotel they had booked for us was unsatisfactory to Roger. It was one of those hastily built establishments filled with young people determined to vacation for two weeks twenty four hours a day. It was flimsy, noisy, and sandwiched in between two other hotels exactly like it. Somehow the Hawaii people had gotten the message from me that we were on a tight budget. The long flight, the sugary drinks, and the budget hotel all combined to make Roger grumpy. When our hosts asked what they could do to make him feel more comfortable I suggested the best Japanese dinner they could conjure up, because I wanted a Japanese dinner. Meanwhile, Roger managed to book one double room for the next night at the Royal Hawaiian Hotel.

The dinner was absolutely superb. It was at an authentic Japanese restaurant with about eight of the arts leaders of the islands. Roger passed on sushi and tried to use chop sticks and drink saki. His mood improved as the twenty-six courses were served.

The next day we checked into the Royal Hawaiian, attended the conference and both made our speeches. The next morning we swam and I left at noon to fly to Seattle, change clothes in the men's room, and catch a flight to Fairbanks, Alaska, where the temperature was 20 degrees. Roger stayed on in Honolulu another day.

A week later we got a big break. Bristol-Meyers made a $300,000 contribution to the Treasury Fund, the first large sum we received. The fact that Treasury Fund money was now earmarked for specific projects had made the difference as Roger predicted. Bristol-Meyers wanted to support the arts through public television and by this arrangement could double their contribution. We immediately called down the matching Treasury Fund money and funded several television programs. This of course was before the Corporation for Public Broadcasting Act had passed. It was also the first time in history that a corporation and the federal government had entered into a partnership in the arts. After that, corporations began to use the Treasury Fund as a simple way to fund their intended projects and double their money.

Also about this time David Rockefeller made a speech on the subject of corporate support for the arts. It is generally agreed his speech was the impetus that inspired the formation of the Business Committee for the Arts that has led corporate sponsorship from minuscule to nearly adequate. In an in-house history of the Endowment written at the end of the Johnson Administration it says, ". . . it is hoped that eventually business support for the arts will progress from its current sporadic and limited status to providing significant assistance." Business support did grow enormously because of the matching requirements of Endowment grants and close cooperation with the business community from the beginning of the federal program.

The first class of Council members had departed and on December 12, 1966, President Johnson released the names of those artists appointed to the Council to replace the departed members: Soprano Marian Anderson, fashion editor Nancy White, actress Helen Hayes, sculptor Jimilu Mason, landscape architect Lawrence Halprin, actor Charlton Heston, actor Sidney Poitier, and humanities professor Donald Weismann were appointed to six year terms.

The following evening, in the midst of a raging blizzard, President and Mrs. Johnson held a White House dinner for the new and former members of the Council. In his remarks that night the President said:

> *"We have learned that beauty and truth are the gold coins of international currency that make all nations richer for exchanging them. . . . Your government's pledge is now established as this nation's policy: to encourage the fullest growth of our artistic talents, to spread the fruits of that talent to all Americans, rich and poor. . . . We can call our task complete when the spotlight of our concern and the glow of our success fall equally on the top half and the grassroots. . . . So I ask those of you who came through the cold this evening to now join me in a toast to that great day, to a truly democratic culture, greater in glory for the arts, and to our best hope for both, the National Council on the Arts."*

> —LBJ Library; History of the
> National Endowment for the Arts

The next day the Council went into a two day meeting at the State Department. Reports on projects underway gave an insight into those which were later judged successful, those which were dropped for various reasons, and those which failed. For instance, $100,000 was allocated for an elaborate study and plans for a National Institute of Design which would include architecture, environmental design, as well as graphics, commercial products, etc. The study proved the project would be too complicated and expensive to be undertaken at this time. When increased funds were appropriated subsequent Endowment Chairmen did not revive the idea.

Projects in progress in dance were successful beyond expectations. Choreographers Alvin Ailey, Merce Cunningham, Martha Graham, Jose Limon, Alwin Nikolias, Anna Sokolow, Paul Taylor, and Anthony Tudor all produced works of quality with the small grants awarded them. By this time Martha Graham had completed her first tour of the country in 15 years. She played 32 cities from coast to coast and received rare reviews everywhere. The Council was also frequently mentioned.

Anna Sokolow was given a $10,000 grant to choreograph a new work. This was more money than she was accustomed to handling. When she went to her bank with the check to deposit it, the bank refused to believe her. It was necessary for her to have the bank call the Endowment offices to verify that indeed she was legally entitled to a $10,000 government check. Such were the conditions under which dancers and choreographers existed before the 1970s and 80s.

Literary programs were also doing well. The Poetry-in-the-Schools project was one year old at this time and had been so successful the Council had already voted additional funds to expand and extend it. Virtually every student in the New York City schools had had contact with this program. Nassau County in the New York suburbs was added. Pittsburgh and Detroit were beginning their sessions shortly. Poets W. H. Auden, Stanley Kunitz and Allen Tate were active in these pilot projects. The first ever individual grants to writers wholly for their own creative efforts by our government had been made. (WPA Writers Project paid writers to write state histories.)

Music programs were most active. The ill-fated Metropolitan Opera National Opera Company, a junior touring company, was kept alive by a $150,000 grant to play to high school and labor union audiences. The Boston Opera was in possession of a $50,000 emergency grant and the Young Musical Artists project was starting.

The first training program in arts management was a cooperative effort with the Office of Education Arts and Humanities Branch. Harvard was the site of the two week seminar on the management problems of arts institutions. The project to give sabbatical leaves to artists in residence on campuses to relieve them of academic obligations was well underway. The list included artists whose reputations have increased in later years. Among those in art, literature and music were Tom Cornell, Muriel Rukeyser, Vance Bourjailly, Mark Harris, W. D. Snodgrass, Edward Dahlberg, James Landau, Vincent Persichetti, Vladimir Ussachevsky, and Richard G. Stern.

Of the sabbatical awards in the visual arts, *Art News* had this to say: ''the best list of grants (or prizes or honors, call them what you will) that we have seen in this field. It reveals a sophisticated knowledge on the part of the regional advisory panels which made the recommendations and, even rarer, the facts have been tempered with tact, fitness, and a humane understanding of individual needs. The money has gone to artists at a point in their careers when it can make a real financial or psychological difference, possibly a crucial one. . . . For almost all of them, the grant is a meaningful act of recognition and the whole enterprise is a major contribution to our culture.''

The first grants from federal funds were paid to the resident professional theatres. Front Street Theatre in Memphis, Theatre Company of Boston, Hartford Stage, Seattle Repertory Theatre, Actor's Theatre of Louisville and the Theatre of the Living Arts in Philadelphia all received grants for various production purposes or stabilization.

Other visual arts projects were not as yet moving as fast as the others. Most were under study, in the process of organizing advisory panels, or held up for some reason. Roger had temporarily withdrawn from the artists' housing plan due to the difficulties of establishing procedures. It was revived later.

An allocation for individual grants to visual artists was made from unallocated funds ($300,000). These were to be the first of many such $5,000 grants to artists of merit. Included in the group were names that became better known in later years, but at this time the grants were welcome as spurs to their careers. Included were: Lennart Anderson, Gene Davis, Mark Di Suvero, Dan Flavin, William Geis, Robert Goodnough, Ed Mieczkowski, Robert Morris, Ed Ruscha, Tony Smith, Theodore Stamos, Richard Stankiewicz, George Sugarman, H.C. Westerman, Jack Youngerman, and Sam Gilliam.

A Master Artists Teaching Program had its roots in the May, 1966 meeting, but at the December, 1966 meeting the idea was fleshed out. It resembled the Presidential Arts Medals that were begun under the Reagan Administration years later, but with one important difference. Under this proposal, the awards were to be given at a Presidential ceremony, as with the Reagan scheme, but the honorees were obligated to spend three weeks at an arts training institution of their choice teaching the next generation of artists in their art form. The program never became a reality because of later problems with the White House, but it remains one of the finest ideas for passing artistic knowledge from generation to generation.

Another idea that germinated at this meeting was a study of artists rights. The study pointed out laws in other countries that protect the artist. The right to protection of a work of art from modification or abridgement, copyright protection, and sharing in the profit from the re-sale of a work were all shown as desirable and well-established in France and other countries. Twenty years later, in 1986, Sen. Edward Kennedy introduced a bill in Congress to accomplish this protection for works of art. Senator Kennedy was still introducing the bill in the 1990 Congress.

A full half day was scheduled for a visual aid presentation by the Stanford Research Institute of the $100,000 study for an American Film Institute. The Council eagerly awaited the results of this elaborate study and report as the three researchers set up their equipment in a conference room of the State Department. These experts on the art of film had spent nearly a year working on the study. Ironically, they didn't know how to work their own equipment. Eventually, they did master the machinery and presented a positive report.

The proposed American Film Institute was to be funded with one third of the money coming from the Council, one third from private foundations, and one third from the movie industry itself. The Ford Foundation provided the $1 million needed from private sources to the Treasury Fund which accounted for the Council's promised funds.

However, the movie industry money was not forthcoming and the Institute had hard times when the initial capital was disbursed. Eventually, the film people saw the advantage and began supporting it.

Our programs for architecture, planning, landscape architecture, and design had not really begun by this time. At this December meeting a comprehensive outline of proposed programs was offered the Council for decision. It was well organized into four sections; professional education, public information, design innovation, and design research.

Under professional education only one of three proposals was approved: that of internships for students in these disciplines.

Public education proposals numbered seven, but only two passed the Council debates. One valuable contribution to our heritage was the approved book of Guidelines of American Architecture, Planning and Landscape Architecture—a sort of map to the best historical and contemporary work in the country. This was the forerunner of the Historic Landmarks program which had just passed in the Congress. The second funded project was a book of photographs of significant American architecture and landscape design.

Under design innovation were six proposals of which two were funded. One of them, the Tock's Island Recreational Area Study, seemed almost as important as any project funded by the Council. The federal forces were planning to dam the Delaware River and create a giant 37 mile long lake. Millions of people in the mid-Atlantic region would be flocking to this recreational area in both winter and summer. The land speculation had already begun and despoilment was inevitable. The Council passed a $10,000 grant for a study and indicated more funds would be made available to stem the tide of fast-food facilities in the forest and souvenirs by the lake. Tock's Island Dam never was built.

Funds were provided for a study aimed at preserving the natural beauty of Hawaii and, under design research, $10,000 was awarded for a study of highway signs and graphics.

By the spring and summer of 1967, the time of the summer race riots and civil rights activities, four grants had come under my responsibility as the catcher of catch-all projects. Character actor Frank Silvera had begun the American Theatre of Being dedicated to making "the Negro as a full and equal participant" in the American theatre. He was asking up to $25,000 for touring productions to the ghetto high schools of Los Angeles. Chicago's Hull House was asking $30,000 to financially catch up to its expanding theatre program. The St. James Community House School of the Arts needed $24,000 to launch a theatre program for teenagers. The school was run by former opera star Dorothy Maynor who successfully converted the school in her husband's church into the now famous Harlem School of the Arts. All these projects were voted full funding.

The fourth proposed project was a personal one for author Budd Schulberg. After the riots in Watts, California, during the summer of 1965, Budd Schulberg went to Watts and tried to interest adult residents in learning to write creatively. It was the one gift he had to give. After weeks of patient waiting for students to appear, a few timidly approached him. He was eventually successful enough to lease a house in Watts for his writing project. The project needed funds for typewriters, a library of reference books, and writing supplies. Schulberg was asking for $25,000 to be matched by writers he would contact. John Steinbeck brought the project to the Council. It was funded.

Our Literature Director, Carolyn Kizer, worked with me on this project. We went to Watts and met with the students and Schulberg. Eventually, an anthology of the writing produced by this workshop was published, *Out of the Ashes,* and we were credited with the funding.

Another "Civil Rights Meets the Arts" gesture came through former Council member Gregory Peck. It was for the third planned Lab Theatre, the one in the West that hadn't been established. This was the Inner City Cultural Center applying. They wanted to have the repertory theatre as the core of an operation celebrating all of the arts in a minority inhabited area of central Los Angeles. Peck was personally interested in this project and contributed substantial funds that were needed to buy an abandoned movie palace as headquarters.

Attending a performance at the Inner City Cultural Center was a unique experience. At that time the company was not professional, though they would occasionally have established actors as guest stars. I remember one performance of "Room Service." The villainous hotel manager was black, the fast-talking con man producer was white, the naive playwright was oriental, and the audience was a mixture of all minorities. When the black hotel manager tried to evict the others, the audience of blacks booed. When the white producer tricked the manager the black audience cheered. The Hispanics in the audience cheered the oriental for everything for some reason. No one identified by race, but rather by the empathic response to the characters. The audiences also talked back to the actors frequently, particularly Hispanic audiences during Hispanic plays.

Later Greg Peck became disenchanted with the Inner City Cultural Center and suggested the Council withdraw its support. He simply couldn't accept color-blind casting of roles. He flew to a meeting in Tarrytown in 1968, and he said, "Tennessee Williams did not write *The Glass Menagerie* for a black mother, a white daughter, an oriental brother, and a Hispanic gentleman caller." The Council did not withdraw its commitment. In fact, at this meeting the Council set aside future funds for the Inner City Cultural Center.

The day following the December meeting in Washington was the annual meeting of the state council people. The Council members were urged to stay in town and attend and several did. In fact, Isaac Stern spoke to them in his usual dramatically eloquent manner and received a thunderous ovation. But not all went well.

The state people were in a rebellious mood. They listened to the latest federal requirements with little comment. When that part of the meeting was over they began an agenda of their own. They wanted minor changes in the guidelines to which I agreed, if they were not legally required by federal law. They wanted more recognition from the

Council. We had already decided a state council representative should attend all Council meetings. That pleased them. Then, they wanted the Endowment to send a copy of all applications to the state from which the request originated. I tried to explain that the volume and administrative burden would overwhelm them. They said they wanted to avoid double funding of organizations. I said they would be notified of all grants so they could avoid this happening. They said the timing might be wrong and they might act at the same time. The meeting was fast developing a state-federal confrontation when Roger entered the meeting. I turned the problem over to him.

Roger listened to the arguments, which by now were quite heated, and then he spoke. He said we would not inform them of applicants and if they didn't like it they could simply not apply for their allotment in the future. That was it, but it left the state people with a negative attitude, though no other decision was possible from our point of view.

The state executive director from Texas, Pat O'Keefe, was given to sudden, spontaneous orations completely removed from the discussion. He would rise and loudly tell rambling, unrelated stories that were almost incoherent and then suddenly sit down. After Roger forcefully refused their request, O'Keefe rose and delivered a fiery patriotic speech on the theme of "my country right or wrong." He praised Roger and me for our protection of the Constitution, the sanctity of the home, compared us to Abraham Lincoln, and ended by quoting "America the Beautiful." The other states were stunned into silence. O'Keefe had been one of the chief advocates on the states side of the debate. Almost out of a lack of understanding, someone began applauding. Everyone joined in out of habit and the swelling of antagonism started to diminish.

The other state problem I was having was with Virginia. Leslie Cheek, the director of the Virginia Museum of Fine Arts, possessed enormous influence with the governors of the state and persuaded the present governor to recognize the museum as the official state arts council. All the arts organizations in the state resented this action. Regularly, delegations would appear in my office from different parts of Virginia pleading with me to remove the museum as the state arts council. I basically agreed with their arguments that the money would stay in the museum and in Richmond, but I was powerless to change the status quo. I would urge these delegations to work through their elected officials to bring about change. Cheek would periodically appear and always offered a conspiratorial wink indicating that he and I together had outwitted the peasants of the state. Eventually, the cultural leaders managed to gather enough votes in the legislature to move the state council out of the museum.

It was now the end of 1966. The law required a report to the President and the Speaker of the House within six months after the close of the fiscal year. And so, on January 15, 1967, we submitted our annual report covering from July 1, 1965 to June 30, 1966. All of the programs and grants for that period have been reported here or are in the appendix. The report does document the forty-three speeches Roger made during that period and the 300,000 miles he traveled at his own expense. I traveled at government expense and made at least an equal number of speeches, mostly at state conferences on the arts.

137

Worth quoting is Roger's statement in the first annual report.

"In its first fiscal year, covering nine months from the enactment of the enabling legislation, the National Endowment for the Arts has initiated experimental projects to determine the feasibility of innovative programs in the arts. It has encouraged individuals and organizations to assume the responsibility for cultural progress. It has developed a program in which Federal, State, and local governments are cooperating to broaden opportunities for artists and audiences. It has sought to stimulate new sources of funds and services for the arts. It has attempted to meet the needs and to foster an appreciation of the individual creative artist in America today, and it has made comprehensive plans for the future.

"It should also be pointed out that the Endowment is cooperating in every way possible with the National Endowment for the Humanities, the twin partner in the new Foundation. We are constantly exchanging information with each other. We participate in each other's Council meetings. The two endowment staffs maintain a close liaison, so that progress in the arts and humanities can be mutually beneficial with respect to the important cultural areas set forth in our enabling legislation."

It was a true statement, except for the last paragraph. The Humanities Endowment staff and Council had been jealous of the Arts Endowment from the beginning. Before the bill was passed, when the hearings were being held, the humanists came to Washington to testify that the arts should be one branch of the humanities program. They were told to change their testimony or be left out of the legislation completely. Resentment seemed to stem from that time. And then when the legislation passed, the arts programs received much favorable press while the humanities people had to beg reporters to come to their press conferences.

We also differed on the approach to Congress. Chairman Barnaby Keeney believed in constantly requesting more staff positions, while we believed in program funds administered by the smallest possible staff. I was the liaison officer that dealt with the humanities staff on the budget each year. I would meet with the two or three designated humanities people and we would argue for hours about the joint staff positions. They were convinced that Congress paid more attention to the agencies with large staffs. I usually gave up after a while and let the committees in Congress handle their plans for aggrandizement.

The statement in Roger's annual report that stretches the truth is the one about attending each others Council meetings. He went once and came back completely bored. After that, Roger would find a convenient excuse to send me to represent him.

Our coming problems were anything but boring.

The Best of Times, the Worst of Times The Spring of 1967

The process through which federal agencies must travel in order to obtain funds to operate is arduous, time consuming and frustrating. It begins with the writing of a budget that outlines the needs for the coming year. From 1965 to 1969 I set aside the month of September for compiling the budget with the other staff members. First, Roger would meet with each staff member and review their ideas and the ideas passed to them from Council members. He and I would then have a final meeting and fix the programs and projects slated for the next fiscal year. Then I would spend most of the month writing prose to defend the projects. The eventual document would be 75 to 100 pages in length.

The next step was to defend our requests before the Bureau of the Budget, the President's Jewish mother. (It is now called the Office of Budget and Management.) This occurred in November. Their job was to carefully examine our needs as we stated them and decide whether we really needed our needs to the extent requested. The BOB Director either concurred or rejected his staff recommendations and took his opinion to the President, who made the final decision about what amount to request of the Congress in January. Sometimes the budget had to be drastically re-written after the President made a final determination.

Then came the House and Senate subcommittee hearings; in those days hearing were held in March and April. Then the full Appropriations Committee in each house passed on the work of the subcommittees. Usually the two houses had different opinions and each house voted on budgets which differed. In our case, we were a small part of the bill covering the Interior Department. When different versions of funding were voted, a conference committee was set up with members of both houses. When they compromised and agreed, the compromise bill was sent back to the floor and voted on by each house.

Finally, the President would sign or veto. If he signed, we could count on that amount of money for those slated purposes for the coming fiscal year. If he vetoed, the Congress would have to vote to override or compromise with the President.

Understating this process is important because of a major problem that developed later, but that's ahead.

Soon after the beginning of 1967 a personal issue was resolved for me. In the spring of 1966 I had received a strange letter from the State Department. Why the letter didn't go directly to Roger I never knew. The letter asked me to recommend a person who would be a candidate for an executive position with UNESCO in Paris. After thinking about it carefully and discussing it in confidence with Roger, I decided the best person to recommend would be me. The position available was one of organizing cultural projects around the world. I had training in community organization, had worked at the community level, organized states, and worked at the federal level. The only level lacking, I thought, was the world level. I notified the State Department to enter me as a candidate. I then learned of a whole new world of politics.

I met with the State Department official in charge of watching UNESCO and was told the U.S. was eager to put up a candidate for this job for a number of reasons. UNESCO received one-third of its budget from the U.S. but the U.S. was under-represented at the executive level. A qualified candidate would allow our people to pressure UNESCO on the reasons for not having more U.S. personnel. Secondly, the U.S. had never proposed a cultural project of benefit to the U.S., therefore we could be most objective in the administration of projects. The implied meaning of this was that UNESCO officials tended to steer projects into their own countries even though they were supposedly objective world citizens.

Lastly, I was told the U.S. intends to go all out on this position, so that even failing to secure the job the U.S. would be in an advantageous position for the next opening.

I felt like a pawn in a worldwide chess game. The first step was the elimination of all candidates except three. This short list would be given to the Secretary General of UNESCO who would then pick one of the three, or he could name someone who wasn't on any list, if he chose to do so.

I tried to put the job at the back of my mind, but the thought of living in Paris and traveling the world crept in to my thoughts. I learned that the salary was about equal to the salary I was earning, but tax free. In addition, there was a living allowance, an allowance for each child, and all sorts of fringe benefits. I was excited about it in a restrained way.

In early summer I was invited to a four nation conference on administering the arts to take place at Ditchley Park in Great Britain. It was my first trip to Europe. I notified the State Department and they said it might be advantageous to drop in on the UNESCO Secretary General. I heard nothing further about it and went off to England.

Ditchley Park is like something out of Tom Jones, complete with ancestral portraits by Reynolds and furniture from the seventeenth century. I occupied the room sometimes used by Winston Churchill, or so the butler claimed. I enjoyed addressing the Chairman and visiting dignitaries as "M'lord."

I was informed on arrival that I had a message to call the American Ambassador to France. It turned out all messages are sent in the Ambassador's name, but that doesn't mean he wants to talk personally. My message was that I had an appointment with the State Department's UNESCO watcher on the site and the Secretary General after the Ditchley conference. I was also told I had made the short list and a final decision by the Secretary General was expected soon.

After the conference I flew to Paris and met with the State Department's permanent delegate to UNESCO. He confirmed that I was one of three final candidates along with an Afghan and a Soviet. He said the Afghan was totally unqualified and only put on the list for window dressing, but that the Soviet was a serious possibility. He then took from his desk drawer a folder with some teletype-looking paper and proceeded to read the biography of the Soviet candidate. Our embassy in Moscow had done a thorough job. We knew the high school he went to, the kind of student he was, where he went to college, his major, his outside interests, his family, personal life, positions held, and publications published. He was a professor. I listened with fascination and then suddenly was overcome with giggling. The UNESCO watcher looked disdainful.

It had suddenly occurred to me that the Soviets undoubtedly had done the same job on me. I imagined them sitting around the Kremlin wondering about my flunking geometry four times, dropping out of college, coming back, getting a masters. How would they react to my having worked as an ice man, an attendant in an insane asylum, a window trimmer, construction laborer, and a dozen other occupations? I was amused and the UNESCO delegate was not, even when I explained it. I pointed out that the Secretary General certainly had a clear contrast between the academic, scholarly Soviet and me.

After lunch I met with the Secretary General, M. Maheu, in his office. He was a tall, rather handsome Frenchman with a friendly manner. We talked about my background, the position and my present job. At one point I mentioned my almost nonexistent knowledge of French, one of the two official languages of UNESCO (the other is English). He said that was no problem. He said he was saddled with too many Russians who weren't understandable in either language. I thought that a good sign.

Sometime in the fall I received a call from the State Department. Secretary General Maheu visited Canada and while there our embassy people had mentioned my candidacy. The Secretary General had replied that I wasn't interested in the job. Was that true? What had I said to give him that impression? I said I had been most enthusiastic about the possibility. The State Department treated the mix up as if it were an international incident.

And so, as 1967 began, I received word through the State Department that the job went not to the Soviet or me, but to an old World War II Resistance friend of M. Maheu who was already on the UNESCO staff in a much lower position. They said they had learned that the reason was because Maheu wanted his friend to retire at a higher pension. I felt neither relief nor disappointment. It had been an adventure, but I was perfectly happy to remain with the Endowment.

During the early months of 1967 we concentrated on the workings of the Congress and securing our fiscal 1968 appropriations. Once again, the President had requested the full amount authorized by our legislation and once again the wisdom of the Congress gave much less: $4.5 million for general programs, $2 million for the state program, and only $674,291 for the Treasury Fund. Our administrative budget for personnel had grown to $1.2 million, mostly to accommodate the full staff that had become employed by the Humanities Endowment. The Treasury Fund amount was an in-house division between the two Endowments; we got the larger share of the $1 million total because we had been able to attract more funds from private sources. In total, the attitude of Congress at this time was one of concern about the growing cost of the Viet Nam War and inflation at home; the arts and humanities did not enjoy a high priority on the federal shopping list.

Roger had a marvelous sales pitch that he used on new Senators and Congressmen. After the elections of 1966, he went around the Hill calling on all the newly elected. He would challenge the newly elected Senator or Congressman to compare his list of campaign contributors to a list of trustees of the larger arts institutions in their state or district. Invariably, the lesson was clear. Roger would point out these people needed federal help with the institutions on which they served.

In the 1966 elections we lost the Chairman of the House appropriations subcommittee; Mr. Denton of Indiana was defeated in his bid for re-election. He had indicated to Roger that any help he could get would be welcomed because he knew he would have a tough battle. Roger managed to get him some editorial help from a newspaper that was influential in his district, and a $5,000 campaign contribution through Herman Kenin and the American Federation of Musicians. Still, he was defeated.

The new Chairman was a great improvement: Julia Butler Hansen of Washington. She had a lively interest in the arts and was a fierce protector of the agencies under her authority.

One year Rep. Mahon, who was Chairman of the full House Appropriations Committee, proposed a cut in the budget of our agency without consulting her. This was a serious breach of professional behavior on his part. He did this on the floor, but aides took the word to her in her subcommittee meeting. I was in the gallery at the time. The house was in session, when suddenly the big, leather, swinging doors burst open and into the chamber flew Rep. Hansen, her bosoms cutting through the air like the prow of a clipper ship, her spectacles swinging from side to side on the ever present ribbon around her neck. Mahon saw her coming and began back peddling toward the rear door of the chamber, but it was no use. She covered the distance between them, bounced up against him, finger raised, rage in evidence. I couldn't hear her words, but later I asked her what she said. Her exact words were, "Mahon, you sonofabitch, you lowlife bastard you, and then I got really rough."

The National Council on the Arts met for the eighth time on May 12–14, 1967. The big event was the formal approval of the American Film Institute (AFI). The funding was now official: $1.3 million from our Treasury Fund, $1.3 million from the Ford Foundation and $1.3 million from the member companies of the Motion Picture Association. The Ford Foundation funds and our funds allowed the AFI to begin operation.

With this priority out of the way the Council voted new ones for restricted gifts to the Treasury Fund; grants were subsequently awarded to two theatre companies, the Association of Producing Artists (APA), and the New York Shakespeare Festival. The Shakespeare Festival grant was specifically for the establishment of the new Public Theatre building which was opened in October 1966, and eventually gave birth to such hits as "Colored Girls" and "A Chorus Line." Ten years later Joe Papp produced a play I wrote in that building. A third use of the Treasury Fund would be another grant to the American Ballet Theatre.

The Council also voted to establish a new opera company, the American National Opera Company, with Sarah Caldwell, artistic director of the Opera Company of Boston, as artistic director. The company was more or less the successor of the failed Metropolitan Opera National Company.

The Council approved a grant to the Music Critics Association to develop a prototype for an *American Musical Digest.* The hidden purpose of this project, which was to reprint the best reviews of musical events, was to spotlight the better music critics and hopefully influence the entire print media toward improving standards in all of arts criticism. The *Digest* was scuttled after a number of issues due to in-fighting among the staff and board of advisors, and poor circulation.

The music panel composed of 18 distinguished individuals from the music field under the chairmanship of Aaron Copland was quite active and proposed a number of projects for approval at this meeting. The panel had been established in the wake of the fiasco surrounding the ill-fated master chamber orchestra.

Several literature projects were approved, notably one to enable black and white writers to visit the developing colleges of the South which had primarily black students. These visiting writers gave classroom lectures and workshop sessions on the art of writing and gave public readings of their work. Student and local writers were also involved. Some of these visiting and local writers became "writers-in-residence" at colleges. The program was later given more support by the Council because of the success.

This was the meeting at which a representative of the Glide Foundation of San Francisco, Mr. McIlvenna, made the Council acquainted with the programs in the Haight-Ashbury area of San Francisco. He gave a short talk at dinner on Saturday night and a discussion followed in the session on Sunday. These were the days of the Hippies and the communes populated by runaway children from all over the country. Haight-Ashbury had become a center for these children who were living in "crash pads" and on the street.

The Council was divided on the issue of supporting the arts activity in this area. Some of the Council believed this was not professional art or even serious amateurism.

Others believed help of some kind was necessary to influence these children in re-joining the mainstream of society and that the arts were a powerful tool of such influence.

Charlton Heston was opposed to any support for this rootless movement. After lunch on Sunday when the Council reconvened, he asked Roger's permission to read a poem written by an inhabitant of Haight-Ashbury. Roger was pleased; a famous actor reading poetry at a National Council of the Arts meeting, what could be more appropriate? The first stanza of this "poem" contained every profane and scatological word possible and described every normal and perverted sex act. As Heston read Roger squeezed the Chairman's gavel tighter and tighter and his face grew more white. When the end was finally reached, the Council members sat in stunned silence. Heston had obviously attempted to scuttle consideration of any grant through this method.

After a long silence, Helen Hayes pushed her glasses up onto her forehead and with her ringing, cultivated voice said. "If I had thought *he* was going to bring *his* material, *I* would have brought *mine*." With this, she dramatically pushed back her chair and left the room.

No grant was ever awarded, but later council member Philip Hanes personally sponsored an art exhibition which was quite successful.

Grants that the Council made at this meeting to the experimental theatres in New York and elsewhere prompted *Variety* later to comment:

> *"The decision of the National Endowment for the Arts to dispense . . . grants to nine experimental theatres is a built-in rebuttal to critics who feared that Federal subsidy might result in exclusive nurturing of 'safe' or 'Establishment' legit . . . the experimental legits produce new and sometimes provocative, occasionally challenging work, besides providing a practical workshop for budding playwrights."*

This is but one editorial out of many that indicated we were winning over those who expected government control and "super safe" programming from the feds.

This was also the meeting when several members tried to interest the majority in saving the old Metropolitan Opera House from destruction as the new one at Lincoln Center was almost ready to open. Roger refused to take a position on the issue because he was on the board of directors of the Met as was Tony Bliss. However, the issue was pressed onto the agenda. Roger could have settled everything by pointing out that the old Met needed to be sold to provide money for continued operation, but he let the controversy run its course.

The discussion was reasonable and intelligent, unlike the Haight-Ashbury debate. However, it was not heading toward a resolution. During a pause Roger turned to Ralph Ellison, who was attending this meeting as a guest.

Ralph said he had listened with interest to the passion on both sides, but that he couldn't really understand the preservationist's arguments. He then talked about the Savoy Ballroom in Harlem and how so many of our composers from Copland to Gershwin listened and learned from the jazz greats who played there. Then he asked, if they were so anxious to preserve the great musical landmarks, why didn't they campaign to save the Savoy Ballroom when it was torn down. It was an eloquent and passionate speech that struck a vital chord with everyone. The debate died with Ralph's last words.

(For a complete list of grants for this period see the Appendix.)

Shortly after this meeting, Mrs. Blum from Louisiana asked me to have lunch at the office of the Majority Whip, Rep. Hale Boggs. When I arrived at the office I was told to wait while I watched a parade of people, including Mrs. Blum and Mrs. Boggs, ushered into the inner office. Finally, I was told I could enter. Everyone was seated at the beautifully prepared table—perhaps 20 or 25 people—but no empty place beckoned me. Mrs. Blum waved me to her side and indicated I was to sit on a chair three feet behind her and away from the table; obviously not to eat.

I sat there only long enough to see the situation and then told Mrs. Blum there was obviously a mistake and I would be in my office if she wanted to see me. I left.

A few years later when I told Ray Mesler, the executive director of the Louisiana State Arts Council, the story of how Mrs. Blum tried to humiliate me he said it was not unusual. He claimed she had an extension phone in her house so the executive was subject to monitoring of his phone conversations at any time.

The Council held a special meeting in Los Angeles on July 17, 1967. It was merely to handle a few grants and announce some news. The Council voted to give the first 1968 Treasury Fund gifts to the American Conservatory Theatre of San Francisco which was in crisis because of the expanded program of performance and the training of theatre artists. Roger also announced that the Bell Laboratories building on the lower West Side of New York was for sale and would make an excellent artists' housing project. If the Council would vote the necessary funds to the J. M. Kaplan Fund, Roger would pursue the goal of buying it and converting it into the first federally funded artists' housing project in history. The Council was delighted with the prospect. It was recommended that when complete the building be named after David Smith.

Three weeks later Roger made a public announcement that the Kaplan Fund, the Council, and the Department of Housing and Urban Development (HUD) would go forward with the project and purchase the Bell Laboratories building. Robert Weaver, Secretary of HUD, said of the announcement, "I am happy that the Federal Housing Administration's (FHA) program has proved flexible enough to house both people and the arts. This is in keeping with our emphasis on developing cities which serve the soul as well as the body."

Sen. Robert Kennedy sent a statement to the press conference, regretting his inability to be present. His statement said in part:

> "The fact that this imaginative and creative project is becoming a reality is a concrete and encouraging result of Congress' enactment of the National Arts and Humanities Act. It is tangible evidence that this legislation created a governmental concern for the arts which will make a great difference. And it is evidence, too, that

the drafters of the Act were right when they contemplated cooperation of private foundations in the projects which they authorized.''

Speaking of "imaginative and creative acts," the project was to house middle income families. The FHA could define the limits of middle income, but a definition of a family was difficult in the case of artists. We finally settled on "two or more adults, with or without children, residing together." No mention of marriage or designation of sex was included.

Little did we know at the time of the problems and obstacles we would face very soon as the artists' housing project developed.

Two Dance Anecdotes with
Roots in 1966
That Blossomed in 1967

When Agnes de Mille was a member of the Council and a few small grants had been made to young choreographers, she and one or two others left a Council meeting early to go into New York to see the premiere of one of these works. In fact, it was the first public work by this choreographer. The next morning they reported to the Council at large that they had witnessed the birth of a major talent. Agnes de Mille had no doubt in her mind the Eliot Feld's first ballet, "Harbinger" would propel him into the major ranks of dance.

Soon after that, he came to us for help in founding his own company, which was granted on a modest level. He soon went bankrupt because he wanted to have a major company instantly and didn't realize reputations were not instantly acquired. Once again, he turned to the Endowment for help. This time he was given a grant with the understanding that he would build his reputation and productions more slowly without a full orchestra and fewer dancers. He had learned his lesson and built one of the most creative companies in the dance world.

When Martha Graham was proposing her first national tour in fifteen years I found the estimated budget to be grossly underestimated. I had called the Gertrude Macy, who was handling the business affairs for the company, and told her she should submit more accurate figures. She said she had just talked with Sol Hurok and he had also told her she was too low in her estimate. She said she had never dreamed the federal government would actually tell her to ask for more money. She did. It was granted, and I forgot all about it.

Much later I was honored to be asked to be the third member of a panel at a dance luncheon along with Sol Hurok and Martha Graham. It was a memorable experience. I sat between them at the head table. Mr. Hurok dominated the conversation at first. His attention at the moment was focused on his perception that the concert business had deteriorated. He was then near 80, but he recited all the concert halls in existence when he first started in business so many years ago.

"Then we had stars. Melba, Mary Garden, Rubenstein," he said, and went on to name twenty or more artists of the days gone by.

"But," I protested, "look at the stars you have made."

"There are no stars today. Not like then."

"But sir," I said, "there are, and you made them stars."

"Like who?"

"Like Isaac Stern, for instance."

"Phee, a kid. Played for $400 in Manhattan, Kansas."

On that day, at least, he could not believe in his own empire and the authority he possessed. He only remembered those who were stars when he fought to sign them to S. Hurok Presents.

After that exchange I turned to Martha Graham who had been mostly silent during the luncheon. She asked me my name and when I told her she asked me to stand up. I did as I was told. She held me by the shoulders and kissed me tenderly on both cheeks. I was taken completely by surprise.

She said, "Gertrude Macy told me that if I ever met you I should give you a kiss for insisting we ask for more money. Now, its done."

Some years later, Eliot Feld was appealing to the New York State Council on the Arts for an additional grant. He was told that the only funds not obligated were the funds earmarked for distribution on a per capital basis to the countries of the state. However, all the funds for Manhattan County institutions had been distributed, and since he had his office in Manhattan, nothing could be done; unless of course he moved his office to Queens County where per capita funds were still available.

Eliot Feld replied: "You warned me I would sometimes have "queens" in my office, and now you tell me I have to have my office in Queens."

New Personnel, Projects
and Problems
Fall and Winter of 1967–68

The characters of this comedy of eras were beginning to change. Our Deputy Chairman, Liv Biddle, was offered a position at Fordham University which was forging a new program in the arts and he departed. William Cannon, who had been one of the upper level career officials at the Bureau of the Budget (BOB), agreed to come in as Deputy for six months. He had accepted a position at the University of Chicago as a vice president that was to begin in the fall, so his tenure with us would be short but effective. Roger wanted Bill Cannon to accomplish a number of specific tasks. One was to tighten the lines of communication between the programs and the finances which had gotten haphazard as the programs became more complicated, improve relations with the BOB, and handle certain specific personnel problems.

Roger's secretary, Luna Diamond, was excellent as a secretary, but didn't grasp the complexities that were developing and the pace that was increasing. She was the Jewish mother to the staff and the Council members, but Roger was not the kind of man who appreciated a Jewish mother. His solution had been to hire another secretary who met his needs Charlotte Woolard, and not replace Luna. Bill Cannon's job was to find some means of moving Luna away from Roger's close proximity. Meanwhile, Charlotte was getting all the work and doing an exceptional job of diplomatically relating to Luna. She would receive assignments directly from Roger, and then would enlist Luna in the execution.

When Bill Cannon became Deputy, he and I talked about the Luna problem frequently, but no solution presented itself. One day we were remarking how Luna did such a good job of mothering the Council members; making last minute airline reservations, hiring limousines, arranging luncheons, and so forth. Suddenly the solution appeared before me. Why not create a position for her as Secretary to the Council? Everyone, including Luna, would be happy with that arrangement. It was done, and she served in that capacity with great distinction for ten years until retirement.

The other personnel problem evaded us completely. The assignment was to replace Frank Crowther, or at least keep him away from the staff and the Council members. He was constantly making troublesome phone calls to the Council members and begging favors, and when Roger wasn't around, he would try to command the staff.

When Cannon was near the end of his tenure with us he wrote a memo about Frank. Frank stole a look at the memo and learned Roger considered him an excellent speech writer but a complete nuisance in every other way. The memo also mentioned that all the members of the National Council had requested Frank's termination. Frank abruptly resigned. Roger was unable to replace him before the end of his term.

Still another personnel problem faced Roger. I was burnt out. The state arts council program kept me traveling and constantly talking on the phone, and Roger kept asking me to take on various projects in addition. I went on fact finding trips. I would be working in my office sometimes planning a full day of catching up on paper work when Roger would appear. He would ask me to run out to Denver, or Atlanta, or New York immediately to check on some project. I would do my paper work on the plane and then work through the weekend to catch up.

In addition, I was handling all the projects involving more than one art form and more applications were arriving every day on my desk, all of which had to be checked and evaluated for the Council. Also, Roger was becoming over burdened with details so he told the program directors to first come to me with their problems.

Friends, staff, Council members, and wife all approached Roger about the state of my health and almost constant testiness. Finally, he and I sat down to talk about it.

With great reluctance, I decided the one aspect of the job I could reasonably give up was the state arts council program; it was now off and running smoothly. After some thought, I invented a new title and built in a promotion to a GS 17; I would be the Director of Planning and Analysis.

The next task was to find a successor for the state council job. One of the best state arts council executive directors was in Missouri, Clark Mitze. I cleared it with Roger and picked up the phone. Clark accepted immediately and began work in the spring of 1968.

It was amusing that whenever we created a new position, the Humanities Endowment would create the same position. When Luna became Secretary to the Council, the Humanities hired someone to fill that new position, also. When I invented a new job for myself, they, too, suddenly decided they needed a Director of Planning and Analysis.

Finally, the last change in staff was the resignation of Fannie Taylor as Director of Music Programs. Fannie wanted to go back to Madison, Wisconsin, to live. She stayed on as a consultant.

But here we were at the tenth meeting of the Council. A number of programs and projects voted at this meeting are worthy of special note. For one, the Poetry-in-the-Schools project that was so successful in New York, Pittsburgh and Detroit, was expanded at this meeting to Chicago, Los Angeles, Minneapolis and the Southwest. Two years later the program expanded further to involve all the arts and a year or two after that, it became a national program blanketing all the states.

This was the meeting when the American National Opera was formally launched. The Council voted that the first unrestricted money given to the Treasury Fund would be used to fund the company. That meant that Roger was free to go looking for money for the new opera project. Nearly $50,000 was raised from private sources and the company was organized and sent on tour. Sarah Caldwell's productions received excellent reviews and were applauded by audiences wherever they sang. However, the company lacked a strong financial manager capable of controlling the mercurial Sarah, who thought the Council a generous patron with unlimited funds.

One day I received a call from the White House asking why they received a bill for $1,500 from a firm in the midwest for an opera performance. I didn't know. I called the firm and found out Sarah had been there at our request to do a performance as part of Mrs. Johnson's national arts study tour.

In 1968, Lady Bird Johnson expressed a desire to see what impact our agency had had on the country. We worked out a short tour for her that allowed for stops at various projects we had funded. Included was a performance by the Sarah Caldwell opera company. The Company was not playing at a place where it was possible for Mrs. Johnson to see a performance so we moved the company to another city and asked a local arts-oriented firm to supervise and act as host. Apparently, since this was a performance essentially for the First Lady, Sarah Caldwell thought the extra expenses incurred should be charged to the White House. But the White House didn't think so. We paid the $1,500 and deducted it from the company's next budget payment.

Then the IRS moved in. It seems the opera company hadn't been sending in withholding taxes on its employees. As I recall, the amount of missing taxes was nearly $200,000. Consequently, the IRS obtained a seizure order and was about to confiscate all the costumes and scenery. To avoid this, arts patron Sam Rubin, one of the contributors to founding the opera, and Roger bought the costumes and scenery and moved them to a warehouse in Los Angeles. That was the end of a critically successful but badly controlled opera company which could have made a significant contribution to our national cultural life. I don't know what happened to the physical property.

At this November meeting a small grant was proposed for another new opera company sponsored by the Walker Art Center of Minneapolis. The company wished to specialize in new operas and neglected older works. In the discussion, which was favorable, Isaac Stern suggested the grant be cut in half: a $10,000 grant instead of $20,000. That didn't make sense to me; it was like building half a house, or providing a pick-up when a dump truck was needed. I countered and said the Council should either give the company the full amount or nothing. The vote was in favor of the full amount. That company is now called the Minnesota Opera.

One of the problems of the commercial theatre is the fact that some very worthy productions with good reviews simply can't remain open long enough to build an audience. Sometimes it is an unknown playwright, or the play lacks a well known actor, that restricts the advance sale of tickets. There are dozens of stories about shows which were closing when suddenly the word of mouth started building audiences just in time to save the day.

Roger of course had been aware of this problem for a long time. In fact, he had been a victim of this kind of "good play no audience" situation several times with some of the 150 productions he had produced.

At this meeting he tried an idea on the Council. Supposing, he said, there was a place in midtown Manhattan where a theatre goer could buy a half-priced ticket to a good play for that night's performance. The number of tickets would be estimated by the show's producer and sent to the half-price booth. This would fill the empty seats and increase the word of mouth opinions, and it would provide enough income to keep the show running until the audience built. The Council voted to try the project, if Treasury Funds were made available.

That vote of confidence was all Roger needed. He raised $100,000 from three private foundations, matched that with Treasury Funds and the Theatre Development Fund was established. However, not all the newspapers thought this was a good idea, in fact, some distorted the idea and attacked Roger personally. Headlines appeared shortly after the program was announced; "FUNDS WILL AID SHAKY PLAYS ON BROADWAY," "$200,000 FUND TO HELP SAGGING STAGE SHOWS," and "FEDERAL FUNDS TO AID BROADWAY LAGGERS." It was obvious the writers didn't understand the purpose of the program and didn't bother to find out. They had a story at last that could be slanted to make us look bad.

Congress got into the act and we learned of several speeches on the floor of both Houses, but Roger stuck to the original plan.

Today, the Theatre Development Fund (TDF) is the single most important nonprofit agency assisting quality commercial theatrical productions. It not only buys blocks of tickets to quality plays before they open, but millions of tickets for theatre and dance and opera are handled through the famous TKTS booth on Times Square. In addition, special performances are provided for the handicapped. Recently, TDF has established a telephone network available across the country at no charge that will give the caller a complete picture of the performing arts attractions available in New York on a daily basis. The half-priced ticket idea has spread to several other cities and is doing well.

This tenth meeting was held in private in the lounge of the National Gallery of Art. Sidney Poitier had flown by chartered plane from a desert location somewhere in the West in order to get to the meeting. He had slept little or not at all. Consequently, he was irritable, candid, impatient in his manner. In short, he was being human. The lounge is immediately next to the main entrance to the Gallery. When the meeting recessed and we stepped into the entrance area, Poitier was immediately recognized and approached by eager fans. This grumpy, sleepy, human being instantly became the movie star we all know. The boyish grin, the shy smile, the sparkling eyes, all appeared as if someone had shouted lights, camera, action. He signed autographs, and joked with his fans.

When I commented on his complete transformation to him he smiled again—a tired smile—and said, "When they stop asking for autographs, then you worry and get crabby."

Sidney Poitier reported on the American Film Institute. He announced that 75 percent of the necessary money had been raised; 66 percent had come from the Council and the Ford Foundation. George Stevens, Jr. had been chosen as the executive director. He had been director of the film unit of the U.S. Information Agency. A temporary office had been established in D.C.

Several other programs had their genesis at this meeting. The Dance Touring Program began here with a small grant to the Illinois Arts Council ($25,000) and an individual grant to Charles Reinhart ($5,000) to develop a program whereby a modern dance company not only performed but stayed in residence at the site of the performance and gave master classes and/or lecture/demonstrations. This program grew tremendously over the years to include all the states and many of the ballet and modern dance companies. Charles Reinhart headed the program for several years and then became the director of the American Dance Festival.

A project to influence the labor unions favorably toward the arts had its beginning at this time. The AFL/CIO Council for Scientific, Professional and Cultural Employees (SPACE) was awarded a grant to work with the unions and cultural organizations of New York, Buffalo, Minneapolis and Louisville. The aim was to increase union member participation in arts events and classes. The project was continued for two years, but then dropped under the Nixon Administration.

Another significant project which continues to this day is the Art in Public Places program. (The transcription of the Congressional appropriations hearings called it "art in pubic places.") The first approved application under this program was from the city of Grand Rapids. Alexander Calder was commissioned to create a stabile, "La Grande Vitesse." Another commission was given to Isamu Noguchi for his "Black Sun" to be placed in front of the Seattle Art Museum.

Some time later Rep. Gerald Ford visited his home town of Grand Rapids, Michigan, and understood how the Calder piece had become a point of unity and joy to the inhabitants. He often referred back to that experience as being the moment of his conversion to the federal arts program. As President he was an advocate, though during the Johnson Administration he was Minority Leader of the House and much opposed to every bill benefiting the arts.

No one knew at the time, but the Council's next meeting and much of the staff time in the near future would be devoted to survival tactics.

Gregory Peck, Agnes de Mille and Elizabeth Ashley.

Guns and Butter and Other
Explosive and Slippery Situations
Winter of 1967–68

The federal government does not establish agencies which continue in perpetuity. Often, when a new program is established, a time limit is built into the legislation. This is called an authorization. At the end of one, two, or more years the program dies unless the Congress sees fit to continue it. This was our problem; we were due for re-authorization.

We had many favorable reactions and much support around the country, especially in the states, but this was the time of the expanding Viet Nam War and the red hot "guns and butter" debate. President Johnson was trying to fight two wars at the same time—the War on Poverty at home and an escalating conflict in Southeast Asia. Inflation was rising, the first opposition to the Viet Nam situation was beginning, and reports of race riots were on the front pages. The plight of opera and dance companies, museums and musicians, was not paramount in the eyes of the politicians, or the public. It was our luck to pop up just at that moment and ask to be renewed, and at a more generous level.

Senator Pell introduced the re-authorization bill in late June. Rep. Ogden Reid (R>NY) introduced a similar bill in the House in early July. Joint House-Senate Hearings were held shortly after that and then a separate one later in the summer.

It was after the November meeting of the Council that the House bill was reported out of committee.

Until then we did not foresee any problems.

In November of 1967 I was invited to represent the U.S. at a UNESCO Round-table Conference on Cultural Policy in Monaco. This was a direct result of my name and background being known to UNESCO through my candidacy for the staff position there. Roger was also invited. The meeting was convening just before Christmas.

Roger and Christine Stevens were to meet me in Monaco, so I few over alone. I was to attend a preliminary meeting in Paris at UNESCO headquarters before flying down to the larger meeting at Monaco. The plane couldn't land in Paris because of

155

terrible weather and some engine trouble, so it flew to the next scheduled stop which was Rome. Consequently, I got no sleep and arrived at my Paris meeting late and groggy. For the next ten days I was awake at night and groggy all day.

My experience at the Roundtable made me happy I didn't get the job with UNESCO —so much protocol is involved, so much tolerance of nonsense, and so little movement. For instance, if one wanted to respond to a speaker, a hand was raised and the secretary would write one's name on a list. Thirty minutes later, when one was called on, the response seemed anachronistic. I learned the trick of raising my hand arbitrarily, knowing I would have some response to something when I was called on to speak.

I fully believed the final report was written by the staff before the meeting took place. When the report was published I saw little resemblance to the discussions that transpired. At one point during the meeting I made an impatient little speech. It happened to be appreciated and my remarks were voted to be transcribed from the audio tape into both English and French. When I read the transcription, I hardly recognized my own words, especially in French. In both languages it was an interpretation of my words with the salt taken out and sugar added.

However, in terms of hospitality, the experience was most pleasant. We were housed at the famous Hotel de Paris and given an allowance of francs as a per diem. (I promptly lost mine at roulette while Roger kept on winning.) The daily sessions began at ten in the morning followed by a champagne break at about eleven. Then we worked until one and took a two hour lunch break, during which the Swedish delegate and I went for a sauna and nap after a quick but delicious lunch beside the indoor pool. At three we went back to work and worked until seven, then a reception and dinner hosted by some Monegasque official, or a private meal.

Prince Rainier appeared at one of our sessions. We were required to crowd closer around the huge square table so he had no one within six feet. His chair was placed a precise three feet from the table and a hat rack was placed next to the chair. The Prince entered with valet, who received hat, gloves, and top coat, which were ceremoniously placed on the hat rack. We waited in silence for this. The Prince sat and listened to the discussion for about twenty minutes, and then we waited in silence again while the dressing ritual was reversed.

One day at our lunch break, we were invited to the palace to formally meet the Prince and Princess. Roger and Christine Stevens had another appointment and didn't go. We were ushered into the palace and waited in the ante room outside the throne room. Then, because Princess Grace was American, I was told to head the reception line and be the first to meet the royal couple. An attendant told me to say nothing, but to nod or bow in acknowledgment when they nodded. I decided not to bow; it would be too subservient. Besides, I was still a bit annoyed by being crunched so the Prince could avoid being near us commoners. They nodded from their elevated throne and I nodded.

We were sped from the throne room into another reception room where we were given excellent champagne. The same attendant told us the Prince and Princess would enter and she would stand just here, and he just there. In the order in which we were introduced we were to approach one or the other and chat for two minutes. No longer. Ready, set, go.

I decided the Princess was prettier and I didn't speak French, so when she was standing just there, I approached. Knowing she was from Philadelphia, I said since I already knew the royalty of Philadelphia it was only fitting I know the royalty of Monaco. She asked who I meant and I said Liv Biddle had been our Deputy Chairman. She acknowledged the Biddles were indeed the royalty of Philadelphia. We then chatted about Roger Stevens, whom she had met previously, and then we got on the subject of theatre and summer stock. She told about a summer company in Colorado where she once acted and I talked about one in Wisconsin. I was greatly impressed with the shine on the floors of the palace, so I asked her if she knew what was used to make them shine. She said she didn't. I told her if she was in charge of the Palace she ought to know. She laughed. I laughed and said good-bye.

But we had chatted four minutes instead of the protocol two. By this I almost ruptured the 200 year relationship with France. The french delegate, the Director of the Ministry of Culture, was next in line and he was greatly annoyed that Princess Grace didn't give him equal time. He and I went to lunch with Nigel Abercrombie, the British delegate, and we all became friends.

Later, I went to the casino with the French delegate. Princess Grace had installed Black Jack and a Craps table to introduce American gambling into Europe. The Director of the Ministry of Culture asked me to explain Craps to him, and I went into detail about the complicated rules. Then he asked if all Americans understood the game. I said most males have learned the game by the sixth grade. He said, "No wonder the Americans are such good engineers."

As 1968 entered, our only worry was the Congressional attack on the Theatre Development Fund, but this was soon to change. We were confident we would be helped by the press as the authorization bill became known. Cleveland's *The Plain Dealer* said: "The biggest thing the foundation has done is to prove that fears of bureaucracy and political influence were unfounded. The foundation's activities have allayed fears . . . that the government might infringe on artistic freedom."

The Milwaukee Journal, another conservative newspaper, had this to say about our program: "Vietnamese war demands have cut sharply into vital poverty programs and sparked the recurring 'guns or butter' debate on priorities. But Congress must look to the future. There is more to life than guns or butter or even both; provision must be made for a bit of essential nourishment for the creative spirit, too. The Arts and Humanities Foundation must not be killed off and should get a reasonable refunding."

The House Committee on Education and Labor under Adam Clayton Powell agreed with the media and voted for a two year funding cycle that would have given the Arts Endowment $67.5 million, and an equal amount to the Humanities Endowment, plus funds for the Treasury Fund and an administration budget. But when the bill hit the floor it was a different story.

The first speakers were eloquent in our behalf. Reps. Thompson, Reid, Moorhead, and Brademas spoke lovingly of our program. Then Rep. Gross went to the Well of the House to speak. My wife was there for the first time and I explained that Gross was aptly named and a clown, in my opinion. I told her he would just make inane suggestions for a short time. I will never forget his first words.

He said, "I rise to call for the resignation of one Charles C. Mark from the National Endowment for the Arts."

It seems that I had called Mr. Gross and one or two other Congressman "Neanderthals" when I appeared before a closed door meeting of the major orchestra managers. The manager of the National Symphony disliked me, though I had never said more than a few words to him. He sent the confidential verbatim transcription of my remarks to Rep. Gross, who then invoked the Hatch Act concerning lobbying by Civil Service employees. Gross harangued me for several minutes. My wife sank lower and lower into her seat in the gallery. Our staff began laughing and pointing their fingers at me. Roger was laughing over in the Speaker's gallery, and I was alternately blushing with anger and sporting a cold sweat of fear. Nothing, however, came of the attack, since I had a Presidential appointment and was technically allowed to lobby.

Then, suddenly, Rep. Anderson (R>IL) was on his feet calling for a reduction in the authorized total proposed. He said it was past time to establish priorities responsive to what he considered the most pressing needs of American life, and it was obvious to him the arts and humanities were not high on that list. Other Congressmen joined in opposing the bill. Rep. Bow (R>OH) remarked; "Certainly at this time there is not a soul on this floor who does not realize that we are at war . . . we cannot have guns and butter. And this (Endowment) is guns with strawberry shortcake covered with whipped cream and a cherry on top."

A long debate ensued with the pro arts people losing ground by the minute. Finally, Rep. Mahon (D>TX), Chairman of the all-powerful House Appropriations Committee rose to speak. He urged "fiscal responsibility" and went on to say this was "the first key vote of the year on a bill to continue authorization for an ongoing program. We are on trial as a nation as to whether or not we have the discipline and the courage and the leadership to pay our way. . . . Today we have a test vote and I hope that we will measure up to the demands of the moment." It was unfortunate that we were a test vote on the first key issue of the year.

The rest of the House took the hint from their fiscal leader and voted 272 to 123 to drastically amend downward H.R. 11308, the bill to control our lives for the next year.

Two Congressmen who voted against us were named George Bush and Robert Dole. Gerald Ford, the minority leader, of course voted with his party.

It wasn't until May of 1968 that the Senate Committee on Labor and Public Welfare reported on a revised version of the original bill introduced by Sen. Pell. The House had reduced the life of the new authorization to one year; the Senate restored the original two years. The House had forbidden grants to individuals; the Senate restored that provision. The more liberal version passed the full Senate almost immediately after it was reported out of committee, a tribute to Sen. Pell's leadership.

Then, the House and Senate appointed members to a Conference Committee to reconcile differences. It wasn't until June 5, that a final bill was passed that allowed us to definitely plan for the next year beginning July 1. President Johnson made it official by signing it into law on June 18. However, because of the long and sometimes bitter debate concerning our future, neither House nor Senate had bothered to appropriate funds for the 1969 fiscal year and we were at the end of the 1968 year.

Here is how it all came out. We were authorized to be appropriated up to $6 million for programs and $2 million for the states. The second year each were supposed to increase $500,000.

The law was changed as Roger wanted it to be so that restricted gifts to the Treasury Fund were now legal; we no longer had to say "If we get a gift we will probably use it for this purpose." Anyone could now say, "I give this to you provided you match it and give it to institution X." Also, the Treasury Fund was increased to a total of $13.5 million for both the Arts and Humanities Endowments for the two years.

Individual grants has been restored, but the meaningless words "of exceptional talent" were added as a precaution.

Roger had also asked and got authority to award grants up to $10,000 without taking proposals to the Council in advance. He did, however, have to report to the Council afterwards.

This was a far cry from the $135 million of the first Senate version. Still, it was a little better than the $4.5 million and the one year authorization with no individual grants which the House tried to impose. But more importantly, it was a blow to our morale. Every member of the Council and every staff member had given their best effort to proving that the state of the arts in the country was in great need of some form of assistance. Everyone had tried their best, and succeeded in proving that federal aid did not mean control or bureaucratic fumbling. We tried to be imaginative, innovative, sound in judgement and creative in solutions. We tried to show the Congress and the President that programs fostered by government would attract additional funding from the states and private resources. All this seemed to us to be accomplished in a vacuum. We were swept up in a maelstrom that had nothing to do with our programs or goals and almost brushed aside by the "guns or butter" debate. The whole experience gave everyone the belief that the arts and the humanities were incidentals in the minds of those who controlled our fate. True, we had a few stout friends, but their rhetoric was shouted into the opposing wind of short-sighted pragmatism. Arguments about enriched lives, the quality of life, and our cultural heritage could only persuade when the agenda carried no threat of any emergency. The impotence of the arts with public bodies was exposed in this first test of understanding. We could accept the negative attitude when we were trying to establish a program, but we had accomplished a viable and much praised program. Now, we realized our successes meant nothing in the final analysis.

The realization that our popularity with the Congress depended on the war in Viet Nam and the size of the federal deficit was only the first blow.

I was taking a shower in Los Angeles on a sunny morning when Roger called. He had the uncanny ability of often calling when I was in the shower and then asking some complicated question. This time it was, "Where can we get $400,000 out of this year's budget?"

"Should I ask for what?"

"I let Humphrey talk me into putting $400,000 into summer arts projects in the inner cities to help combat violence. That man can talk you into anything. I never should have accepted a ride from him. He had me all alone in that plane for two hours."

I asked a few more questions to give me time to think about where to find the money. Then I remembered that we hadn't spent any of the architecture and design budget for the year as yet. Roger said that would do. We could put off those projects until next year.

He said, "When you get back tell the architects on the Council and Spreiregen the story."

"I can't do that. I'm not the Chairman."

"But you're the planning and analysis director. Tell them your plans have changed."

"I really think you have to break bad news, especially to Council members."

Roger didn't like to bring bad news to anyone, but he agreed it was his job.

The procedure was simple. When an agency head wanted to change a program in mid-year he simply notified the appropriations committee in both houses, and permission was granted. I wrote the necessary letters and we received instant approval from the House subcommittee. Meanwhile, the original plan was to offer the mayors of the fifty cities in the Vice President's program $8,000 for summer arts programs in the inner city. The mayors would be obliged to match the grant on a two-for-one basis, creating a local fund of $24,000.

Upon closer examination, it was decided the size of the grant was too small to be effective, and a new plan would award 16 cities grants of $25,000, making a $75,000 program. Vice President Humphrey was asked to choose the 16 most volatile cities. Telegrams were sent to those mayors and all accepted the grant and the conditions. The 16 cities considered most likely to erupt in the summer of 1968 were Atlanta, Baltimore, Boston, Buffalo, Chicago, Cleveland, Detroit, Los Angeles, Milwaukee, Minneapolis, Newark, New York, Philadelphia, San Francisco, St. Louis, and Washington.

Then came the giant obstacle. With the mayors expecting the grants, they began planning for the summer. It was now spring of 1968. Suddenly, the Senate answered our request to shift programs. They said that if we couldn't launch architecture programs within the framework of the current year, and since the country needed all its resources for the war and domestic programs, we should leave the funds in the Treasury and let them be used for essential purposes. Permission denied. Another case of telling us we were low priority.

The Council had to approve the idea. April 19, the Council was in session and all the telegrams had been returned with a positive response. Junius Eddy, who was serving with the President's Council on Youth Opportunity, came to the Council meeting and explained the program. The Council voted to spend up to $600,000 on the program, but this was before the Senate denied our transferring funds for this project.

We had also planned a conference on organizing and operating an inner city arts program at the Wingspread Foundation in Wisconsin. I had suggested it after hearing from people who had definite ideas about such programs; such people as Junius Eddy, Howard Whitaker, Dorothy Maynor, and Katherine Dunham. I thought they could teach the people who were starting programs. We had sent letters to the mayors inviting their coordinators to Wingspread on May 8.

What to do? I had an appointment out of town someplace. When I got back into my office the entire staff descended on me; one of the women was in tears. It seems Roger got this brilliant idea of having a benefit for the Endowment to raise the $400,000. If $200,000 could be raised through a gala and donated to the Treasury Fund, then the money would be matched and available for the inner city program. It was an idea typically creative of Roger. However, he called a meeting of the staff and asked them to sell the tickets to the proposed gala. He wanted to sell 200 tables at $1,000 per table with ten places. He told the staff to start calling grantees and anyone in the arts, or outside the arts, who could afford $1,000. Individual tickets were $150, with $100 a tax deductible contribution, the rest to cover costs.

Leaving aside the issue of the legality of federal officials soliciting money from recipients of federal funds, the people who ran the various programs were not fund-raisers. They had been on the phone to their grantees and were being largely rejected in unkind phrases.

The staff begged me to talk Roger out of using them. I thought the benefit idea was brilliant, if it was legal, but using the professional staff as solicitors was not. Charlotte Woolard told me Roger was arriving at Dulles Airport in an hour. Perfect. I called for a White House limousine for the first and only time.

The staff people had told me they tried to talk Roger out of using them as sales-people, but the more they talked the more insistent he became. I knew from experience that Roger would set his heels if he was challenged in public, but in private he was as reasonable as anyone I had ever known. Getting him alone on the long ride into town from Dulles Airport was a heaven sent opportunity. In his office the door was always open and people thought nothing of interrupting.

When he came through the gate he was smiling and seemed pleased I was there with a limousine. As we rode, I told him what a great idea the benefit was and that if Chuck Ruttenberg, our legal counsel, said it was legal it was the answer to our prayers. However, I said, it wouldn't do to use the staff to sell because it's probably illegal and they won't do the job you want. "If you want the benefit to be a success you will have to spend the next few days on the phone and do it. Otherwise, it's an idea whose time isn't in the right hands."

When we arrived at the office I told the staff to forget their role as solicitors.

Roger sold all the tables in two days time, all by phone.

The benefit was held at the Pierre Hotel in New York on June 26th as a celebration of re-authorization. It was called "Salute to H.R. 11308, As Amended". Co-Chairmen of the dinner-dance were Alvin Ailey, Bill Cosby, T. Edward Hambleton, Thomas Hoving, Peter Mennin, Robert Motherwell, Gregory Peck and George Plimpton. The music, supplied gratis through Herman Kenin and the Music Performance Trust Fund, was Peter Duchin's Orchestra and the New York Rock and Roll Ensemble. Robert Indiana designed the invitation and Sasha Schneider had a string quartet to play during dinner. It was a lovely and profitable party.

The conference at Wingspread to train the people who would be working on the inner city arts projects started badly and ended superbly, thanks to Katherine Dunham. Most of the conferees sent by the mayors were neophytes. Our deputy chairman, Bill Cannon, was to preside for the first day and I, the second day.

Immediately, Topper Carew intimidated Cannon by interrupting him every five minutes with scatological remarks.

When Bill mentioned a program in the ghetto, Topper Carew interrupted to say, "Man, you live in a ghetto, we live in a community." When Bill mentioned low-income, Topper would say, "You mean those who don't demean themselves to work for what the Honkies want to pay." The language was much saltier.

When it came to telling of their plans for the summer program, most of the people told of plans to present symphony orchestras and field trips to art museums. In 1970, Junius Eddy wrote about those misguided plans in an article for *Public Administration Review*. Eddy described these programs as "a kind of loosely organized exposure of poor youngsters (mainly nonwhite) to enriching experiences from the Western middle-class cultural tradition, intended to compensate for presumed deprivation in their lives and backgrounds. One does not have to deny the true richness of the Western cultural tradition to point out the presumptuousness, arrogance, and racism inherent in this simplistic approach to the culturally different person in our pluralistic society."

The dinner speaker that first night was Katherine Dunham, who had been completely silent that whole day. She was introduced as the first black dancer to take modern and ethnic dance to Broadway and Hollywood and who now had an enormously successful program in the inner city of East St. Louis in one of the toughest neighborhoods in America. She rose and stood silent for several long moments. Then she said she had listened patiently to all that was said that day and commented that she had never heard such bullshit in her life. Then she proceeded to tell each person how wrong their particular proposed programs were and how they could be improved. She scolded Topper Carew for extremely rude behavior and told him to behave and contribute or leave. When she finished, a long silence was broken by loud applause and my turn at presiding the next day was extremely pleasant.

In Eddy's article in 1970, he wrote about how that conference, and the projects the Endowment endorsed, changed the attitude of many arts funding agencies, including the Endowment itself in later years:

"It was this counterthrust (ethnic cultural programs) already beginning to emerge in some of the cities themselves, that the Endowment's 1968 summer workshop program recognized, strengthened, and sustained, with far more than the monetary value of the grants themselves. Its true significance needs elaboration.

"First, until the 16-city program was undertaken no federal agency had put its money squarely on the principle of direct involvement in the processes of the arts by young people in poverty neighborhoods . . . no funds mandated for this purpose, with few strings attached, and intended to support a multi-city program, had been forthcoming from any federal agency prior to this time."

Eddy's article was a prize winner in 1971 and on the strength of it he was invited to consult with the Arts Endowment under the Chairmanship of Nancy Hanks. He was thereby instrumental in the formation of the Endowment's Expansion Arts Program. Eddy suggested to Nancy Hanks that Vantile Whitfield be named the first director of that program.

It is important to understand the tension in the country at that time in order to appreciate the atmosphere in which we were working. Martin Luther King, Jr. was murdered on April 5th of that year. Full page ads were running in the major newspapers every week condemning the Johnson policies in Viet Nam and many were signed by prominent artists. At one point President Johnson explained his withdrawal of support for our programs. He said no president had done more for artists than he had, and they turned against him. He believed in loyalty at all costs.

Much dissension existed within the staff, particularly during and after the Martin Luther King riots. Some of the staff wanted to protest publicly, some felt civil rights was none of their business. Those who were outraged by the King murder were almost equally outraged by the attitude of their colleagues. My position was that my private sympathies should remain private unless I was prepared to transfer my full energies to the civil rights cause: merely protesting wasn't going to accomplish anything, except make me feel better and diminish my effectiveness with the arts program.

The days of the King riots were lessons in human nature. News of the assassination was spread through that first night, but the general population of Washington remained alert but calm. Everyone came to work the next morning without exceptional apprehension. However, by early afternoon employees of one agency were calling friends in other agencies and comparing riot news. I sat in my office and heard the level of panic rise from a whisper to a crescendo. It began to sound like an aviary disturbed by a prowling cat. Rumors were transmitted from secretary to secretary. Smoke appeared on the streets below. Agencies were being closed for the day and that news was spread rapidly. Finally, we agreed to dismiss our people even though the radio stations were reporting that horrendous traffic jams were forming.

I continued to work. By four in the afternoon I realized I was alone in our offices. Suddenly a man appeared in my doorway. He suggested I go home and stay there. I said I had work to do here. He showed me an FBI identification and ordered me out of the building.

As I left the building I saw another FBI agent sitting in a chair in front of the entrance with a submachine gun across his lap. I learned later that our building housed an unpublicized communications center which they were protecting.

April 5th and 6th were days which changed the lives of many people. Friends who were black and worked in Congress were going into the riot areas to observe. They agreed it was the black civil service workers, docile up until now, who were enraged at King's murder and joining the frustrated youths in looting and burning. It was the turning point of the civil rights movement.

My friend and neighbor, the writer Chuck Stone, told of entering a liquor store being looted and encountering well dressed black men selectively taking the best scotch and bourbons from the shelves.

Also, white owned businesses in black neighborhoods which had refused to hire black clerks, or which had charged usurious interest, were targeted for burning.

Warner Lawson, who was the only black member of the National Council on the Arts at the time, and a friend and neighbor, was highly critical of another black neighbor who was a militant. He and I had had several discussions about the black militant movement in which we disagreed. After the riots Warner made a point of telling me he no longer thought our neighbor wrong and became highly critical of colleagues who were passive.

I think we all were made aware during those few days how fragile our open society could be when rage rises in a segment of the community. To see convoys of armed troops speeding down neighborhood streets, and then seeing these soldiers stationed at local gas stations and drug stores, is an indelible experience.

At the Wingspread Conference on the summer programs in the inner city, Katherine Dunham told of her experience during the King insurgence. She was at her arts center in East St. Louis, one of the most repressed black communities in the country when the announcement came. Slowly, over the next hour, the young men who had been coming to the center drifted in from the streets. They were stunned, enraged, frustrated beyond reason, and about to explode. Katherine Dunham silently gave them the drums they had been learning to play. And they drummed. They drummed into the night. Other young men and women heard the sound and came in the doors. They joined in. When there were no more drums to distribute, they beat on the floor and clapped their hands. By morning the rage and frustration were spent and at least that part of East St. Louis didn't burn that night.

We weathered two crises during the spring and summer of 1968, but there was still one ahead; this one had to do with our artists' housing project.

Actually, the problems started before the Great Benefit Operation of 1968. When the decision was made to acquire the Bell Labs Building in Lower Manhattan it wasn't known that a small portion of that building stood on leased land. That small parcel was owned by a family who negotiated a lease with AT&T every ten years. As Roger said, that was like having a key to Fort Knox. If AT&T didn't want to pay the price asked for any ten year period, the family could tell them to remove the building from their land. Naturally, the family did not want to sell.

It was then learned that FHA could not enter into a financing deal for any property that was involved with leased land. The whole deal depended on obtaining the deed to that land.

Even with the support of the President, the Secretary of HUD, Governor Rockefeller of New York, and Mayor Lindsey of New York, the project was going nowhere; the family did not wish to sell. The only advantage on our side was that the building was up for sale and the family would not have AT&T to kick around every ten years. Finally, when the Governor and the Mayor said the state and city would buy the building and condemn the land for a park, the family listened to reason and sold.

It should be pointed out that probably no one in the country could have successfully completed this project, except Roger Stevens. Only a man who had bought and sold half of midtown Manhattan's real estate, including the Empire State Building, a man who intimately understood the artist temperament, as well as the political mind, could have brought the deal to conclusion. When Roger met with HUD Secretary Weaver he wanted me along so I would understand the deal. I almost never took notes at a meeting, but depended on my memory. This time I practically wrote every word spoken because I didn't understand what they were saying; it was all real estate technical language. Later, I had to ask Roger to explain all those anagrams and number designations. As time went on the deal became even more involuted.

The land was acquired and the purchase made. The next blow was the requirement of the FHA that a cash payment be made and held until full financing was arranged. The Kaplan Fund, which was the funneling source and generous partner in the deal, couldn't handle such an arrangement and it fell to us to find the large sum, or drop the project. What to do?

The obstacle was overcome by de-obligating funds we had already awarded to various arts institutions. To explain: a grant of $100,000 to American Ballet Theatre, for instance, would be obligated with the Treasury Department. ABT would then request partial payments as needed from us and we would notify the Treasury Department to draw a check for that amount. At any one time, there is a lag between fund obligated and funds requested and paid. By de-obligating some of these unpaid funds we could obligate them for the down payment on the artists' housing project. The problem would arise when the grantees asked for some of their grant money and we could not oblige.

Handling the complex problems became so difficult that we split it into three parts. Roger took care of the overall project and the real estate technicalities, Chuck Ruttenberg dealt with the legal requirements, and I had the financial problems. In order to avoid mistakes, the three of us met every morning to review each other's problems and actions to date.

165

The down payment was supposed to be reimbursed within a month or six weeks, so de-obligating a large sum for a short while should have proved no problem. However, the financing took more time. The staff directors were told to refer all requests for grant payments to me and I would stall and plead with the grantee for another week.

The ground breaking actually took place June 21, 1968, though the down payment wasn't re-imbursed to us until August. All the rightful money was re-obligated, the project went forward, and today artists are housed in the Westbeth Center as they have been since early in 1970. Because of the exceptionally strong construction, the high ceilings, and the heavy electrical wiring in the original laboratory building, it is considered a choice location for studio-living space for visual artists.

Just as the fiscal year was ending I learned that the Humanities Endowment would not be using all of their Treasury Fund money. Since these funds were appropriated to both Endowments as a single amount and divided in-house, I asked Roger if he could convince Chairman Keeney to relinquish his claim to some Treasury money and let us try to find gifts to benefit the arts. Roger convinced Keeney that not using the money would encourage Congress to appropriate less in the future and that would be bad for both Endowments.

However, we had only two days to find donors and have them actually provide the money in cash to us. Roger made a list of the most likely people and institutions to have spare cash and the authority to rush it to us. We would promise them the Treasury Fund would double it and send back to them. We divided the list between us.

On my list was John Crosby, the patron saint of the Santa Fe Opera. I couldn't locate him at first, though I left messages at several places. Finally, he called on the morning of the deadline. I asked him if he could find $50,000 immediately. It was six in the morning in Santa Fe when he called. He was delighted, but a bit annoyed at the timetable. Nevertheless, he said he would try his best. He persuaded his banker in Santa Fe to open the bank for him and personally draw up a note and wired the money to us. It was an arduous process, but one he felt would be profitable for the Opera.

When I went into Roger's office to triumphantly tell him I had gotten $50,000 for Santa Fe Opera, Roger told me it was too late. The one aspect we didn't coordinate was the amount of the Treasury Fund still available as we generated the contributions. He had secured the last $50,000 from someone else while Crosby was rousing his banker. I had to call Crosby back and tell him he was too late. I was treated to considerable invective and advice on how we could run a tighter ship. I felt I was unjustly punished.

Another unjust punishment came at the hands of puppeteer Bil Baird. Occasionally, Roger was asked to supply the entertainment for the White House because he was the President's Assistant for the Arts. On one occasion, he suggested Bil Baird and the new project he was developing with a grant from the Council. I was assigned to work with Baird. At the last minute, someone in the White House decided that puppets were the wrong image—they were for kids, not grown up politicians—and the appearance was cancelled. When I called Baird and told him he was livid. He had created special puppets and written a complete script for the presentation at the White House. He had spent money that was wasted.

One more event of the spring of 1968 affected our future.

I was in Texas attending The Governor's Conference on the Arts. It was the final night and several successful Texans had been invited to entertain. Carol Burnett, pianist James Dick, and Trini Lopez had all appeared. I was sitting on the aisle directly behind Governor Connally. Suddenly, a huge Texas Ranger walked down the aisle, kneeled next to the Governor, and whispered in his ear. Connally jerked upright and bolted from his seat. This was the time of assassinations and turmoil; I immediately thought of tragedy. The program was essentially over when the Governor appeared on stage. In emotionless tones he said that President Johnson had just announced on television that he would not run for re-election. The entire audience of several hundred rose and filed from the auditorium in silence, except for one man somewhere who beat his hands together in a solitary, slow cadence until the hall was empty. Later, at the reception I asked the Governor if he had any idea the President would withdraw. He said Johnson had asked advice of him two months before, but he couldn't offer any help. It was March 21, 1968.

President Johnson had become grossly disillusioned with the needs of artists because of the vocal protests and newspaper ads opposing his war policy. As a result, during the last few months of the Johnson Administration we received little help from the White House staff or the President himself. During the days before the passage of our legislation President Johnson assigned about a dozen White House staff members to lobby House members. During the re-authorization fight, no White House personnel ever appeared on Capitol Hill on our behalf. The President continued to appreciate Roger's work, but washed his hands of personally lending support to artistic causes.

The influence of the President cannot be over estimated, especially a president who is an expert politician as Johnson was. His withdrawal of support was read on the Hill as a clear sign of his indifference and historically the arts were neglected until Leonard Garment convinced Nixon to give Nancy Hanks support with Congress. Once the arts and humanities were embraced by the Republicans as well as most Democrats, prosperity reigned. President Reagan, of course, reversed the friendly attitude and sowed the seeds of disapproval which flowered in 1989.

John Steinbeck and Ralph Ellison.

Winding Down and Out
The End of 1968 and into 1969

The twelfth meeting of the Council was held on June 14th, 1968 in New York. This was two weeks before the famous benefit at the Pierre Hotel. For the last several months the Bureau of the Budget (BOB) had been requesting that we conform to what came to be called the Gospel According to Saint McNamara, invented by Robert McNamara, the Secretary of Defense. This was a theory of management the Administration had embraced requiring every agency to file a statement of objectives. In our case, all grants would have had to fall under specifically stated objectives. Roger opposed the BOB by ignoring their directives. For some unknown reason, the BOB people kept pressure on me to keep pressure on Roger to conform to the regulations forced on all agencies. Roger's argument was that the Department of Defense could have one objective such as "provide for the common defense" and get on with their work. Conversely, our objectives were broad and varied and couldn't be pinned down because of the nature of the arts and because we were a new agency.

The BOB wouldn't accept the argument and kept insisting. I wrote several versions of possible objectives, all of which Roger threw out immediately. Finally, with my last and best effort, he threw the papers across the room. He was angry and frustrated. At that point we had our most serious disagreement. I wasn't about to scrabble about the floor picking up the papers. I explained we had no choice but to conform and that I had written a set of objectives that would cover any grant he could think of. He sat glaring at me. I waited. After seemingly endless minutes Roger silently rose and picked up the papers from the floor and said, "I want to see if you've covered every possibility."

With the latest set of objectives in hand we went over a list of recent grants and I placed each one under one of the objectives. Reluctantly, Roger agreed to the seven objectives and we were back in stride with the rest of the government, as the BOB people put it. From then on, each grant had to be reported as part of one of the objectives; so broad were they that we never had trouble deciding where to place each one.

A report at the twelfth meeting said that the proposed National Design Institute was further delayed. This was to be a permanent agency dedicated to preserving good design, encouraging better design in all federal enterprises from letterhead to architecture, and offering fellowships to talented designers. The report commissioned by the Council did not meet the satisfaction of the Council committee of architects. Further, reduced funding for fiscal year 1969 made a major new project unrealistic. (The Institute was scrapped in later years, though an effective design project within the federal establishment was launched.)

Each director presented proposed projects and programs within the new objectives. In dance, for instance, a grant to the Joffrey Ballet was put under Aid to Artistic Institutions. Funding of the successful Dance Touring Project was listed under Wider Distribution of the Arts. A grant to San Francisco Ballet to commission four choreographers was, of course, Aid to the Individual Artist and Aid to Artistic Institutions.

Affiliate Artists was assisted in becoming established with a $50,000 grant to become the leading agency for connecting performing artists with non-traditional audiences. The respected American Playhouse public television series had its beginning with a 1968 grant to National Educational Television. In theatre, the now highly successful Eugene O'Neill Foundation which nurtures new plays and directors received $2,500 to begin an experimental workshop for directors that led to its present operation today.

Roger announced the bankruptcy of the American National Opera Company, but pointed to the need for a permanent "opera institute" to assist opera companies and young professional opera singers. A year or so later he managed to organize the service organization now known as the National Institute for Music Theatre.

It was announced that *The American Literary Anthology/1* was available and that the publisher, Farrar Strauss, had absorbed all production costs which reduced the Council's obligation for funds. The anthology was well reviewed; the New York Times being typical:

> *"This first volume of 'best' fiction, poetry, and essays culled from the 1966 issues of nearly 300 magazines of limited circulation marks the first official recognition of the important role played by noncommercial magazines in the discovery and development of authentic literary talent. A substantial grant from the National Endowment for the Arts . . . not only makes possible an annual anthology judged by well known writers and critics, but is the occasion for financially rewarding worthy 'little' magazines, their editors, and outstanding contributors."*

The report on the Museum Purchase Plan was encouraging. Living American artists were being helped by the $10,000 fund available to each of 15 smaller art museums across the country. The museums were enriching their collections and the public was exposed to the work of living artists.

This was to be the last meeting for eight Council members: Leonard Bernstein, Anthony Bliss, Herman Kenin, Warner Lawson, William Pereira, Richard Rogers, John Steinbeck, and James Johnson Sweeney. It was to be the last meeting for another member, Rene d'Harnoncourt. Several months later he retired as Director of the Museum of Modern Art, and six weeks after that he was struck and killed by a drunken driver at ten in the morning.

Leonard Bernstein and Isaac Stern competed for control of the music programs with Stern usually winning because he paid closer attention to the affairs of the endowment. Tony Bliss usually brought a broad perspective to any discussion. Herman Kenin was always helpful on music problems and not always narrowly interested in only union matters. Warner Lawson was the conductor of the famous Howard University Chorus and the Dean of Fine Arts there, so he was most active in arts education, minority, and music projects. William Pereira, the architect, had experience in movie making and design, and was one of the leaders in discussions affecting these fields as well as his own. Richard Rogers never attended. John Steinbeck said little in meetings, but was an effective lobbyist with individual members. Jim Sweeney knew the visual arts and stayed in his field in discussions.

Because of the atmosphere of war, civil strife, and inflation, our appropriation was cut back for the first time. We were reduced in fiscal 1969 from $5 million to $3.7 million for programs, and the funds for the states were reduced from $2 million to $1.7 million. However, the states were taking the arts seriously and in terms of generating new support for the arts this was our most successful venture. State appropriations had increased from $2.6 million in 1966 when only 23 state legislatures provided funds, to $6.85 million in 1969 with 44 states providing state funds. The states dragging their fiscal feet were Arizona, Delaware, Florida, Indiana, Mississippi, Nevada, North Dakota, Wisconsin, Wyoming, American Samoa, and Guam. State appropriations ranged from $7,500 in New Hampshire and $10,000 in Idaho to $2.5 million in New York and $1.35 million in Puerto Rico. Also, it should be noted that during our fight for re-authorization the state politicians and cultural leaders were almost our only advocates actively beating the drums in Washington.

A number of Council members, and some of the staff, had been unenthusiastic toward the state program to this point. Some thought it amateur night out there in the provinces, some thought the money should be spent to bring the major institutions to the hinterlands, some were just snobbish about it. After the re-authorization fight, I noticed colleagues looking at my old program with new respect. Clark Mitze, who was now the Director of State and Community Operations, found it difficult to believe when I told him some of our own people had been less than supportive of the state program.

In fact, Roger was now such an advocate of the work of the states that he accepted an invitation to attend an Indian festival in South Dakota that was sponsored by the state. At the last minute he had a conflict and I took his place. One of the highlights of the program was a series of native American dances. Black Eagle was the emcee and I sat passively on a log bench watching the show. The Rabbit Dance was introduced as the only dance in Indian culture in which the ladies choose their partners. Suddenly I was tapped on the shoulder and turned to see an ancient, toothless, scraggly haired woman; I was to be her dance partner. I danced, but as I danced I thought of dignified

171

Roger with his chronic bad back and city ways. What if he had made the trip. Seeing him doing an Indian dance with this original Native American would have been priceless. When I was asked why I was laughing hysterically while dancing, I couldn't tell them.

In early summer I received an unexpected letter. UNESCO was asking me to write a 25,000 word monograph about American cultural policy for a series they were sponsoring on the subject. As I remember five countries were commissioned at that time. Two of the others were the USSR and Brazil. Roger and I had also been invited to attend a UNESCO meeting in Budapest on the subject of cultural centers. While at that meeting I discussed the proposed monograph with the director of the cultural policy program, hoping I could refuse the honor.

I said the U.S. had no cultural policy, that we all did our own thing and hoped for the best. I told him how the arts and humanities programs were established as a political expediency and how the state program was the price of support from certain Senators. But then, the UNESCO official convinced me I was wrong.

The UNESCO official said everyone recognizes the U.S. cultural policy as laisser-faire, even pluralistic laisser-faire. He said we had so many facets to our cultural support system no single resource could ever control the arts. I said you mean that so many pipers are calling the tune that it doesn't ruin the song if one piper plays off key or refuses to play? He said it probably worked something like that. I thought about it and decided to tackle the assignment.

The book had to be written according to a standard outline; all the monographs were to be comparable. The fine Gallic logic of the outline was the greatest hurdle. I stayed home for a week to write the monograph and spent Monday through Wednesday studying the outline. Thursday I began writing and turned the manuscript over to my secretary on Monday. It turned out to be only a 43 page booklet, but it was accepted and UNESCO had it translated into several languages.

Every time they would send me a copy of my work in a new foreign language I would look at one of the early statements. I had written that Ulysses S. Grant once said he only knew two tunes, one was "Yankee Doodle" and the other wasn't. In every language Ulysses and Yankee Doodle couldn't be translated.

The last statement in the booklet (1969) is worth noting:

"Lastly, it would be a mistake to interpret United States cultural policy simply as the rise of federal support in replacement of failing private resources. The entrance of Federal interest in the cultural scene in 1965 was of paramount importance because that action decisively thrust culture into the center of American life. It was the final step in an evolutionary process. It was done with the support of business, science, and labor as these elements reflected their growing concern for increased leisure-time. However, the presence of a federal agency does not mean a subsequent relaxation on the part of other public and private sectors. As it was explained earlier, the states were prompted by the federal programme to establish arts councils. Private individual corporation and foundation contributions have increased because of the focus provided by the federal action. The federal funds expended

during the first three years by the National Endowment for the Arts had amounted to $22.9 million, but $31.4 million in state and private funds were generated to carry out the projects largely initiated at the federal level. In short, the federal action has come to be as it was intended: a stimulating force for cultural development."

—*UNESCO: Cultural Policy in the*
United States, 1969, Paris.

And so it was, and is.

The visit to Budapest in those days was almost like a middle-European operetta. Before I could get a visa for my wife to accompany me, I had to secure a Hungarian money order for $70 to insure she would not become a ward of the state. Who was authorized to issue a Hungarian money order? Why, only the Hungarian Ambassador of course. He charged 10 percent for the service. The exchange rate was 30 forints to the dollar.

When we got to Budapest I was anxious to cash the money order immediately. The hotel clerk obliged and offered me 32 forints per dollar. I said, "Thirty-two forints?"

He said, "Alright, 34."

I learned that forints were Monopoly money and protesting the rate always produced a higher exchange.

UNESCO followed its customary practice of giving each delegate a per diem amount in the currency of the country. By the time the meeting was over we still had a pocketful of forints. Then, we were told, we couldn't take forints out of the country; we had to spend them or turn them in.

On the last day, we managed to grab one of the few taxis in Budapest and go on a shopping spree, buying hand carved chess sets, embroidered placemats and handkerchiefs. Finally, with the last forints I bought a harmonia in a music store; the instrument with a keyboard about a foot long that one blows into to make a sound.

On the train to Vienna I examined the instrument and found it was made in Pennsylvania. The price in Hungary was less than it would have been here. The next time I saw my Hungarian delegate friend I asked him why. He told me the government encourages music and subsidizes the price of instruments. At that time the U.S. had an excise tax on musical instruments as a luxury item. A different attitude toward art.

Roger had invited Mrs. Auchincloss, the mother of Jacqueline Kennedy, to join him on this trip. The Hungarian hosts kept us busy every day when the UNESCO meeting adjourned and she generally accompanied us to these activities and in the evening. I was constantly amused that she always referred to her family by familial designation. For instance, she would say, "My oldest daughter sang quite beautifully." Or "My oldest daughter's husband had a lively interest in Hungarian food."

On September 11, 1968, President Johnson appointed eight new members to the National Council on the Arts; veteran theatrical producer Jean Dalrymple, Duke Ellington, Architect O'Neil Ford, sculptor Richard Hunt, singer Robert Merrill, Gregory Peck for his second term, Rudolph Serkin, and dancer Edward Villella.

We also had a new Deputy Chairman, Douglas MacAgy, a Canadian who gave up his citizenship to accept the job. He was an art historian by training. Our new Music Program Director was Walter Anderson, a pianist and administrator from Antioch University. Frank Crowther by this time had announced he was leaving by the first of the new year. From the minutes of that meeting:

"With new Council and staff members present, Chairman Stevens took the opportunity of reviewing the policies which were developed during the first three years:

> *"Namely, that as a general rule, the Council will recommend projects with national implications or those which are part of a national support program (such as the program of assistance to resident professional theatres across the country); that due to budgetary limitations, the Council will not entertain requests for construction or rehabilitation of arts facilities; and that the Council is generally not in favor of covering deficits of arts organizations. The Chairman noted that there had been a few exceptions to these general guidelines, made at the Council's recommendation, and that the overriding principle was to enable the Council to be flexible in its approach, and to retain its ability to move with speed when necessary."*

Flexibility was illustrated by the grant made to the Alvin Ailey Dance Theatre. Roger had received a call from London from Alvin Ailey. The company had undertaken the European tour with advanced bookings across the continent. A number of their bookings were cancelled after they had arrived. They were, in effect, stranded in England and had no way of getting back home. Ailey had called all the private foundations, but no one could free up funds fast enough to be of help. Roger was the last resort.

On the phone Roger negotiated for two new choreographed works by Ailey for a $10,000 Chairman's grant and the money was dispatched the next day. (Our funds could not be spent for overseas ventures, that's why the grant was in the form of a choreographer's commission.)

Another Chairman's grant was for one of my projects. A marble quarry in Vermont wanted to invite sculptors from all over the world to come there and use their tools and marble to create whatever the artists wanted. It would be an international sculpture symposium for eight weeks. The sculptors could keep the works created, destroy them, or leave them there.

I thought it a tremendous project. Henry Geldzahler, director of Visual Arts, didn't like it at all. He thought sculptors who wanted to work in marble were all hacks. I tried David Stewart, our Education Director, saying it was an educational project and belonged to him. He said he had other uses for his allotment of funds. So, I said I would put it into the "Variety of Art Forms" category which was under my jurisdiction, but Roger said that wouldn't do. He liked the project also, and decided to make a Chairman's grant.

The project was successful with the Vermont Marble Company and with the sculptors. They voted to leave all their work in place at the quarry and it is now a sculpture park.

During this fall period preceding the 13th meeting of the Council I was assigned the task of writing the official history of the Council and Endowment. The President had ordered these histories to be written and stressed that mistakes and failures, as well as successes, were to be included. My other assignments—writing next year's program and budget, handling personnel problems—kept me from diligent work on the history. The White House deadline for a first draft was upon me and I hadn't gone over the work with Roger. I made two copies of the draft, sent one to the White House and put the other on Roger's desk.

When he read it he was astonished to find the mistakes and failures. He told me he didn't want that material to be permanently part of the record in the President's archives. I tried to explain the specific orders I had been given, but he demanded I retrieve the other copy from the White House immediately. I called and asked for the return of the draft. Will Sparks, one of the President's speech writers in charge of the project, was perfectly willing to return the draft, but he said I should know they liked what I had written so much that they had sent copies to other agencies as an example of a proper history.

I showed Roger the returned copy and never told him of the wider distribution of the history he didn't like. My heart was no longer in writing the history, so staff member Ana Steele took over the project and rewrote from my manuscript.

The 13th meeting was both joyful and sad. Richard Nixon was the President-Elect and that meant Roger would not be appointed to a second term. However, it also meant the Endowment would be funded at much higher amounts, because it would now be an Administration program. Democrats in Congress would continue to support it because it was their program originally. Further, as Roger pointed out so many times, the major institutions' boards of trustees had many Republicans on them. Word would reach the Administration that the arts are good politics. But who could replace Roger? Was there such a thing as a knowledgeable person in the arts who was Republican? Naming Roger's successor became both a serious consideration and a humorous game.

Sad, too, was the loss of the second group of original members; only five of the founding members were still serving, plus Gregory Peck serving his second term. But then, the new members were well-qualified, so the future seemed to be in good hands.

Overriding all other emotions was the realization the smallest appropriation ever for a full year was available as we met for the 13th time.

So many of the programs were becoming completely accepted by the respective fields that the prospect of not being able to continue funding was out of the question. In dance, the Residency Touring Program as a pilot program in Illinois was so successful it needed to be expanded. The Merce Cunningham Dance Company had been given a parade to the airport when they left Normal, Illinois, an honor usually reserved for football teams. In literature, *The American Literary Anthology/2* was ready to be published.

In music, the first program of aid to symphony orchestras was being readied for support. Affiliate Artists, Inc., was being launched at 15 colleges and universities. The project to study the Kodaly method of music instruction for children was exceeding expectations with the Americans in Hungary receiving complete cooperation. At the Budapest UNESCO meeting, Roger and I were overwhelmed by the performances of junior high school aged performers, both choral and instrumental. The youngsters seemed to have complete confidence in their sense of pitch and rhythm.

The Corporation for Public Broadcasting had been established by Congress giving strength to the programs the Council had launched with public television and radio.

Theatre programs were booming. A festival of new plays in the Berkshires resulted in four of the plays being produced on Broadway the next season.

Though the states program only had a maximum of $30,909 per state instead of a possible $50,000, the state legislatures continued to increase state appropriations.

The Artists' Housing Project, now known as Westbeth, would be ready for occupancy within a year.

All of these programs were completed or continued despite the cut in funds, and additional projects were launched. (See appendix for all grants made in the first five years).

Finally, the highlight of this meeting was a proposal by Roger that the Council accept the ANTA Theatre on West 52nd Street in New York as a gift. If the Council would advance the funds to pay off a second mortgage of $375,000 the theatre would be given to the Endowment and thereby qualify as a $1.1 million gift to the Treasury Fund. The Treasury Fund had $500,000 available for the match. The total value of the theatre was $2.1 million. It was a complicated deal that only a real estate expert such as Roger fully understood. The Council voted to undertake the deal.

The social highlight was a White House dinner for the Council as a gesture of gratitude as the Johnsons were leaving office. Roger wanted the professional staff invited also, but the White House refused. However, he said he could insist the most senior staff— Deputy MacAgy, Legal Counsel Ruttenberg, and myself—be included. I said if the rest of the staff wasn't invited I didn't think we should go. Why did I do that?

Roger's speech that night introducing the President so moved the Council members they voted the next day to have it permanently entered into the record. He said:

"Mr. President, Mrs. Johnson, members of the Arts Council, distinguished guests:

"I am pleased to have this occasion to introduce the President to the members of the National Council on the Arts, because it gives me a moment to say publicly what many of us have expressed privately in the past few years.

"Without President Johnson's firm and unwavering support, we would not have an Arts Council today.

"Three years ago last summer, I remember sitting all day in the House Gallery during a session of the 89th Congress. The Democratic leadership was attempting to extract seven bills from the House Committee on Rules. There was quite a pull and haul, and the opposition used every stalling tactic in the book. Late that night, it appeared as if they would only be able to get the first three of the seven bills out of Rules. The bill on the establishment of the National Foundation on the Arts and the Humanities was number four.

"I am told by reliable friends that, as we sat there facing what appeared to be the doom of the arts bill, word came from the White House that the leadership was to get that fourth bill out of the Rules Committee if they had to keep the House in session half the night.

"So I think it would be well for the artistic community to remember that none of the programs initiated over the past few years by our Council would have been possible if it had not been for the personal efforts of the President. If we review the many other accomplishments of his Administration during these years, it is quite evident that, as I have said on other occasions, President Johnson has done more for the arts than any other President in the history of the United States.

"We all know that the arts are, if anything, controversial. But through all these years, the President has left us alone to make our own decisions. He has offered us only encouragement and complete support. Because of this, I believe we can say today that the artistic world no longer fears, as some did at the beginning, that the heavy hand of government will somehow interfere in the freedom of the arts. Let us hope that fear has been firmly set aside.

"During all these years, there was one evening here at the White House I shall remember especially. I was talking quietly with the President when he introduced me to someone saying, 'This is my friend Roger Stevens, who causes me no trouble and gives me great pleasure.' That was the kindest thing said to me in all my days here in Washington, and I think the President knows how much it meant to me, personally.

"This evening, therefore, I have the distinct honor of introducing to you a man who, during his term of office, to use your own words, Mr. President, far from ever having caused us trouble, has given the members of the National Council on the Arts a great deal of pleasure. I am very proud to have served him, and have known him.

"Ladies and gentlemen, the President of the United States."

Leonard Bernstein and Isaac Stern.

The Curtain Falls
1969 and Out

Richard Nixon was sworn in as President on January 20, 1969, and the last meeting of the National Council on the Arts under Roger's chairmanship was held January 27–28. We met in the board room of the Museum of Modern Art with a large number of invited guests. Representatives from the Business Committee for the Arts were present, mostly the corporate officers responsible for charitable contributions, representatives of the state arts councils, deans of fine arts at universities, and members of the press.

By this time it was generally known that Roger and I would both be leaving, though several prominent Republicans attempted to influence the Nixon people to reappoint Roger to a second term as Chairman. In the middle of this meeting I was handed a message that I should call a person from the Times-Mirror Corporation. During a break I called. I was told that Mrs. Dorothy Chandler would like to talk to me about the Los Angeles Music Center. I said I'd be happy to. When could I come to Los Angeles? I said I didn't have any plans at the moment to come West. Would I mind if they kept in touch? Not at all.

At the meeting two new members were introduced. Mrs. Ruth Carter Johnson of Fort Worth was appointed by President Johnson to replace Rene d'Harnoncourt. Sculptor Robert Berks replaced Minoro Yamasaki, who resigned pleading press of work.

One of the projects that I had been single handedly advocating since the first meeting was that of organized graduate training for future arts managers. The Council was not friendly to the concept. To the performing artist like Isaac Stern, an arts manager was someone who took 10 or 15 percent of your money for doing a very simple job. To the creative artists, a manager was the same as the agent who peddled your work. They failed to grasp the complexities of building audiences and organizing communities to support cultural enterprises.

At this last meeting I could report that the small grant awarded for two conferences, one on each coast, organized by UCLA had received the support of leading managers of orchestras, theatres, dance companies, and arts councils. A unanimous request was addressed to UCLA by the Council to establish an arts management program in the Graduate School of Management. The Council yawned, but I was happy.

As events happened, I moved to Los Angeles in April of 1969 and served on the organizing committee for the arts management program and later taught during the first year. It never became the program I envisioned, but it was the first of the more than twenty that have sprung up at the universities since that time.

In general, the Council concerned itself with major programs into the future, realizing increased funding was a necessity before many additional programs could be undertaken. They re-affirmed their conviction that grants to individual artists was an essential part of the entire federal effort.

The states program was now enjoying full support from the Council and staff. Clark Mitze could report increased cooperation between states and the Endowment as well as regional cooperation among the states. Considerable support was present for an increased authorization for the states when next the Congress addressed reauthorization; $5.5 million was mentioned.

The next few weeks were chaotic at the office. Roger's term expired on March 11, 1969. Doug MacAgy was a willing enough Acting Chairman, but he was a Canadian and didn't understand the subtleties of our government, he was new on the job, and he wasn't a forceful leader. The major burden of running the agency fell to me. The press reaction to Roger's leaving was critical of the Nixon Administration, and the rumors of his successor were flying around the country. The calls from the press were referred to me. I was told by the White House to assure the press "the Endowment would continue and that they were searching for a replacement for Roger."

If the Nixon White House actually offered the job to everyone who says they were asked, they were a busy bunch. Supermarket heir and art collector Huntington Hartford, Metropolitan Museum of Art Director Thomas Hoving, Los Angeles art patroness Dorothy Chandler, art patron George Irwin, and Morton D. May of the May Company department store chain all claimed they turned it down. I know Morton "Buster" May was asked because the White House asked me to write a recommendation for him.

His appointment, in fact, was imminent. He was to act as Chairman, but on a part-time basis and John MacFadyen was to be the full time deputy and actually operate the Endowment. Our Democratic friends in Congress put a stop to that ineffective arrangement.

Meanwhile, the staff and Council members were reacting to Roger leaving and to Nixon in the White House. Richard Diebenkorn resigned with a flat out statement that he didn't want to work for the present Administration. Public Media director David Stewart jumped to the new Corporation for Public Broadcasting. Literature Director Carolyn Kizer merely said she wanted more time for her poetry and stepped into a consultant's role. Later, Helen Hayes quietly resigned from the Council; I don't know why.

I had gotten at least three more telephone calls from different people in the Times-Mirror organization, all saying Mrs. Dorothy Chandler wanted to talk to me about a position with the Los Angeles Music Center. Finally, I said I would be in Las Vegas for a regional conference of state arts councils and if Mrs. Chandler wanted to pay my expenses from there to L.A. I could oblige her. It was promptly arranged.

Mrs. Chandler had a charming feminine office in the Times-Mirror building near the Music Center. We drank tea and talked. What she had in mind, she said, was retirement. I would be the president of the Music Center Arts Council, primarily responsible for the Center's fundraising, but also programming with the constituent groups: the Philharmonic, Mark Taper Forum, Ahmanson Theatre, L.A. Civic Light Opera, and the Master Chorale. As she described the different layers of authority over the Center I envisioned a Balkan country. Los Angeles County had the routine maintenance responsibility, the Operating Company took care of nonconstituent bookings and certain central services such as box office and accounting. In addition, each constituent group had its own board. The job sounded challenging, but not like much fun.

Then she asked under what conditions I would take the job. I described everything I could think of as a salary or a fringe benefit. When I finished she suggested a few more items she would like to give me and I said I'd accept.

Back in Washington the Nixon people had been doing everything to get me to resign. They published a list each week that the Republicans called "The Plum Book" and the Democrats called "The Doomsday Book." In it were the 2,000 top jobs in the government. Every week my job would be listed as "currently vacant." I would call and ask them to correct it, but they never did. One day I came back from a meeting and some of my furniture had been taken from my office. My secretary said the White House took it because it was on the White House inventory. It probably was theirs, but it was harassment none the less.

Back from California, I sent my letter of resignation to President Nixon. Since a President had appointed me I thought a President should let me resign. The letter was gleefully accepted, I assumed.

Congressional hearings for the next year's budget were coming up and I was scheduled to leave before then. Suddenly, the White House realized Doug MacAgy was inadequate to testify. I had written the appropriations material, knew all the programs, and knew the subcommittee members. The White House called and asked me to rescind my resignation until after the hearings. I was greatly tempted to say, "Sayonara fellas, you wanted me out, so I'm out." However, the agency meant more than pettiness; I rescinded and testified.

The Subcommittee Chairwoman, Julia Butler Hansen, asked me to ask Roger to testify. I didn't know whether that was allowed or whether that would prejudice the new powers. I had no one to turn to. MacAgy's plan was to make an opening statement, which I was to write, and turn the hearings over to me on the grounds that he was too new to do a good job. Roger would be in attendance as a consultant.

In the statement I wrote for MacAgy, I said, "The Subcommittee has requested Roger Stevens be present and testify. The Endowment is pleased to accede to the committee's wishes." That was a mistake.

When MacAgy read those words at the opening of the hearing, Rep. Hansen jumped to full attention and looked straight at me.

She said, "Chuck, what do you mean accede?" She went on to lecture me in a loud and tense voice that I was insulting, arrogant, and stupid to think that one could merely accede to the Congress's wishes. She said I had no choice but to produce Roger Stevens if the Committee asked for him. She went on for some five or more minutes before telling MacAgy that he could continue.

He couldn't speak. He sat there staring at her with a glazed look while we all waited. His face was colorless and he was breathing in shallow gulps. Finally, Rep. Hansen said we would proceed by entering his full statement into the record. She cautioned me to remove the offensive statement before allowing it to be a permanent part of the record.

I explained that MacAgy did not feel adequate to testify and that Roger would act as a consultant, answering any questions the committee put to him. MacAgy uttered not one more word during the three or four hours of testimony.

I was gone by the time the appropriations process ground out a final amount. Ironically, it was the largest appropriation to date: $4.25 million for programs, $2 million for the states and $2 million for the Treasury Fund. Even the administrative budget was increased by $200,000. As Adlai Stevenson once said, "You have to vote like a Democrat to live like a Republican." By 1976, when the Democrats once more captured the White House, the Arts Endowment budget was ten times the 1970 amount; $8 million to $82 million. Most of the increased funds went to the major arts institutions.

The last annual report of Roger's tenure was submitted to the President on January 15, 1969. In it he said in part:

"We often hear about the 'cultural explosion' or the American Renaissance. I have used these phrases myself. But in reflection, after this first experience with Federal assistance to the arts on a national basis, what I believe we need is neither an 'explosion' nor a renaissance. An explosion implies quick and destructive revolution, and that I do not favor. A renaissance means 'rebirth,' and that rather misses the point. (Rebirth of what, the Hudson River School of painting, or silent motion pictures.)

"Rather, I think we need, as a society, an artistic revolution and regeneration, but not so quietly nor so slowly as in the past. We must be able to give our talented young people the encouragement and the means to enter the artistic life. Slowly, but inexorably, the arts must become part of our daily lives. The desire, even the demand, is there. I have seen it in children's eyes, in a man's work of massive sculpture, and in a woman's company of dancers. I have heard it in bright questions posed by students to established writers, and I have read it in the many pleading letters that have crossed my desk these past several years."

National Endowment for the Arts
Fourth Annual Report

And so had I. But the journey that began with a telephone call in St. Louis had come to an end. The National Endowment for the Arts would grow to become the largest single source of assistance to the arts in the history of the country, but it wouldn't be the same. The eminent artists who served during those first few years were the ones who made history. They set the pattern and brought to fruition the imaginative programs that have continued until today. It was the late David Smith who first talked about more sculpture in public places, not to sell his work, but to expose the public to the beauties of this art form. Isaac Stern and Leonard Bernstein were concerned about the burden borne by composers when having works copied. I will never forget Bernstein's words when he spoke in favor of a rural arts project; "This project has nothing to do with art, but it has everything to do with why we are sitting here."

The final untold story actually took place in 1968. I was in my office when a call came from Liz Carpenter, Lady Bird Johnson's Press Secretary. "Hey, Chuck," she said. I had never met her, but she acted as though we were old friends. "I'm told you know everything about the arts in St. Louis." I modestly admitted I had spent three and half years there trying to organize the arts.

"Well, I was wondering if you would like to help the President out with a little problem he has that involves St. Louis."

"Certainly. I would—"

"Well, come on over to my office and we'll talk about it."

I entered the East Wing where her office was located and was immediately ushered into her presence. Hers was one of the most pleasant staff offices in that sanctuary.

She explained the problem in concise declarative sentences. President Johnson wanted to congratulate August Busch, owner of the St. Louis Cardinals, on winning the 1967 World Series. The occasion was a testimonial dinner the next night. At a recent governor's conference which was held on a cruise ship, a Presidential telegram had been leaked to the press and all the governors, before it arrived at the governor to whom it was addressed. For the past week, the leak, Johnson's angry reaction to the leak, and so forth, had been much in the news.

President Johnson's idea for a funny joke was to send congratulations to "Gussie" Busch in the form of a singing telegram with some reference to the leak. Liz Carpenter looked up at me and said:

"Our job is to add something to make it actually funny."

I felt like someone was asking me to give a ten minute outline of total human knowledge. I asked for a minute to think about it. She said to take my time, but she kept drumming with a pencil while I stood before her desk like an errant school boy.

"What is the song of the singing telegram?"

"What could it be but 'Take Me Out to the Ball Game?' "

Finally, I said, "Maybe if it was sung as a madrigal that would make it funnier."

"A what?"

"A madrigal."

"What's that?"

"Well, it's a kind of renaissance vocal musical style based on contrapuntal arrangements. It was very popular during Shakespeare's day. You know, a lot of fa la las and hey nonny nonnies."

"How would one go?"

"I don't understand."

"Sing one."

Few people know that I actually sang in the White House, but this was the moment of my debut. I sang "Take Me Out to the Ball Game" in contrapuntal style with a few fa las and hey nonnies thrown in.

Liz Carpenter squinted her eyes at me, remained serious in her demeanor, and said, "You mean it's like a round; like 'Row, Row, Row Your Boat.'"

"Exactly."

"That may do it. I'll get back to you. You know how to get ahold of singers who can do this stuff?"

I nodded and she said she would get back to me.

I went back to my office. About an hour later I was called back. She handed me a piece of foolscap with my idea hastily typed. In the margin in pencil was the notation, "Good idea, LBJ." I wanted more than anything to ask if I could keep that piece of paper to show my grandchildren, but I merely nodded and handed it back. She wanted me to contact the people in St. Louis and have them rehearse.

The man responsible for the madrigal group in St. Louis was the Chairman of the Music Department at Washington University and a man of superb, but very fussy taste. He spoke with precision, dressed with precision, had esoteric musical and literary taste, and I always thought he considered me to be slightly crude and a bit too earthy to be in the arts.

Mrs. Carpenter's secretary got him on the phone. I was told to pick up the other phone. She said:

"Listen, Doctor, an old friend of yours, Chuck Mark, and I are sitting around here in the White House trying to help the President play a little joke on Gussie Busch and we wondered if you might want to help us out. Say hello to Chuck, Doctor."

"Oh. OH! Hi Chuck. How are you?"

From the way she talked it sounded as if I sat around the Oval Office with LBJ every afternoon and plotted little fun things to do.

I explained the situation to him and asked if he could have his group prepared on such short notice. He seemed so flattered to be asked and so nervous I felt a residual satisfaction dating back to encounters in St. Louis when he displayed his esoteric knowledge at my expense. Then I said I definitely wanted his people to be wearing Western Union hats, and he should take care of that personally. It was mean of me, but the image of him going to the grimy Western Union office in his neat ensemble to beg for the dirty old hats somehow brought out a mean streak.

"Oh, yes Chuck, yes. I'll do it personally."

"And let me know how it works out."

"Oh, yes. I'll call you first thing the following morning. Anything I can do to help President Johnson I will do."

"You're a great American," I said, suppressing a spontaneous smile.

I thought that was the end of the incident. Two weeks later Roger had his usual party for the Council. Senators, Representatives, and cabinet members were there. Artists love to meet politicians and politicians love to meet artists. Lady Bird Johnson had promised to come and that word gets around Washington faster than scandal in high places. But she was late in arriving, which was unusual. Apparently, most people at the party knew that when the First Lady was exceptionally late it meant that she was waiting for her husband to finish work so he could accompany her, but I didn't know it.

I was talking shop to people and having my end of the day cocktail when I decided to check on my wife's comfort. She was not comfortable at these large celebrity parties nor was Gregory Peck's wife, Vernique. They usually sat in a quiet place and talked. On my way to find her I approached the front door. Suddenly the door opened and two or three men in black tie pushed people away from the entrance, me included. President Johnson then entered. As it happened, the President was forced to stop his progress right in front of me. He shook my hand and asked my name like a good politician. I answered him and then I said,

"How did your joke go over with Gussie Busch the other night?"

He said, "It went fine. How do you know about that?"

I said that I had helped Liz Carpenter with devising the joke. I was so impressed with the physical domination of the man I could hardly think.

For some reason, President Johnson was interested. He put his arm around me and began asking me about how I got the idea, about what I did with the Endowment, and thanking me over and over for helping him out, all the while moving us toward the main living room.

At the entrance to Roger's living room was a flight of stairs. Here was the President of the United States making his well anticipated entrance with his arm around an obscure civil service worker. Our entire professional staff stood with mouths open. LBJ was in serious conversation with me with Lady Bird trailing behind. He patted me on the back, made his round of handshaking, had a cocktail and some food from the buffet table. In half an hour he was ready to leave.

An interesting sidelight was the fact that from the moment they entered he and Lady Bird split up, each working the crowd separately.

The bar at the house was at the foot of the living room stairs. As LBJ was leaving he passed the bar, saw me, and again took notice. He said, "There you are again." He took my arm and pulled me along to the door, shook my hand and left.

Naturally, the staff descended on me and asked what he had said, why did he single me out, what did I say to capture his attention. I said it was between the President and me and I didn't want to talk about it. Some of the staff was quite envious. I never did tell anyone on the staff the reason why the President was so friendly, nor did I know why he didn't just pass me by. It has occurred to me since that perhaps LBJ liked to hang on to some obscure person at a party to dramatize his role, or maybe feel more comfortable himself. I really don't know why.

After that, every time I went to St. Louis, people were always asking me for inside information from Washington, so certain were they that I was part of the inner circle.

Epilogue

I was an observing witness to history. I was there at the conception of the many great civilized and progressive actions of the Johnson years. Those brief years brought more than government recognition of the arts and humanities. They also brought public television, historic preservation, the first national park entirely devoted to the arts, federal aid to education, the Peace Corps, Headstart, civil rights, voting rights, and more than one hundred other beneficial pieces of legislation.

I was there and rejoiced with friends and colleagues when a new program hurdled the obstacles and passed through the Congress. And they rejoiced with me when we overcame the opposition and put the arts and humanities in the public consciousness.

I was there when Roger Stevens was assigned the task of developing a plan to establish a federal program to assist the arts. I experienced running out of funds in the White House; the richest nation in the world. I remember the casual Saturday morning meeting when it was decided that the arts and humanities needed to be politically married to triumph in Congress. I remember Rep. Thompson coming toward us in the corridor behind the House after midnight when our bill was assured of passage. He was gray with fatigue and his hands shook with tension. He said not to ask him to do it again. I remember Senator Claiborne Pell telling Roger not to mention him as the father of the arts bill, if he wanted to help his re-election in 1966. During Pell's next campaign in 1972, his work in the arts was mentioned in all his campaign literature and he organized a committee of artists to support him.

I was there when the indefatigable Rep. Gross was once again clowning at our expense and Rep. Adam Clayton Powell walked across the aisle to the Republican side and whispered in Gerald Ford's ear. Ford moved to Gross's side, placed two hands on the spouting man's shoulders and forced him back into his seat.

I sat in the room at the first Council meetings and heard great artists, patrons, and scholars tell of their visions for the arts in America. Brilliant minds were guided by the brilliant mind of the Chairman toward viable programs that stretched a few millions of federal funds into programs of important and permanent impact. I saw large personalities clash, mesh, soar, and contemplate. I saw many programs blossom, some die, and watched from a distance as succeeding Councils and Chairmen dismantled programs which deserved to be continued.

Roger Stevens and the National Council on the Arts dispensed approximately only $25 million in federal funds in three and one-half years. Most of those funds required state or private matching funds to complete the projects which the Council initiated. A total of approximately $70 million in nonfederal money was generated for the arts in that period; less than half the annual budget of the present day Arts Endowment. Yet that money stimulated the quiet revolution Roger Stevens referred to in his annual report of 1968. Quite simply, it gave artists hope and a feeling that they were valued.

As the appropriations grew in the 1970s, the bureaucracy grew. The Council could no longer look at each application in detail, programs were no longer tailored to particular problems. Instead, needs were addressed with a wholesale approach. Larger grants were given to orchestras, opera companies, theatres and ballet troupes on an annual basis. Galloping inflation ate away at the solvency of the arts institutions so that more funds meant only treading water and not artistic progress. Then, in 1980, came the first really organized attack by the conservatives, an attempt to abolish the agency. Failing that, the Reagan Administration managed to keep funding from increasing, which actually meant a decrease in support because of inflation and rising costs.

Congress had learned to protect the arts because the members had been shown that the people wanted a fruitful cultural life and were willing to pay for it. But the 1980 attack has had a permanent effect on the Endowment. It has given the opposition an agenda which will not be easily shaken from their purpose. The knowledge that forces are present which would move the arts backward has chilled the creative spirit. The Endowment has become more conservative since that first cold challenge, conservative in policy and conservative in the nature of appointments to senior posts and the National Council on the Arts. The arts institutions have also embraced a cautious attitude, both because survival has become more difficult and because they fear controversy could curtail support even more. Arts and institutions which have shown boldness have stirred gigantic and disproportionate conservative reaction, nearly toppling an entire edifice because of one misplaced brick.

What began as a bold vision and grand design has become a routine bureaucracy, an elaborate mechanism for producing the ordinary, a funnel for federal funds flowing to the bank balances of arts institutions to forestall bankruptcy in many cases. This may have been inevitable—the creeping stiffness of age and the emergence of a conservative national consciousness—yet, if ever a government agency had a mandate to remain flexible and imaginative it was the National Endowment for the Arts. Today, the Endowment is the largest, single source of survival money in the country, but it is not as innovative, imaginative, or aggressive as it was in the beginning. And if an arts agency does not have those qualities, what can be expected from other federal programs established to be concerned with our problems?

Not all has disappeared from the early days. The modest rural arts study has expanded into elaborate outreach programs within the state arts agencies. The pilot program to put poets in the schools has become one of the major programs and has greatly influenced arts education. The summer inner-city workshop became a major division of the Endowment for multi-cultural arts development. Writers, composers, visual artists and choreographers are still assisted, but not at a level commensurate with present costs of living. And no longer does the agency move quickly to prevent troubled organizations from collapse, or back the talented young with consistency.

Precious little of our tax dollars are being used to bring pure pleasure to our citizens. Our National Parks do, our wildlife conservation programs do, and our arts and humanities programs do. Should we not fight vigorously to make these programs flexible and bold, and not let them be as bogged down in bureaucracy as other government agencies? It is possible. It only takes intelligence, imagination, and devotion, all of which the people in the arts have in abundance; in other words strong leadership.

I have related all I know about the struggle to establish the National Endowment for the Arts and its early years. As I cited in the Preface, I haven't written a book at all: I have merely cleaned house.

Roger Stevens and Charles Christopher Mark.

Programs of the National Council on the Arts

and the

National Endowment for the Arts

October 1965 through April 1970

◆ **Environmental Design Program:** Non-matching grants of up to $5,000 to 32 individuals, and matching grants of up to $10,000 to 8 organizations have been made in a major continuing program of assistance for a variety of projects in various fields of environmental design: architecture, planning, landscape architecture, and interior and industrial design. Grants totalling $219,500 have been made to the following individuals and organizations:

Sidney Cohn	$ 5,000
William Cooper	4,900
James R. Cothran	2,000
Laurence S. Cutler	5,000
Alton De Long	5,000
Frederick Eichenberger	3,000
Franklin L. Elmer, Jr.	5,000
Francis Ferguson	5,000
John F. Furlong	4,600
Myron Guran	5,000
Eugene Kremer	5,000
R. Randolph Langenback	4,000
John B. MacKinlay, Jr.	5,000
Hal M. Moseley, Jr.	3,000
Gary O. Robinette	4,800
Donald C. Royse	5,000
Robert M. Sarly	5,000
Roger D. Sherwood	5,000
Nathan Silver	5,000
Leonard D. Singer	5,000
Michael Southworth	5,000
Carl F. Steinitz	5,000
Erma B. Striner	5,000
Richard Tatlock	5,000
Philip Thiel	4,900
Robert Vickery	4,200
Donald R. Watson	5,000
Joseph Watterson	1,500
Douglas S. Way	5,000
Harry J. Wexler	5,000

Myer R. Wolfe	4,000
David L. Young	4,900
America The Beautiful Fund	10,000
Boston Architectural Center	10,000
Kent State University	10,000
Massachusetts Institute of Technology	10,000
Metropolitan Museum of Art	5,000
Philadelphia Museum of Art	10,000
Tocks Island Regional Advisory Council	10,000
University of Florida	8,700

♦ **Exhibition and Book on American Architecture:** A joint grant with the Graham Foundation for Advanced Studies in the Fine Arts in Chicago helped support a two-year program under which G. E. Kidder Smith is preparing material for an exhibition and book of photographs of American architecture, landscape architecture and planning. ($25,000)

♦ **Professor E. A. Gutkind:** A matching grant was made to the University of Pennsylvania to enable Gabriel Gutkind to prepare for publication the last five volumes of a seven-volume series entitled International History of City Development, written by the late Professor E. A. Gutkind. The first four volumes have already been published and the fifth volume is to be published shortly. This series, when complete, will be a principal source of knowledge in urban development and design. ($23,000)

♦ **Schools of Architecture and Design:** A program of matching grants provided up to $30,000 each to schools of architecture and design to undertake environmental design projects of significant scale and relevance; the site areas are in the schools' regions, and the projects are being conducted by teams of faculty, students, and outside experts. The following nine schools were awarded grants totalling $265,992:

Institute for Architecture and Urban Studies (New York City): A matching grant to study the design potentials of the city street as a fundamental element of urban open space design. ($30,000)

Massachusetts Institute of Technology (Cambridge): A matching grant to develop a design training program in which ghetto talent will be sought and developed. ($30,000)

Tulane University (New Orleans): A matching grant to further investigate design possibilities for the Vieux Carre riverfront expressway in New Orleans. ($30,000)

University of Kentucky (Lexington): A matching grant to investigate methods of strip mining that leave landscape intact for alternative future developments. ($30,000)

University of Minnesota (Minneapolis): A matching grant to study alternative forms of suburban growth. ($30,000)

University of Notre Dame (South Bend): A matching grant to study new forms of land use resulting from advanced scientific and technical information in geology. ($30,000)

University of Pennsylvania (Philadelphia): A matching grant to pursue advanced studies in ecological analysis and regional design. ($30,000)

University of Southern California (Los Angeles): A matching grant to design a new town in a mountain valley, utilizing new methods of design analysis and synthesis. ($30,000)

University of Tennessee (Knoxville): A matching grant to design a regional transportation town which will serve the future transportation needs of a group of small towns in eastern Tennessee. ($25,992)

♦ **Undergraduate Student Travel:** In Fiscal 1967, 75 grants-in-aid of $500 each were provided to undergraduate students recommended by schools of architecture, planning, and landscape architecture, for research and travel during the summer of 1967, before their final year of study.

This program was continued by the Endowment in Fiscal 1969 as 106 undergraduate students received $250 each for research and travel during the summer of 1969. (Total: $64,000)

♦ **American Guide Series:** A grant was made to Carl Feiss, FAIA, AIP, member of the Board of the National Trust for Historic Preservation, to develop a program for producing an *American Guide Series* on significant architecture, landscape architecture and planning. ($26,000)

♦ **Basic Design Manual:** A grant was made to Professor Ralph Knowles of the University of Southern California to develop a basic design manual based on his courses and experiments with the effects of natural forces on three-dimensional architectural and urban forms, for distribution in schools of architecture, planning, and landscape architecture. ($25,000)

♦ **Design Internships:** A matching grant to the Natural Area Council of New York and the America the Beautiful Fund of Washington, D.C. enabled students of architecture, planning, and landscape architecture to obtain practical experience through work in selected public agencies on nearly 50 significant design projects throughout the country. ($42,000)

♦ **Festival Foundation, Inc.:** In conjunction with Southern Illinois University, a matching grant enabled the display of Richard Buckminister Fuller's geodesic domes and other materials at the Festival of Two Worlds in Spoleto, Italy during the summer of 1967. ($12,500)

♦ **Hawaii State Foundation on Culture and the Arts:** The Endowment funded a project to develop effective design techniques and means for preserving Hawaii's natural beauty by supporting a series of studies by the Oahu Development Conference and other community action groups working with professional designers. ($50,850)

♦ **Highway Signs and Graphics:** An Endowment grant enabled Ronald Beckman of the Institute of Research and Design in Providence, Rhode Island, to conduct a study aimed at the improvement of highway signs and graphics to enhance the safety and appearance of the highway. Mr. Beckman's report was presented in a most interesting form—utilizing computer data cards to cross-reference the numerous items of information. ($10,000)

♦ **National Institute for Design:** The Council investigated the feasibility of establishing a national institute for design. Its responsibilities would include efforts to increase designer capabilities as well as public receptivity to excellence in architecture, planning and design. (Robert R. Nathan Associates, Inc., Washington, D.C., received an $83,708 study grant to develop a plan for a national institute.)

♦ **New Technologies and Architecture:** A grant was made to Professor John Eberhard of the University of Buffalo to prepare the basic research for a book on the potential applications of "new technologies" on environmental design. The book, to be published shortly, will be entitled *Systems Design and Urban Places.* ($7,000)

♦ **Redesign of an Old Industrial River Area:** A matching grant assisted the Lake Michigan Region Planning Council to develop an exemplary design plan for Little Calumet River Basin in southern Illinois and northwestern Indiana. The concept here, as in other projects in this category of the arts, is to develop a prototype useful to other areas of the country. ($10,000)

♦ **Tocks Island Regional Advisory Council:** A matching grant supported a design action conference which permitted local officials, civic leaders, and citizens to confer with leading designers on environmental design excellence in the areas bordering the new national park—the areas impacted by the creation of the park. The area includes portions of six counties in New Jersey, New York, and Pennsylvania. The park and the areas surrounding it will serve the recreational needs of the people in a portion of the eastern seaboard of "megalopolis," extending from New York to Philadelphia. It is anticipated that this will be the most popular and most heavily used national park in the United States. ($10,000)

▶

Choreography

♦ **Alvin Ailey American Dance Theatre** (1968). A matching grant was made for the commissioning of two new works. The works have been premiered and are titled *Quintet* and *Knoxville*. ($10,000)

♦ **American Dance Foundation/American Ballet Company** (1970): A matching grant was made for the Company's new ballet entitled *Early Songs* by Eliot Feld. This grant was made possible by donations to the Endowment from private sources amounting to $5,000, matched by $5,000 from Endowment funds. (Endowment funds: $5,000; private funds: $5,000)

♦ **Challenge Grants for Productions** (1970): Matching grants totalling $153,300 were made to enable major dance companies to create, rehearse and perform new works. This program includes the stipulation that matching funds be raised from new sources, thus assisting the creation of new dance works while stimulating a broadened base of support for America's major companies. Grants were made to the following companies:

American Ballet Theatre	$133,300
City Center Joffrey Ballet	20,000*

*Future funding will raise this amount to $133,400; and the New York City Ballet will also receive $133,300.

♦ **Choreographers' Grants** (1966): Individual grants under the first broad choreographers' commission program ever undertaken by an American foundation, enabled the following seven choreographers to create, rehearse, and produce important works in the field of dance: Alvin Ailey, *Come Get the Beauty of it Hot, Lament, A Music for Sighs* ($5,000); Merce Cunningham, *Place* ($5,000); Martha Graham, *Cortege of Eagles, Dancing Ground* ($39,100); Jose Limon, *Psalm* ($23,400); Alwin Nikolais, *Imago* ($5,000); Anna Sokolow, *Deserts* ($10,000); and Paul Taylor, *Orbs* ($5,000). (Total: $92,500)

♦ **Choreographers' Grants** (1969): Individual grants to 15 choreographers included a personal award to the choreographer plus 4 weeks rehearsal salaries for an appropriate number of dancers. Choreographers with less than 10 years professional experience received personal awards of $2,500. Choreographers with 10 years or more of professional experience received $5,000. The choreographers and their works are as follows: Merce Cunningham, *Canfield* ($10,760); Richard Englund, *Odes (of the Mysterious Accord)* ($9,220); Eliot Feld, *Pagan*

Spring ($10,500); Ann Halprin, *A Ceremony of Us* ($10,560); Lucas Hoving, *Assemblage '69* ($8,840); Pauline Koner, *Fragments* ($5,000); Richard Kuch, *Chaos* ($2,500); Jose Limon, *The Unsung* ($10,760); Murray Louis, *Proximities, Intersection* ($8,360); Alwin Nikolais, *Echo* ($9,800); Don Redlich, *Slouching Towards Bethlehem* ($3,940); Anna Sokolow, *Memories* ($10,760); Paul Taylor, *Private Domain* ($10,720); Glen Tetley, *Ziggurat* ($11,240); Charles Weidman, *A69-I-123* ($9,800). (Total: $132,760)

♦ **Foundation for American Dance/City Center Joffrey Ballet** (1967): A matching grant permitted the company to conduct a six-week rehearsal period and produce several new works for the 1967–68 season in the Pacific Northwest and at the New York City Center. Original works added to the company's repertoire were: *Cello Concerto,* Arpino; *Elegy,* Arpino; and *Astarte,* Joffrey. The company also added four new productions: *Moves,* Jerome Robbins; *Pas de Dix,* George Balanchine; *Pas de Trois,* George Balanchine; and *Rooms,* Anna Sokolow. ($100,000)

♦ **Martha Graham Company** (1968): A matching grant enabled the creation of three new works: *A Time of Snow, The Plain of Prayer,* and *The Lady of the House of Sleep,* for the 1968 season. ($25,000)

♦ **San Francisco Ballet** (1969): A matching grant enabled the Ballet to commission nationally recognized choreographers, including Merce Cunningham, John Clifford, and Gerald Arpino, to mount new works for the company. ($35,800)

Workshops

♦ **Kansas Dance Councils** (1970): A matching grant helped support the 1969 American Dance Symposium held in Wichita, Kansas. ($7,500)

♦ **National Association for Regional Ballet:** Matching grants in Fiscal 1968 ($18,130) and Fiscal 1970 ($16,200) assisted four week-long Craft of Choreography Conferences during the summers of 1968 and 1969 in four regions of the country (Northeast, Southeast, Pacific Western, and Southwestern). These workshops offer professional advice and expertise to the directors and members of approximately 200 dance companies. (Total: $34,330)

♦ **Northeast Regional Ballet Festival Association** (1967 pilot project): A matching grant assisted the Association to provide honorariums for the professional staff, and to invite representatives from other regional ballet associations to observe the Association's annual *Craft of Choreography Workshop.* ($1,725)

Touring

♦ **Ballet Theatre Foundation/American Ballet Theatre** (1966): A matching grant helped support nationwide tours. ($250,000)

♦ **Ballet Theatre Foundation/American Ballet Theatre** (1970): A matching grant was made for support of the 1969–70 touring program beginning at the Brooklyn Academy of Music and including engagements in Los Angeles, San Francisco, Chicago, and Urbana. ($120,000)

♦ **College Circuit Tour** (1968): With an individual grant, Alexander Ewing, President of the Board of Directors of the Foundation for American Dance, developed a six-college circuit for an experimental in-residence tour by the City Center Joffrey Ballet. ($5,000)

♦ **City Center Joffrey Ballet** (1969): Based on the College Circuit Tour developed by Alexander Ewing, a matching grant was made to the City Center Joffrey Ballet for an experimental in-residence tour during the 1968–69 season, including the following campuses: Michigan State University, University of Arizona, University of Cincinnati, University of New Mexico, University of Oklahoma, and the University of Vermont. ($97,200)

♦ **Coordinated Residency Touring Program:** This program, initiated in Illinois for the 1967–68 season, is aimed at improving touring practices for the benefit of both dance companies and audiences. The method is to develop regional circuits of local sponsors through the cooperation of State arts councils. Each local sponsor engages at least two companies for at least a half week each, during which time the dance company provide a variety of services such as master classes, lecture demonstrations, music and design workshops, and teachers' classes. Grants made under this program are as follows:

1968: *Illinois Arts Council* received a matching grant ($25,000) to support a pilot project involving four dance companies in six cities for 8 weeks. Companies were Alwin Nikolais, Merce Cunningham, Paul Taylor and Glen Tetley. Charles Reinhart received an individual grant to develop several regional circuits based on the pilot project in Illinois ($5,000).

1969: Three regional circuits were developed for the second year with the following companies: Merce Cunningham, Erick Hawkins, Lucas Hoving, Jose Limon, Donald McKayle, Alwin Nikolais, Anna Sokolow, Paul Taylor and Glen Tetley (Total: $110,533)

Illinois Arts Council for the Great Lakes Circuit ($67,333) with eight companies playing 21 1/2 weeks in Illinois, Indiana, Minnesota, Missouri, Wisconsin, and Ohio.

Vermont Council on the Arts for the New England Circuit for six companies playing eleven weeks in Vermont, Connecticut, New Hampshire, Rhode Island and New Jersey. ($35,900)

North Carolina Arts Council for an in-state circuit for four companies playing two and one-half weeks in four cities. ($7,300)

1970: Six regional circuits covering 22 states for 67 1/2 weeks of programming by the following 10 companies: Alwin Nikolais, Paul Taylor, Merce Cunningham, Murray Louis, Alvin Ailey, Don Redlich, Lucas Hoving, Pearl Lang, First Chamber Dance Quartet, Jose Limon. ($215,400)

Utah State Institute of Fine Arts for the West Coast including California, Colorado, Montana and Utah. ($42,600)

Oklahoma Arts and Humanities Council for the Midwest Circuit including Missouri and Oklahoma. ($26,800)

Maryland Arts Council for the Mid-Atlantic Circuit including North Carolina, New Jersey, Pennsylvania, Virginia, Maryland, and the District of Columbia. ($31,500)

Michigan State Council on the Arts for the Great Lakes Circuit including Minnesota, Indiana, Wisconsin, Illinois and Michigan. ($79,000)

Maine State Commission on the Arts and the Humanities for the New England Circuit including Rhode Island, Massachusetts, Connecticut and Maine. ($23,900)

Florida Arts Council for in-state engagements. ($11,600)

♦ **Martha Graham Company** (1966): A matching grant permitted the Company to make an eight-week national tour in the fall of 1966, its first American tour in 15 years. ($142,250)

♦ **Washington State Arts Commission** (1967): A matching grant made it possible to establish a summer residence in the Pacific Northwest for the City Center Joffrey Ballet Company. ($25,000)

♦ **Pacific Northwest Ballet Association** (1968 and 1970): Matching grants supported the second ($75,000) and third ($100,000) summer residency programs in the Pacific Northwest for the City Center Joffrey Ballet Company. (Total: $175,000)

♦ **Saratoga Performing Arts Center** (1969): A matching grant helped defray travel expenses of the Repertory Dance Theatre (Salt Lake City, Utah) in connection with its tour to Saratoga, New York, the first East Coast appearance of this company. ($3,800)

Support for Institutions

♦ **American Dance Festival—Connecticut College** (1967): A matching grant supported the Festival's summer 1967 20th season special program of new works made possible by previous Endowment grants to choreographers Martha Graham, Jose Limon, Paul Taylor, and Merce Cunningham. ($15,000)

♦ **American Dance Festival—Connecticut College** (1969): A matching grant was made to the School of Dance to expand its fellowship program and to engage the Jose Limon Company in residence during the summer 1968 Festival. ($11,534)

♦ **American Dance Festival—Connecticut College** (1969): A matching grant provided partial support for the residencies of four dance companies during the summer 1969 Festival. ($25,000)

♦ **Association of American Dance Companies:** An initial study grant of $11,450 and matching grant of $13,550 (1967), followed by an additional $15,000 matching grant (1968), supported this newly-formed organization's program of services and information for the AADC's more than 400 member professional and regional dance companies. (Total: $40,000)

♦ **Ballet Theatre Foundation/American Ballet Theatre:** An emergency matching grant ($100,000) enabled the company to continue operations (1966); and matching grants ($200,000) for general support were made in Fiscal 1968. In addition to the above, a further grant of $194,830 was made in Fiscal 1968; this latter grant was made possible by donations to the Endowment from private sources amounting to $97,415, matched by $97,415 from Endowment funds. (Endowment funds: $397,415; private funds: $97,415)

♦ **Brooklyn Academy of Music** (1970): A matching grant was made for support of the three companies in residence—Alvin Ailey American Dance Theatre, Merce Cunningham Dance Company, and the American Ballet Company. The grant was made possible by donations to the Endowment amounting to $25,000, matched by $25,000 from Endowment funds. (Endowment funds: $25,000; private funds: $25,000)

♦ **Capitol Ballet Guild** (Washington, D.C.) (1966): An emergency matching grant enabled the company to continue operations. ($5,000)

♦ **Center for Arts of Indian America** (1968): A matching grant enabled the Center to engage the services of a consultant to develop plans for a projected Center for American Indian Dance in the Southwest. ($3,000)

♦ **Dance Theatre Workshop** (New York City) (1970): A matching grant is helping support a performance season for six choreographers and 30 dancers at the Manhattan School of Dance. ($10,000)

♦ **Directors of Development** (1970): Matching grants (2/3 Endowment funds, 1/3 grantees' funds) to American Ballet Theatre ($16,700) and City Center Joffrey Ballet ($16,700) initiated a continuing program to assist major dance companies in hiring professional directors of development to strengthen the financial footing of these companies. (Total: $33,400)

♦ **Foundation for American Dance/City Center Joffrey Ballet** (1969): A matching grant for general support continued the Endowment's assistance to this major American dance company. ($100,000)

♦ **Martha Graham Center of Contemporary Dance** (New York City) (1969): A $100,000 matching grant for general support of the Graham Dance Company was made possible by donations to the Endowment from private sources amounting to $50,000, matched by $50,000 from Endowment funds. (Endowment funds: $50,000: private funds: $50,000)

♦ **Jacob's Pillow Dance Festival** (Lee, Massachusetts) (1969): A non-matching grant was awarded to this theatre, devoted solely to dance, for general support during the summer of 1969. ($25,000)

♦ **Regional Dance Development Project** (1968): A pilot program of matching grants enabled regional dance companies to commission guest choreographers, engage professional performers, acquire additional production or administrative personnel, and expand programming in their regions. The grantees were as follows: Garden State Ballet, Newark ($5,000); Sacramento Ballet Guild ($3,055); Pennsylvania Ballet Company, Philadelphia ($5,000); National Ballet Company, Washington, D.C. ($5,000); State Ballet of Rhode Island, Lincoln ($5,000); Atlanta Civic Ballet ($3,770); Ballet Guild of Cleveland ($5,000); Ballet of San Diego ($5,000); Dayton Civic Ballet ($2,800); Laguna Beach Civic Ballet ($4,710). A touring grant of $3,000 to Ballet West (formerly Utah Civic Ballet) initially developed through this program, was included in another project administered by the Endowment. (Total: $44,335)

♦ **Technical Assistance for Dance Companies** (1966): With an individual grant from the Endowment, dance manager Ralph Black conducted a feasibility study and organized a meeting of dance companies to consider the establishment of a national service association for dance. This meeting resulted in creation of the Association of American Dance Companies. ($5,600)

Research

♦ **Allegra Fuller Snyder** (1968): A consultant's fee was paid to Mrs. Snyder to investigate the field of dance films, collect all relevant material, and submit a plan to the Council for its consideration as a possible outline of procedure in developing a dance film program. ($3,009)

◆ **Central Midwestern Regional Educational Laboratory, Inc. (CEMREL)** (St. Ann, Missouri): A transfer of Fiscal 1969 funds from the Office of Education to the Endowment enabled a $100,000 non-matching grant to be made to CEMREL for administration of a Visual Artist-in-Residence pilot project during the 1969–70 school year in six secondary schools in: San Diego, California; Lakewood, Colorado; West Palm Beach, Florida; St. Paul, Minnesota; University City, Missouri; Philadelphia, Pennsylvania. In Fiscal 1970, an additional $45,000 assisted CEMREL to produce and distribute a film that will examine and document the value of the program and encourage additional school systems to engage artists as an integral part of the educational environment. (Total: $145,000)

◆ **Educational System for the 70's** (E.S. '70) (San Mateo, California): A matching grant was made to cover the salary of the Director of a new program in Arts Curriculum Development, in cooperation with The JDR 3rd Fund and the Office of Education. It is anticipated that the curricula developed under this program may serve as a model for schools all over the country, following their trial in the 18 E.S. '70 school systems. ($25,000)

◆ **Poets in Developing Colleges** (Programs in cooperation with the Endowment Literature Division): A program was administered by the Woodrow Wilson Fellowship Foundation in cooperation with The Poetry Center of the 92nd Street YM-YWHA, in which, in the fall semester of 1967, seven poets, both black and white, toured a circuit of five developing Southern colleges, primarily black in enrollment. For the spring semester, five poets spent five-week terms as Writers-in-Residence at five colleges. In mid-May, a Festival was held at Morehouse College in Atlanta which brought together all the poets involved in the program, in concert with their students, reading and discussing their work. A grant was made to Dr. Stephen Henderson, chairman of the English Department at Morehouse and coordinator of the Festival, to compile an anthology of the work written in the first year of the program. ($29,518)

As a result of the initial success of the program, and to make more permanent its impact, matching grants for support of Writers-in-Residence Programs were made to Miles College in Birmingham, Alabama ($3,700) for 1968–69; to Tougaloo College in Tougaloo, Mississippi ($3,800) for 1968–69 and 1969–70; to Virginia Union University in Richmond, Virginia ($4,500) for 1968–69; and to Talladega College in Tallaega, Alabama ($3,184) for 1969–70. (Total: $15,184) The Council plans continued support of this program in Fiscal 1970.

♦ **Arts Curricula:** The project on a matching basis with the American Association for Higher Education was a comprehensive study of the impact of college entrance exams and admissions requirements on school arts curricula. The study resulted in the publication of a book entitled *The Arts in Higher Education.* ($16,500)

♦ **Colgate University:** A matching grant to Colgate University, Hamilton, New York, supported a two-week student-run arts festival in March 1968, concentrating on music, film, theatre, and graphic art. ($5,300)

♦ **Dance Recording Methods:** A study grant was made to improve the preservation and instruction of choreographic works by enabling Douglas Blair Turnbaugh to conduct a one-year survey and make recommendations on current dance recording methods. ($9,120)

♦ **Fordham University:** A matching grant supported a one-year research and demonstration program to develop superior teaching methods using exceptional films dealing with literature, social studies and the arts to stimulate effective communication among secondary school students, particularly those from culturally and economically disadvantaged backgrounds. ($71,780)

♦ **The George Washington University/Workshops for Careers in the Arts** (Washington, D.C.): A matching grant supported a pilot project that brought high school students to the University campus for instruction in the fields of drama, dance, and visual arts during the summer of 1969. The project is continuing during the 1969–70 academic year and may be expanded into a high school for the arts in the District of Columbia. ($5,000)

♦ **Graduation Awards:** Individual grants-in-aid of $1,000 each enabled 77 promising young artists, musicians and creative writers who graduated from college in June, 1966 to visit art centers, museums, institutions or areas of the United States to enrich their cultural experience. ($77,000)

♦ **Great Lakes Colleges Association** (Detroit): A matching grant enabled professional filmmaker Richard Kaplan to consult with and recommend cooperative film programs for the ten participating GLCA colleges: Albion College, Albion, Michigan; Antioch College, Yellow Springs, Ohio; Denison University, Granville, Ohio; Depauw University, Greencastle, Indiana; Hope College, Holland, Michigan; Kalamazoo College, Kalamazoo, Michigan; Oberlin College, Oberlin, Ohio; Ohio Wesleyan University, Delaware, Ohio; Wabash College, Crawfordsville, Indiana, and College of Wooster, Wooster, Ohio. ($5,550)

♦ **Harlem School of the Arts:** A $24,500 matching grant was made in Fiscal 1967 to support dance, art, music, and theatre training programs for ghetto youth in New York City under the supervision of Dorothy Maynor; a second matching grant of $32,700 in Fiscal 1969 continued the Endowment's support of this School, formerly known as the St. James Community House School of the Arts. (Total: $57,200)

♦ **Elma Lewis School of Fine Arts** (Boston): An emergency grant in Fiscal 1967 permitted this outstanding school to continue operation in a period of financial crisis. Now firmly established in the Boston community, this school has developed into the new National Center for Afro-American Artists. ($3,500)

♦ **National Art Education Association:** Continuing the Council's policy of enabling international arts conferences to be held in the United States, a matching grant was made for the 1969 World Assembly of the International Society for Education Through Art (INSEA), held in New York City during August, 1969. ($35,000)

♦ **New Thing Art and Architecture Center:** A matching grant was made on a pilot project basis to assist this workshop school of the arts to continue and expand its activities for inner city residents, particularly the young, in the Nation's Capital. ($25,000)

♦ **North Carolina School of the Arts:** A matching grant for scholarships enabled ten college music majors to attend the School's 1967 summer session at the Accademia Musicale Chigiana in Siena, Italy. ($4,500)

♦ **Pilot Films in Visual Arts:** A grant was made to enable Ralph Steiner to make four short films in color for a proposed series entitled *The Joy of Seeing.* This series will be used by art educators to stimulate heightened perception and appreciation of works of art and to bring art to small communities without direct access to such works. ($15,000)

♦ **Student Arts Festivals:** Christopher Murphy, a senior year student at Notre Dame University in South Bend, Indiana, made a study of the origin, establishment, and administration of student arts festivals at representative colleges and universities throughout the country with an individual grant from the Endowment. ($1,500)

♦ **Teaching Artists:** Grants-in-aid of up to $7,500 each enabled 50 novelists, poets, painters, sculptors, and composers teaching in institutions of higher learning to take one-year leaves, during 1966 and 1967, to pursue creative work in the arts. ($372,500)

▶ ━━━━━━━━━━━━━━━━━━━━━━━━━━━━━━━━━━

♦ **The American Literary Anthology/2:** The second annual Anthology of the best poetry, fiction, essays and criticism from American literary magazines of limited circulation was released by Random House in February 1969. Of $52,412, $42,750 went to the 75 chosen authors and to the editors, on behalf of their magazines, who originally published the material: $1,000 for fiction and non-fiction writers, $500 maximum to their editors; $500 for poets, and $250 maximum to their editors. The rest was used for administrative costs, including fees and mailing to nine judges and a panel of preliminary readers. *Anthology/1* was published by Farrar, Straus & Giroux in June 1968 ($61,497, of which $44,500 went to authors and editors). Funds for *Anthology/3* include $55,000 for authors and editors and $11,041 for administration. All publication costs are borne by the major publishing houses; Endowment funds are used solely to compensate the writers and editors for their contributions, with a small portion of funds assisting with administration of the project. (Total: $179,950)

♦ **Association of American University Presses:** A matching grant was made for a program which assists university presses to publish up to 15 projects which will supplement existing publication schedules of the presses. The projects involve poetry (particularly first books), short fiction, the novella, or works of creative criticism; each author whose work is selected receives $500, in addition to the standard royalties. ($28,500)

♦ **Authors League Fund:** A matching grant has enabled the Authors League Committee to make emergency grants to authors in need. ($30,000)

♦ **Coordinating Council of Literary Magazines:** A $50,000 matching grant in Fiscal 1967 helped the National Institute of Public Affairs to establish the Coordinating Council of Literary Magazines, representing all of the major and many of the smaller literary magazines in the country, created to make selective grants to these publications to match private support, assist special projects, or provide direct subsidies. CCLM received another $50,000 matching grant in Fiscal 1968; and additional grants of $100,000 in Fiscal 1969 and $150,000 in Fiscal 1970 are providing continuing support of CCLM, now an independent organization headquartered in New York City. (Total: $350,000)

♦ **Discovery Awards:** This program was initiated in Fiscal 1968 with Endowment grants enabling six prominent writer-teachers to form a Literary Study Group which investigated ways of discovering and assisting young and unknown writing talents. The group included Max Steele of Chapel Hill, North Carolina; William Hairston of Washington, D.C.; Ann Stanford of San Fernando, California; Robert Hayden of Nashville, Tennessee and Terre Haute, Indiana; Thomas Fitzsimmons of Rochester, Michigan; and John Hawkes of Providence, Rhode Island and Stanford University, California ($18,000). As a result of their "talent-scouting" throughout the United States, individual grants of up to $2,000 each assisted 29 exceptionally gifted but unrecognized writers ($37,500).

In Fiscal 1970, a new Literary Study Group was drawn up, composed of Ronald Bayes of Laurinburg, North Carolina; Gus Blaisdell of Albuquerque, New Mexico; Mari Evans of Indianapolis, Indiana; Roderick H. Jellema of College Park, Maryland; Frank MacShane of New York, New York; Frederick Manfred of Luverne, Minnesota; Howard McCord of Pullman, Washington; and Jarvis Thurston of St. Louis, Missouri. As the result of their recommendations, discovery awards of up to $3,000 each were made to 41 emerging writers to encourage future development ($82,000). (Total: $137,500)

♦ **Independent Publishers:** Over a three-year period, a series of grants has been made to the following distinguished noncommercial publishers and printers of fine books: Cummington Press ($20,000), Stone Wall Press ($20,000) and Prairie Press ($20,000), all of Iowa; Kayak Books ($20,000), Four Seasons Foundation ($5,000), Poets Press ($20,000) and Talisman Press ($5,000), all of California; Elizabeth Press ($10,000) of New York; and Jargon Books ($20,000) of North Carolina. (Total: $140,000) Additional grants are expected to be made in Fiscal 1970.

♦ **P.E.N. (Poets, Playwrights, Essayists, Editors, and Novelists) American Center** (New York City): A $20,000 matching grant is helping the organization to expand its services to writers in New York, throughout the country, and abroad; and an additional $3,000 matching grant is enabling the organization to establish its archives by assembling and classifying historical materials. Earlier grants helped it to establish a permanent headquarters, develop a professional staff, establish and strengthen regional chapters, and publish a newsletter ($20,000 matching grant) and to print and distribute 1,000 copies of "List of Grants and Awards Available to American Writers" ($2,100). (Total: $45,100)

♦ **Poetry in the Schools:** A matching grant ($4,600) was made to *The Academy of American Poets* to provide consultant services for expansion of its pilot program ($79,750 in Fiscal 1966 and 1967 matching grants), initiated in the New York City, Long Island, Detroit, San Francisco, and Pittsburgh school systems, entitled "Dialogues on the Art of Poetry." Although the two-part format remains the same, with well-known senior poets discussing how to transmit the vitality of language with elementary and secondary school English teachers, and with younger poets reading and discussing poetry directly with students in their classrooms, the content is changed for the audience. The Endowment in Fiscal 1968 and 1969 made matching grants to the *Illinois Arts Council* for administration of this program in the Chicago area ($15,500); to the *University of Minnesota* to support its program in Minneapolis and surrounding areas ($17,400); to *California State College at Los Angeles* for its program in the Los Angeles area ($15,500) and to the *University of Arizona* to support its program for Spanish-American and Indian students ($15,000).

In Fiscal 1970, matching grants were made to the *Illinois Arts Council* for administration of this program in eight Midwestern states ($50,000); to the *St. Paul Council of Arts and*

Sciences for support of its program in the St. Paul and Minneapolis area ($5,000); to the *New Jersey State Council* on the Arts for support of its program in the State of New Jersey ($2,500); to the *Rhode Island State Council on the Arts* for support of its program in the State of Rhode Island ($2,500); and to *The Academy of American* Poets for support of a pilot project in two New York City junior high schools ($2,000). (Total: $209,750)

♦ **Poets in Developing Colleges:** (Program in cooperation with the Endowment Education Division) A program was administered by the Woodrow Wilson Fellowship Foundation in cooperation with The Poetry Center of the 92nd Street YM-YWHA, in which, in the fall semester of 1967, seven poets, both black and white, toured a circuit of five developing Southern colleges, primarily black in enrollment. For the spring semester, five poets spent five-week terms as Writers-in-Residence at five colleges. In mid-May, a Festival was held at Morehouse College in Atlanta which brought together all the poets involved in the program, in concert with their students, reading and discussing their work. A grant was made to Dr. Stephen Henderson, chairman of the English Department at Morehouse and coordinator of the Festival, to compile an anthology of the work written in the first year of the program. ($29,518)

As a result of the initial success of the program, and to make more permanent its impact, matching grants for support of Writers-in-Residence Programs were made to Miles College in Birmingham, Alabama ($3,700) for 1968–69; to Tougaloo College in Tougaloo, Mississippi ($3,800) for 1968–69 and 1969–70; to Virginia Union University in Richmond, Virginia ($4,500) for 1968–69; and to Talladega College in Talladega, Alabama ($3,184) for 1969–70. (Total: $15,184) The Council plans continued support of this program in Fiscal 1970.

♦ **City College of New York:** Matching funds were provided for a pilot program (Operation SEEK) during the summer of 1968. The prebaccalaureate cultural enrichment program, with particular emphasis on literary materials, is intended to prepare gifted young people from the ghetto for college. ($13,550)

♦ **College Literary Festivals and Conferences:** Matching grants ranging from $250 to $3,900 supported literary conferences or festivals in nine colleges and universities: University of Arkansas, Fayetteville; State University of New York at Stony Brook; University of California at Irvine; Sauk Valley College, Dixon, Illinois; University of Maryland, College Park; Pitzer College, Claremont, California; Eastern Oregon College, La Grande; Providence College/Rhode Island School of Design, Providence; and Beloit College, Beloit, Wisconsin. (Total: $15,386)

♦ **Coordinating Council of Literary Magazines** (New York City): Three matching grants of $1,000 each were made to CCLM: 1) for support of its annual college literary magazine contest; 2) to enable the Committee of Small Magazine Editors and Publishers (COSMEP) to print and distribute a catalogue of small magazines and small press publications; and 3) for support of a national magazine conference held at Michigan State University in June, 1969. (Total: $3,000)

♦ **Corcoran Gallery of Art** (Washington, D.C.): A matching grant supported an exhibit and reading of the works of distinguished American poet Kenneth Patchen in December 1969. ($3,000)

♦ **Distinguished Service Awards:** Awards have been made to eight senior American writers for life-long contributions to American letters: John Berryman, Louise Bogan, Kenneth Burke, Malcolm Cowley, Kenneth Patchen, John Crowe Ransom, Reed Whittemore, and Yvor Winters. (Total: $74,000)

♦ **The Hudson Review:** A matching grant was made to *The Hudson Review* of New York City in support of the November 1968 joint anniversary Symposium of the Review and The Poetry Center of the 92nd Street YM-YWHA. ($1,750)

♦ **Individual Grants to Creative Writers:** Grants-in-aid were made enabling 45 writers to complete works-in-progress or to conduct special research essential to their continuing work. ($362,500)

♦ **M.L.A./P.E.N. Conference on Writers in the Universities:** A matching grant supported a Modern Language Association/American P.E.N. conference which explored means by which successful writers lacking academic degrees might be successfully integrated into college teaching. ($4,222)

♦ **National Book Committee, Inc.:** A matching grant supported an experimental program to extend and expand "Book and Author" community-wide events, to broaden public appreciation of the literary arts and to stimulate readership and the wider and wiser use of books. Held in a number of cities, such as Wichita, Grand Rapids, and Binghamton, these events included participation by high school and college students and municipal and educational officials as well. ($18,058)

♦ **Radcliffe Institute for Independent Study:** A matching grant enabled the Institute to expand its program of fellowships for women writers. Partly as a result of this grant, the Institute was given over $300,000 by a private foundation, so that there was no need for the Endowment to renew its grant. ($25,000)

♦ **Thirty-fourth International P.E.N. Congress:** A matching grant assisted in meeting the administrative costs of the first International P.E.N. Congress to meet on American soil in its 42-year history, in June 1966. ($40,000)

♦ **Westminster Neighborhood Association, Inc./Douglass House Foundation, Inc.:** An initial matching grant ($25,000) helped strengthen Budd Schulberg's Writers' Workshop, now the independent, all-black "Watts Writers House of Respect," in the Watts area of Los Angeles. An additional matching grant ($25,000) maintained and expanded the Workshops into different regions of the country. (Total: $50,000)

♦ **YMHA Poetry Center Festival of Foreign Poets:** A matching grant assisted The Poetry Center of the 92nd Street YM-YWHA to sponsor a program in cooperation with Lincoln Center, of readings by six illustrious foreign poets, not yet familiar to American audiences, and translations of their work, in two sessions in late June, 1968. This was an extraordinarily successful festival with some of the world's leading poets in attendance, many of whom had never before read in, or visited, America. ($3,500)

◆ **Affiliate Artists, Inc.** (New York City): Matching grants in Fiscal 1969 ($50,000) and 1970 ($160,000) were made for the development and administration of a program which establishes a partnership between colleges or community organizations and performing artists; the institution engages the services of the artist as an "affiliate" rather than an artist-in-residence, thus giving the artist the freedom to pursue his professional career, and at the same time assisting the community to obtain the artist's direct services for a maximum of eight weeks a year, for a three-year period. The 1970 grant was made possible by an $80,000 donation to the Endowment from the Sears-Roebuck Foundation, Inc., matched by $80,000 from Endowment funds. (Endowment funds: $130,000; private funds: $80,000)

◆ **American Choral Foundation:** A matching grant ($50,000) supported a summer 1968 institute to provide choral conductors with the practical experience of working with professional choruses and orchestras through workshops held at the State University of New York in Binghamton and the University of Wisconsin in Madison. The Endowment assisted the summer 1969 institute at the University of Oklahoma in Norman ($25,000) and is continuing its support with $25,000 for the summer 1970 institute to be held at Temple University in Philadelphia. Margaret Hillis, Director of the Chicago Symphony Orchestra Chorus, is musical director of these summer institutes. (Total: $100,000)

◆ **American Musical Digest** (New York City): Matching grants in Fiscal 1969 and 1970 have been made to aid publication and distribution of the non-commercial *American Musical Digest* magazine. The Endowment launched this project in Fiscal 1968 through a contract with the Music Critics Association. The new monthly journal, which digests, excerpts, translates, and reprints articles and reviews on American music and artists from publications the world over, is aimed at enhancing the scope and quality of music criticism throughout the country and serving as a model for criticism in other fields of the arts. (Total: $115,000)

◆ **American Symphony Orchestra League** (Vienna, Virginia): A matching grant was made to enable ASOL to administer a pilot project, in conjunction with the Missouri State Council on the Arts, in which communities and orchestras will work together in providing additional performance opportunities and new sources for recruiting experienced personnel. ($40,000)

◆ **American Symphony Orchestra League:** A matching grant was made to enable ASOL to conduct its 1970 Summer Institute for Conductors and Orchestras in Orkney Springs, Virginia. ($10,000)

♦ **Contemporary Music Programs:** A series of matching grants totalling $37,300 was made to groups engaged in significant contemporary music programming. The six grantees are as follows:

Carnegie Hall Corporation (New York City)	$15,000
Contrasts in Contemporary Music/Composers' Showcase (New York City)	6,000
Music In Our Time (New York City)	5,000
Philadelphia Composers' Forum	5,000
Theatre Chamber Players (Washington, D.C.)	3,300
University of Alabama Regional Composers' Forum	3,000

♦ **The Festival Orchestra Society, Inc.:** A matching grant enabled the New York Chamber Soloists, which tours colleges and universities around the country, to extend its stay on each campus and include seminars, master classes, lectures, open rehearsals and additional concerts. ($20,000)

♦ **International Folk Music Council** (New York City): A matching grant was made to assist the U.S. National Committee of the Council with the publication of its Yearbook. ($5,700)

♦ **Music Critics Association, Inc.** (Vienna, Virginia): A matching grant is supporting a pilot project, initiated in September 1968, which is providing for an exchange of music critics between newspapers around the country. ($6,910)

♦ **National Guild of Community Music Schools** (Urbana, Illinois): A $24,700 individual grant and a $7,500 matching grant in Fiscal 1968 enabled the Guild to establish a permanent national office, whose purpose is to stimulate the creation of new community music schools throughout the country and to provide counseling services to established schools. Matching grants in Fiscal 1969 ($15,000) and in Fiscal 1970 ($17,500) have continued the Endowment's support of this organization, under the direction of Dr. Herbert Zipper. (Total: $64,700)

♦ **The National Opera Institute** (Washington, D.C.): A non-matching grant was made to establish and support the Institute whose purpose is to encourage the growth and development of the opera in the United States. Five areas of Institute activity are: 1) to supplement production costs of new or unproduced operas; 2) to commission new operas; 3) to make possible a study of the best methods of developing opera for television, aimed at broadening the audience for opera; 4) to send companies or workshops into sections of the country currently without exposure to live opera; and 5) to provide a limited number of grants for study, training, and living expenses for outstanding young singers. The grant was made possible by donations to the Endowment from private sources amounting to $300,000, matched by $300,000 from Endowment funds. (Endowment funds: $300,000; private funds: $300,000)

♦ **Orchestras and Opera Treasury Fund Program:** A series of 12 Fiscal 1970 grants totalling $706,400 was made for projects to develop and serve broader audiences and to upgrade artistic quality. All of the grants were made possible by private donations to the Endowment; thus, all grant amounts represent one-half private and one-half Federal funds. Grantees were:

Opera Companies

The Center Opera Company (Minneapolis)	$ 40,000
Goldovsky Opera Institute (Brookline, Mass.)	30,000
Philadelphia Grand Opera Company	20,000
Seattle Opera Association	36,000

Orchestras

Buffalo Philharmonic Orchestra	$ 50,000
Chamber Symphony Society of California	40,000
Cincinnati Symphony Orchestra	100,000
Denver Symphony Society	60,000
San Francisco Symphony Association	$100,000
St. Louis Symphony Society	100,000
Utah Symphony	30,400
Washington (D.C.) National Symphony	100,000

♦ **Professional Symphony Orchestras Special Program:** Four major symphony orchestras received grants totalling $142,800 under a program of support enabling major orchestras to develop auxiliary services or special programming. Grants are as follows:

Atlanta Symphony Orchestra*	$15,300
Boston Symphony Orchestra	50,000
Detroit Symphony Orchestra	50,000
Minnesota Orchestra*	27,500

*Future funding will raise these amounts to $50,000 each; and the New York Philharmonic will also receive $50,000.

♦ **Seattle Opera Association, Inc.:** A matching grant was made for support of the Opera Directors' Conference in Washington, D.C. on April 24–25, 1970. ($5,000)

♦ **Young Audiences, Inc.** (New York City): In Fiscal 1969, a matching grant ($60,000) was made for support of this national audience development organization for music, to be utilized in the following areas: part-time music consultants, laboratory research and development of future programs, and development of special techniques for pre-school/third grade audiences. An additional $150,000 matching grant for general support in Fiscal 1970 was made possible by donations to the Endowment from private sources amounting to $75,000, matched by $75,000 from Endowment funds. (Endowment funds: $135,000; private funds: $75,000)

◆ **American International Music Fund, Inc.** (New York City): A non-matching grant was made for the Fund's "Recording Guarantee Project," which involves the collection and national distribution, through libraries and non-commercial radio stations, of tapes of contemporary music performances. ($25,000)

◆ **American National Opera Company:** In an effort to replace the Metropolitan Opera National Company after it was forced to cease operation, matching grants ($350,000) assisted the creation and subsequent national tour of the American National Opera Company under the artistic direction of Sarah Caldwell. An additional $100,000 matching grant to A.N.O.C. was made possible by donations to the Endowment from private sources amounting to $50,000, matched by $50,000 from Endowment funds. (Endowment funds: $400,000; private funds: $50,000)

◆ **American Symphony Orchestra League:** A Fiscal 1966 matching grant assisted this national service organization to establish workshops on orchestra management and related problems, and to render technical assistance to orchestras. ($33,531)

◆ **Audience Development Project—Chamber Music Societies:** Matching grants totalling $9,425 were made in a program enabling chamber music societies across the country to enlarge their schedules. The 12 grantees are as follows:

Auburn Chamber Music Society (Alabama)	$ 875
Birmingham Chamber Music Society	625
Chamber Music Society of Baltimore	1,000
Chamber Music Society of Kalamazoo	850
Ensemble Music Society of Indianapolis	675
Free Library of Philadelphia	650
Friends of Chamber Music (Nashville)	625
Houston Friends of Music	875
New Orleans Friends of Music	900
Phoenix Chamber Music Society	875
Pittsburgh Chamber Music Society	675
Raleigh Chamber Music Guild	800

◆ **Audience Development Project—College and University Concert Series:** A program launched in Fiscal 1968 has provided 145 matching grants of up to $1,000 each to established college and university concert series for fees for additional programs by American artists. (Total: $131,041)

◆ **Audience Development Project—Contemporary Music Societies:** Matching grants were made under a program of assistance to groups concerned with the performance of contemporary music: to Composers' Showcase, Inc./Contrasts in Contemporary Music, Inc. ($5,000) of New York City, and to Contemporary Concerts, Inc. ($3,200) of Barrington, Illinois. (Total: $8,200)

♦ **Audience Development Project—Museum Concert Series:** Matching grants totalling $10,370 were made in a program enabling museum concert series across the country to enlarge their normal schedules with additional programs by American artists. The 12 grantees are as follows:

Carroll Reece Museum (Johnson City, Tennessee)	$1,000
Columbia Museum of Art (South Carolina)	900
M.H. de Young Memorial Museum (San Francisco)	1,000
Hudson River Museum (Yonkers, New York)	1,000
Los Angeles County Museum of Art	875
Minneapolis Society of Fine Arts	1,000
New Jersey State Museum (Trenton)	1,000
Norfolk Museum of Arts and Sciences (Virginia)	920
Old Economy/Pennsylvania Historical Society (Ambridge)	1,000
State Capitol Museum (Olympia, Washington)	400
Tampa Bay Art Center (Florida)	875
Wichita Art Museum (Kansas)	400

♦ **Johann Sebastian Bach International Competitions:** A matching grant was made to support the 1969 Competitions, sponsored by George Washington University in Washington, D.C. and open to piano students of all countries between 17 and 32 years of age. ($1,500)

♦ **Bennington (Vermont) Composers' Conference and Chamber Music Center:** Matching grants expanded fellowship opportunities for young composers to attend the 1967, 1968, and 1969 summer conferences, at which their works were rehearsed, performed, taped and discussed. Works of particular merit receive New York performances, and tapes are distributed to national educational radio stations. (Total: $27,100)

♦ **Boston Opera Company:** An emergency matching grant enabled the Company to meet commitments for the 1966 season, including a major production of Arnold Schoenberg's *Moses and Aaron.* ($50,000)

♦ **Boston Symphony Orchestra:** A matching grant was made to record the Elliott Carter Piano Concerto, for distribution to music schools in the United States and abroad and to U.S.I.S. centers. ($7,500)

♦ **California Youth Symphony Association** (Palo Alto): A matching grant provided partial support for traveling expenses in connection with the Symphony's Australian tour during the summer of 1969. ($10,000)

♦ **Composer Assistance:** Sixty-seven individual grants of up to $2,000 each have enabled composers to defray costs of copying scores and parts for orchestral presentation of their work, and 43 matching grants of up to $2,000 each have enabled orchestras to commission new works and prepare them for performance. The American Symphony Orchestra League and the American Music Center have assisted in administering this program. ($101,467)

♦ **Denver Symphony Orchestra:** A matching grant supported the study of the feasibility of converting the organization from a local to a regional performing group. ($828)

♦ **Eastern Connecticut Symphony Orchestra** (New London): A matching grant was made for support of its activities in connection with the MacDowell Festival of American Music held in New London in October 1969. ($6,700)

♦ **Goldovsky Opera Institute** (Brookline, Massachusetts): Matching grants were made to assist in improving the quality of touring productions during the 1967–68 and 1968–69 seasons, while holding fees to sums which local sponsors can afford and keeping ticket prices moderate. (Total: $115,000)

♦ **Group for Contemporary Music/Columbia University** (New York City): A matching grant was made to support this Columbia University-based group's 1968–69 season of concerts of significant 20th Century compositions. ($10,000)

♦ **Hofstra University** (New York): A matching grant sponsored the first laboratory workshop on the technique of repairing stringed instruments, during the summer of 1967. ($4,650)

♦ **Hunter College** (New York City): Matching grants supported a pilot series of public concerts, The New Image of Sound, held during the 1967–68 season ($5,780) and the 1968–69 season ($10,000). This series is designed to encourage intermedia cooperation and to expand the audience for contemporary music. (Total: $15,780)

♦ **Kodaly Fellowship Program:** An individual grant was made to Alexander Ringer, Professor of Musicology at the University of Illinois, to initiate and direct a limited fellowship program, implemented by additional Endowment grants which enabled ten qualified young musicians to study the Kodaly concept of music education in Hungary during the 1968–69 school year. The young musicians are now teaching in various school systems in the United States. (Total: $91,291)

♦ **Irving Lowens:** A grant was made to enable Mr. Lowens, Music Critic for Washington, D.C.'s *The Evening Star* and Chairman of the Board of Directors of the *American Musical Digest* to take a six-month leave of absence from his regular critic's duties to devote full time to the final preparation and publication of the *Digest.* ($10,000)

♦ **Metropolitan Opera National Company:** A matching grant in Fiscal 1967 assisted a pilot program to develop new audiences for opera by enabling the Company to give additional performances for labor groups and students in many states. ($150,000)

◆ **Montgomery County Youth Orchestra Association** (Maryland): A matching grant helped enable the Orchestra to participate in the First International Festival of Youth Orchestras in Switzerland during the summer of 1969. ($10,000)

◆ **Music Critics Association, Inc.** (Vienna, Virginia): In Fiscal 1968, the Endowment contracted ($64,000) with the Music Critics Association to develop the *American Musical Digest;* additional funds ($38,000) were committed in Fiscal 1969 to assist the Association to complete work on the prototype. Reaction to the magazine and its contents has been very favorable. (Total: $102,000)

◆ **National Music Camp at Interlochen:** A matching grant permitted the United States to host, for the first time, the International Society for Music Education Conference held at Interlochen, Michigan in 1966. ($25,000)

◆ **National Music Council:** A matching grant assisted the Music Council to host the Sixth International Music Council Congress during the fall of 1968 in New York City and Washington, D.C. This marked the first time that the Congress, attended by 600 delegates from 50 countries, was held in the United States. ($32,000)

◆ **New York City Opera** (City Center of Music and Drama): Matching grants for a two-year project enabled director Julius Rudel to expand a training program for assistant conductors and young singers. (Total: $80,000)

◆ **Opera Society of Washington, D.C.:** A $100,000 matching grant was made for general support during the Society's 1968–69 season. This grant was made possible by donations to the Endowment from private sources amounting to $50,000, matched by $50,000 from Endowment funds. (Endowment funds: $50,000; private funds: $50,000)

◆ **Project for Young Musicians:** A grant was made to assist Carnegie Hall-Jeunesses Musicales, Inc. to develop a program which might enable promising young musical artists to participate in national tours. ($31,500)

◆ **Project to Develop String Musicians:** A grant was made to Alexander Schneider, violinist, chamber musician, and conductor, to develop a project to meet the acute shortage of string musicians in the United States and thus assist both music training and orchestral development. ($19,185)

◆ **Regional Opera Project:** A Fiscal 1967 program explored and assisted regional opera activity in the southeastern United States through grants for research and demonstration projects. ($94,116)

◆ **George Russell:** An individual award was made to jazz composer and instrumentalist Russell of New York City in recognition of his outstanding contributions to 20th Century American music. ($5,500)

◆ **San Francisco Opera/Western Opera Theater:** A matching grant ($115,000) in Fiscal 1967 assisted in the creation of the Western Opera Theater, a small, flexible opera ensemble which is performing condensed and full-length opera for audiences in areas in five States (thus far), where opera on a large scale is not feasible. A matching grant ($100,000) in Fiscal 1968 permitted expanded touring activities of this highly successful new group, and another matching grant ($100,000) in Fiscal 1969 continued the Endowment's assistance to the Western Opera Theater, whose annual performance rate increased in three years from 35 to 150. (Total: $315,000)

◆ **Santa Fe Opera** (Opera Association of New Mexico): A $160,000 matching grant was made to assist with the design and construction of newly built opera productions, replacing those destroyed by fire in 1967. This grant was made possible by donations to the Endowment from private sources amounting to $80,000, matched by $80,000 from Endowment funds. (Endowment funds: $80,000; private funds: $80,000)

◆ **Seattle Opera Association:** A matching grant was made for support of this regional opera company's 1968–69 Singer-in-Residence Program, to utilize and develop local talent, as part of a long-range plan of regional development. One part of the program was a tour of 20 communities in the Northwest. ($10,000)

◆ **Symphony of the New World** (New York City): A matching grant permitted the country's first fully integrated orchestra to expand its touring activities during the 1967–68 season. ($25,000)

◆ **Syracuse Friends of Chamber Music:** A matching grant on a pilot project basis assisted in enhancing the 1967–68 season of the Syracuse Friends of Chamber Music. ($1,000)

◆ **Thorne Music Fund** (New York City): A matching grant expanded the Fund's program of fellowships to deserving composers. ($50,000)

◆ **University of Alabama Regional Composers' Forum:** In 1968, and again in 1969, the Endowment supported a regional composers' forum, an annual three- to four-day session devoted exclusively to the reading and performance of new music by composers living in the southeastern United States. (Total: $5,666)

◆ **Violin Finishes:** A grant (matched by the A. W. Mellon Educational and Charitable Trust) was made for experimental analysis of violin varnish believed to have enriched violin quality and resonance more than 200 years ago. ($3,500)

◆ **Walker Art Center** (Minneapolis): A matching grant ($20,000) was made to aid general artistic development of the Center Opera Company of the Walker Act Center during the 1967–68 season. In Fiscal 1969, another matching grant ($15,000) continued the Endowment's support and assisted a new production, Eric Stokes' "Horspfal." The Center Opera Company, a regional experimental venture, avoids standard repertoire and presents contemporary and seldom-done older works of moderate size. (Total: $35,000)

▶

♦ **The American Film Institute:** Through private fund donations made to the Endowment, The American Film Institute was created in June 1967 as a non-government, nonprofit organization to develop excellence in this area of the arts. An initial study was undertaken in 1966 by Stanford Research Institute ($91,019) to determine the needs in this area. The Endowment's share in establishing the Institute was $1.3 million; the Ford Foundation contributed an equal amount, as did the member companies of the Motion Picture Association of America. The Institute, with offices in Washington, Los Angeles, and New York, is operating with an initial three-year budget of at least $5.2 million, with remaining funds coming from private sources, and is concentrating essentially in the following areas of endeavor: archives, education, advanced film studies, production, and research and publication.

♦ **Bay Area Educational Television Association (KOED)** (San Francisco): A matching grant was made to support a fellowship program for the National Center for Experiments in Television. The year-long fellowships will be for individuals who are not necessarily associated with television production but who have demonstrated special talents which may be applied to television as a distinct medium of expression. ($60,000)

♦ **Educational Television Stations/Indiana University Foundation** (Bloomington): As a follow-up to the ETS grants program launched in Fiscal 1967 and 1968, a matching grant was made for a project entitled "Artist in America Public Television Awards." It is an incentive program leading to the production of twenty half-hour television programs, to be produced locally for distribution nationally, which feature the work of local artists and their effects on their communities. ($110,000)

♦ **National Educational Television/American Regional Theatre Project:** Two matching grants were made to support the filming of four plays, selected from the repertories of four American resident professional theatre companies, for inclusion in NET PLAYHOUSE, and national distribution, during the 1968–69 season. The four plays, *A Celebration for William Jennings Bryan* (Theatre Company of Boston), *The New Theatre for Now* (Cen Theatre Group in Los Angeles), *Glory! Hallelujah!* (American Conservatory Theatre in San Francisco), and *Story Theatre* (The Yale School of Drama in New Haven), have been produced and distributed. (NET is also producing two documentary films which examine the work of America's regional theatre. The first grant was made possible by donations to the Endowment from private sources amounting to $37,500, matched by $37,500 from Endowment funds. (Total: Endowment funds: $122,500; private funds: $37,500)

♦ **Chicago Educational Television Association:** A matching grant in 1967 permitted the distribution of 20 programs of WTTW's "Chicago Festival" arts series to all noncommercial educational television stations in the country. ($20,000)

♦ **Costume Design Program:** A matching grant to National Educational Television resulted in two color films, "The Creative Person: Pauline Trigere" and "In Fashion," which explored the world of fashion design. The films received national distribution via the NET Network and were made available to costume-design-teaching schools and cultural groups in an attempt to improve instruction and to create a permanent record of American costume design. ($12,500)

♦ **Educational Broadcasting Corporation:** A matching grant of $625,000 supported the production and national distribution to all educational television stations of 19 arts programs in the SUNDAY SHOWCASE series. This 1967 grant was made possible by donations to the Endowment from the Bristol-Myers Company amounting to $300,000, supplemented by $325,000 from Endowment funds. (Endowment funds: $325,000; private funds: $300,000)

♦ **Educational Television Stations/Indiana University Foundation:** A matching grant of $64,991 to ETS Program Service, a division of the National Association of Educational Broadcasters, launched an incentive grants program in Fiscal 1967 which enabled educational television stations to begin production of arts programs. This grant, made possible by donations to the Endowment from private sources amounting to $17,150, supplemented by $47,841 from Endowment funds, resulted in the selection of 20 original programs for production by local educational television stations. An additional $101,805 matching grant was made in Fiscal 1968 for production of an additional 41 new half-hour arts programs developed during the initial phase of the project by local educational television stations for national distribution by ETS. (Endowment funds: $149,646; private funds: $17,150)

♦ **Film Culture Non-Profit Corporation—Filmmaker's Cinematheque** (New York City): A matching grant was made for operating expenses of this organization's program of services to the growing community of independent and largely noncommercial filmmakers. ($30,000)

♦ **KOED (San Francisco) Television Project:** A matching grant in Fiscal 1968 supported a one-year experimental project enabling creative artists and television production experts to develop new programming concepts and techniques for television. ($70,000)

♦ **KOED (San Francisco) Film:** A matching grant was made to produce a color film about Ghirardelli Square in San Francisco which explores the potentialities of urban living, combining the talents of dancer-choreographer Merce Cunningham, composer John Cage, and filmmaker Richard Moore. NET will distribute the film in the fall of 1970 through the Public Broadcasting Service to all public television stations; some international distribution is also planned. ($50,000)

♦ **National Educational Television:** A matching grant of $75,000 provided partial support of two major dramatic productions for NET PLAYHOUSE, and their national distribution, free of cost, to all educational television stations throughout the country. This 1967 grant was made possible by donations to the Endowment from private sources amounting to $37,500, matched by $37,500 from Endowment funds. (Endowment funds: $37,500; private funds: $37,500)

♦ **New York Film Festival:** A matching grant was made in partial support of the 1969 New York Film Festival at Lincoln Center and for the founding of a new institution for film at Lincoln Center. ($50,000)

♦ **Tony Schwartz:** An individual grant enabled Tony Schwartz to establish a one-year experimental project in the art of sound recording which resulted in the production of a "portrait in sound" of a crosstown strip of blocks in New York City. The results of the project will be disseminated through records and tapes to radio stations, critics, schools, colleges and universities throughout the country. ($24,959)

♦ **WGBH (Boston) Radio Drama Development Project:** A matching grant was made in Fiscal 1968 for a one-year pilot project to establish a repertory group of directors, writers and actors who create and perform high quality radio drama, and to sponsor a nationwide competition to stimulate writing excellence and revived interest in radio drama. The ten outstanding works produced have been distributed via a specially prepared record album to noncommercial radio stations, graduate drama schools, critics, and leading repertory theatre groups throughout the United States. ($56,838)

◆ **American National Theatre and Academy (ANTA):** A contract ($438,000) between the Endowment and ANTA enabled the Endowment, early in 1969, to accept donation of the ANTA Theatre building, located in the Broadway theatre district in New York City, as a gift to the American people. This theatre is being utilized as a forum for performing groups from around the country who perform in the ANTA Theatre for limited periods of time without having to pay prohibitive rental costs. In the fall of 1969, under the new programming developed by ANTA and funded by the Endowment ($694,000), the American Conservatory Theatre (ACT) of San Francisco was the first group to perform in the ANTA Theatre, followed by the American Shakespeare Festival Theatre of Stratford, Connecticut. Other professional theatre companies and experimental groups are appearing for limited engagements during the 1969–70 season. (Total: $1,132,000)

◆ **Arena Stage** (Washington, D.C.): A $300,000 matching grant was made for general support of this theatre, which is one of the major resident professional theatres in the United States and an important contributor to the local and the national theatre scene. This grant was made possible by a $150,000 donation to the Endowment from The Ford Foundation, matched by $150,000 from Endowment funds. (Endowment funds: $150,000; private funds: $150,000)

◆ **Atlanta Arts Alliance, Inc.** (Atlanta Cultural Center): A matching grant supported the 1969–70 activities of its four major constituents—museum, school, symphony orchestra, and theatre. This grant is intended to assist the Alliance in establishing itself as a permanent, viable, and locally-supported entity in the Atlanta community, and was made possible by donations to the Endowment from private sources amounting to $217,500, matched by $217,500 from Endowment funds. (Endowment funds: $217,500; private funds: $217,500). It is anticipated that additional private donations will enable the Endowment to increase the total grant amount.

◆ **Brooklyn College** (New York): A matching grant was made to assist the College's Theatre Artisan Training Program, a new project that trains young people (primarily from disadvantaged backgrounds) for technical careers in professional theatre companies. ($50,000)

◆ **Foundation for the Extension and Development of the American Professional Theatre, Inc.** (New York City): A matching grant for general support was made to this national service organization which offers informational and free consultative services to professional theatres of all types and sizes, as well as to individuals, groups or institutions wishing to organize and/or operate professional theatres. ($7,500)

♦ **International Theatre Institute, U.S. Centre** (New York City): Two matching grants, one in Fiscal 1969 and one in Fiscal 1970, were made for the operation and expansion of this permanent, independent organization, which serves as a communications link between the American theatre and theatre abroad, and conducts a program of services including publications, international conferences, and exchanges of information and theatre experts. (Total: $45,000)

♦ **The Paper Bag Players** (New York City): Matching grants in Fiscal 1969 ($24,000) and Fiscal 1970 ($20,000) have assisted this group, which tours extensively out of its Henry Street Playhouse headquarters, using only original material in a completely new approach to children's theatre. (Total: $44,000)

♦ **Professional Experimental Theatre Development:** A series of matching grants, launched in Fiscal 1968, is being made in a continuing program to provide encouragement and assistance to new playwrights, and to stimulate the production of new works and the development of new forms and techniques. These experimental groups are all committed to the development of the theatre artist; they account for some of the most adventurous and promising work now being done in this country. Advised by a special panel drawn up to assist with this program, the Endowment has thus far made three groups of grants totalling $365,438 to the following 34 theatres:

Academy Theatre (Atlanta)	$ 7,500
Albarwild Theatre Arts, Inc., The Playwrights' Unit (New York City)	10,000
American Place Theatre (New York City) (2 grants)	35,000
The American Playground (Washington, D.C.)	5,000
Barbwire Theatre (San Francisco)	2,500
Caravan Theatre (Boston)	1,500
Chelsea Theatre Center (Brooklyn) (3 grants)	25,000
Chicago City Players	5,000
Company Theatre (Los Angeles)	10,000
Corner Theatre Cafe (Baltimore)	2,500
The Cubiculo (New York City)	2,500
Dancers Studio Foundation (New York City) (2 grants)	7,500
Firehouse Theatre (Minneapolis) (2 grants)	25,000
Free Southern Theatre (New Orleans) (3 grants)	27,000
Free Theatre Fund (Chicago)	5,000
Group Concept (New York City)	2,500
Hull House Playwrights Center (Chicago)	5,000
The Interplayers (San Francisco)	2,500
Judson Poets' Theatre (New York City) (2 grants)	10,000
The Julian Theatre (San Francisco)	2,500

La Mama Experimental Theatre Club
(New York City) (3 grants)   35,000
Loft Theatre Workshop (New York City)   5,000
New Dramatists Committee (New York City) (2 grants)   12,500
New Lafayette Theatre (New York City) (2 grants)   15,000
New York Free Theatre (New York City)   5,000
New Theatre Workshop (New York City)   2,250
Office for Advanced Drama Research,
University of Minnesota (Minneapolis)   9,688
The Open Theatre (New York City) (3 grants)   42,500
The Performance Group (New York City)   15,000
Society Hill Playhouse (Philadelphia)   5,000
Studio Watts Workshop (Los Angeles)   5,000
Theatre Workshop (Boston)   7,500
Thresholds (New York City) (2 grants)   7,500
Two Arts Playhouse (New York City)   5,000

♦ **Resident Professional Theatres:** A series of matching grants, launched in Fiscal 1967, is being made in a continuing program to assist the decentralization of the American theatre and to strengthen the growing resident professional theatre movement across the country. Advised by a special panel of theatre experts, the Endowment has thus far made four groups of grants under this program to encourage the artistic development of these theatres by enabling them to increase actors' salaries and engage guest directors, performers, and technical personnel, as well as to initiate special projects or new productions. To date, grants totalling $1,434,000 have been made to the following 33 theatres:

Actors Theatre of Louisville (4 grants) $ 49,750
Alley Theatre (Houston) (3 grants)   57,500
American Conservatory Theatre (San Francisco)   20,000
Arena Stage (Washington, D.C.) (3 grants)   67,500
Arizona Repertory Theatre (Phoenix)   11,250
Asolo Theatre Festival (Sarasota) (2 grants)   17,500
Center Stage (Baltimore) (4 grants)   72,500
Center Theatre Group (Los Angeles) (2 grants)   45,000
Charles Playhouse (Boston) (2 grants)   37,500
Cleveland Play House (2 grants)   37,500
A Contemporary Theatre (Seattle) (2 grants)   12,500
Dallas Theatre Center (3 grants)   36,000
Front Street Theatre (Memphis)   22,500
Goodman Theatre (Chicago)   12,500
Tyrone Guthrie Theatre (Minneapolis) (3 grants)   92,500
Hartford Stage Company (3 grants)   52,500
Long Wharf Theatre (New Haven) (3 grants)   92,500
Milwaukee Repertory Theatre (3 grants)   67,500
Negro Ensemble Company (New York City)   25,000

Old Globe Theatre (San Diego Shakespeare Festival)	5,000
Olney Theatre (Olney, Maryland) (2 grants)	30,000
Pittsburgh Playhouse	25,000
Playhouse-in-the-Park (Cincinnati) (3 grants)	67,500
Repertory Theatre New Orleans	25,000
Seattle Repertory Theatre (4 grants)	80,000
Stage West (Springfield, Massachusetts)	5,000
Studio Arena Theatre (Buffalo)	15,000
Theatre Atlanta (2 grants)	17,500
Theatre Company of Boston (4 grants)	77,500
Theatre of the Living Arts (Philadelphia) (3 grants)	137,000
Trinity Square Repertory Company (Providence)	25,000
Washington Theatre Club (D.C.) (3 grants)	60,000
Yale Repertory Theatre (New Haven) (2 grants)	35,000

♦ **American Conservatory Theatre** (San Francisco): Two matching grants totalling $510,000 were made in Fiscal 1966 and 1968 for development of the Theatre's professional training program and for general support of the company's activities. The latter grant was made possible by donations to the Endowment from private sources amounting to $175,000, matched by $175,000 from Endowment funds. (Endowment funds: $335,000; private funds: $175,000)

♦ **American Educational Theatre Association:** A grant was made in Fiscal 1967 which enabled secondary school theatre expert William Cleveland to conduct a survey of theatre at the secondary school level. ($7,000)

♦ **American National Theatre and Academy:** A Fiscal 1967 matching grant assisted ANTA in the establishment of two regional offices, one in Arizona and one in Florida. ($27,824)

♦ **American Playwrights Theatre:** A matching grant ($5,467) to APT facilitated the production of a new play (through matching royalty payments) by university, community and resident professional theatres included in the APT membership. Co-authors of the play Jerome Weidman and James Yaffe each received individual grants of $5,000 under this project. (Total: $15,467)

♦ **American Puppet Arts Council/Bill Baird Puppet Theatre** (New York City): Two matching grants, in 1967 and again in 1969, enabled the Baird puppeteers to design, build, stage and rehearse new productions for their permanent theatre. (Total: $41,400)

♦ **American Shakespeare Festival Theatre and Academy** (Stratford, Connecticut): Matching grants in Fiscal 1968 ($21,852) and Fiscal 1970 ($250,000) have assisted the Festival with its repertory season and its training program in classical theatre. The latter grant was made possible by a $125,000 donation to the Endowment from private sources, matched by $125,000 from Endowment funds. (Endowment funds: $146,852; private funds: $125,000)

◆ **American Society for Theatre Research:** A matching grant supported the activities of the Sixth Congress of the International Federation for Theatre Research held in New York City in October, 1969. ($15,000)

◆ **American Theatre of Being:** A matching grant supported this company's presentations of works predominantly by Negro authors in schools and depressed areas of Los Angeles, in 1967, under the direction of Frank Silvera. ($24,000)

◆ **Association of Producing Artists** (APA-Phoenix): A matching grant ($125,000) was made in Fiscal 1966 for general support of the company's activities which had partial seasons in New York, Ann Arbor, and Los Angeles; in Fiscal 1967, and additional $250,000 grant was awarded APA, made possible by donations to the Endowment from private sources amounting to $125,000, matched by $125,000 from Endowment funds. (Endowment funds: $250,000; private funds: $125,000)

◆ **Berkshire Theatre Festival** (Stockbridge, Massachusetts): A matching grant to the Festival supported its operation which included the professional production of four new plays, during the Festival's summer 1968 season. A second matching grant helped to support the Festival's operations during its summer 1969 season. (Total: $80,000)

◆ **Boston University Playwrights Symposium:** Two matching grants to the University supported its summer 1968 and 1969 professional playwrights workshop program, in which scripts are developed and produced at the Berkshire Music Center in Tanglewood, Massachusetts. (Total: $35,980)

◆ **The Forum Theater of The Repertory Theater of Lincoln Center:** In Fiscal 1968 a matching grant of $100,000 was made to initiate support of The Forum's new play program and its free student ticket program during the 1968–69 season. This grant was made possible by donations to the Endowment from private sources amounting to $30,000, supplemented by $70,000 from Endowment funds. In Fiscal 1969 the Endowment's support of this program continued with a matching grant of $50,000. (Endowment funds: $120,000; private funds: $30,000)

◆ **Hull House** (Chicago): A matching grant was made to implement plans for an outdoor theatre and a number of basement theatres in public housing projects. ($30,000)

◆ **International Theatre Institute, U.S. Centre:** A matching grant to the U.S. Centre of the International Theatre Institute helped support the ITI's 12th International Congress in June 1967, the first international theatre event of its kind to be held in the United States. ($34,994)

◆ **Laboratory Theatre Project for Education:** A program launched in 1967, in cooperation with the U.S. Office of Education and local school boards, enabled professional theatre companies in Providence (Trinity Square Repertory Company), New Orleans (Repertory Theatre New Orleans) and Los Angeles (Inner City Cultural Center) to expose secondary school audiences, free of charge, to the impact of live theatre at the same time the plays offered were being studied in the classroom. The program additionally made performances available to the general public at reasonable rates, and developed techniques to improve the instruction of dramatic literature in the schools. As had been planned, the Endowment supported these three projects for a three-year period, finishing in Fiscal 1970. (Total: $1,351,000)

♦ **National Repertory Theatre:** Matching grants in Fiscal 1967 assisted the company to expand its audience development and student educational programs ($75,000), and to perform in New York for a three-week period ($30,000). (Total: $105,000)

♦ **New York Shakespeare Festival:** A matching grant ($100,000) enabled the company to conduct in the summer of 1966 theatre programs throughout the city which otherwise would have been curtailed; and an additional grant ($250,000) partially supported the 1967–68 season of new plays at the Festival's new Public Theatre. This latter grant was made possible by donations to the Endowment from private sources amounting to $125,000, matched by $125,000 from Endowment funds. (Endowment funds: $225,000; private funds: $125,000)

♦ **Olney Theatre** (Olney, Maryland): A matching grant was made for general support of the Theatre during its 1969–70 season. The grant was made possible by donations to the Endowment from private sources amounting to $27,500, matched by $27,500 from Endowment funds. (Endowment funds: $27,500; private funds: $27,500)

♦ **Eugene O'Neill Memorial Theatre Foundation, Inc.:** Two matching grants were made in 1968 and 1969 to the Playwrights' Workshop-Conference (held each summer in Waterford, Connecticut). The purpose of the grants was to permit regional theatre directors from professional companies around the country to observe the works of new playwrights and new trends in the theatre, as demonstrated by the O'Neill Playwrights' Workshop-Conference. (Total: $6,000)

♦ **Playwrights Experimental Theatre:** Matching grants of $25,000 each assisted playwrights by providing high caliber professional productions of new works in resident professional and university theatres, at Arena Stage (Washington, D.C.), Barter Theatre (Abingdon, Virginia), Brandeis University (Waltham, Massachusetts), the Professional Theatre Program of the University of Michigan (Ann Arbor), and Yale University Drama School (New Haven, Connecticut). The plays produced by the theatres, respectively, were: *The Great White Hope, Five in the Afternoon, Does a Tiger Wear a Necktie?, Amazing Grace,* and a new adaptation of *Prometheus Bound.* (Total: $125,000)

♦ **Theatre Development Fund:** A matching grant of $200,000 was made in Fiscal 1968 to stimulate creativity and experimentation in the commercial theatre through financial assistance for plays of merit which are unlikely to be produced or are likely to close prematurely without Fund assistance. This grant was made possible by donations to the Endowment from private sources amounting to $100,000, matched by $100,000 from Endowment funds. Theatre Development Fund is a private nonprofit organization, located in New York City. (Endowment funds: $100,000; private funds: $100,000)

▶

◆ **The American Federation of Arts** (New York City): A matching grant was made to support the spring 1970 Art Critics Workshop. The program provides a working situation with carefully selected writers engaged actively in the production of criticism. Leading critics are brought in to work with the students. ($10,000)

◆ **Artists' Fellowship Program:** A continuing program of direct assistance to painters and sculptors was initiated by the Endowment in Fiscal 1967. To date, individual awards of $5,000 each have been made to 119 painters and sculptors, recommended by special regional panels, to encourage future efforts in the field of visual arts in the United States. (Total: $595,000)

◆ **Artists' Housing/The J. M. Kaplan Fund:** Matching grants in Fiscal 1968 and 1970 enabled The J. M. Kaplan Fund, Inc. to establish the nonprofit Westbeth Corporation which purchased the old Bell Telephone Laboratories on New York's lower West Side for conversion into America's first national artists' housing center. The center (Westbeth), now open and occupied, provides 384 units of studio-living quarters for artists and their families at reasonable rents; in addition, the complex includes film studios, rehearsal rooms, exhibition galleries, sculpture gardens, and adjoining park and playground areas as well. The Fiscal 1970 matching grant was made possible by donations to the Endowment from private sources amounting to $250,000, matched by $250,000 from Endowment funds. (Endowment funds: $1,000,000; private funds; $250,000)

A previous matching grant in Fiscal 1967 assisted The J. M. Kaplan Fund to purchase and convert smaller projects for artists' housing. ($100,000)

◆ **Corcoran Gallery of Art—Workshop Program** (Washington, D.C.): A matching grant was made to continue a model workshop program designed to sustain and gain the support of the local community of artists, as well as subsidize the production of art. Artists are provided fellowship grants, studios, materials and exhibition space in the museum. ($10,000)

◆ **Experiments in Art and Technology (E.A.T.)** (New York City): A matching grant was made to support a spring 1970 exhibition and conference at Automation House, for the purpose of presenting and clarifying the social, environmental and esthetic problems in the area of art and technology. ($25,000)

♦ **Hawaii State Foundation on Culture and the Arts:** A matching grant enabled the Foundation to commission a sculpture by Tony Smith to be located at the University of Hawaii. ($10,000)

♦ **Museum Purchase Plan:** A continuing program of matching grants enabling museums to purchase works of living American artists was initiated in Fiscal 1968. Recipients are recommended by panels of experts in the museum field, and it is required that matching funds be raised from new sources specifically for this purpose. To date, the following 20 museums have received $10,000 grants for a total of $200,000:

> Andrew Dickson White Museum of Art (Ithaca)
> Brooks Memorial Art Gallery (Memphis)
> Dayton Art Institute
> Des Moines Art Center
> Flint Institute of Arts (Michigan)
> The High Museum of Art (Atlanta)
> Huntington Galleries, Inc. (West Virginia)
> Isaac Delgado Museum of Art (New Orleans)
> Milwaukee Art Center
> Newark Museum Association (New Jersey)
> New Jersey State Museum (Trenton)
> North Carolina Museum of Art (Raleigh)
> Oakland Art Museum (California)
> Oberlin College, Allen Memorial Art Museum (Ohio)
> Pasadena Art Museum
> Portland Art Museum (Oregon)
> Rhode Island School of Design, Museum of Art (Providence)
> San Francisco Museum of Art
> Walker Art Center (Minneapolis)
> Wichita Art Museum

♦ **Museums Project:** A series of matching grants has been made over a three-year period for pilot programs to increase public interest in the visual arts through expansion of museum resources. The Boston Institute of Contemporary Art received $60,000 over a two-year period for special educational programs. The Amon Carter Museum of Western Art in Fort Worth received $70,187 and has established The North Texas Museums Resources Council. The program reaches into ten Texas counties. The Detroit Institute of Arts has thus far received $219,851 for its "Project Outreach," which is involving the entire State of Michigan and some neighboring States as well. (Total to date: $350,038)

♦ **Promoting Increased Liaison between Universities and Museums:** A series of $1,500 nonmatching grants has been made under a program aimed at stimulating museum scholarship and raising the reputation of museums in universities, and at interesting the university community in museums and museum scholars. Grants are made to enable university art history departments to hire museum scholars as instructors for one semester. To date, 11 grants totalling $16,500 have been made to the following:

Brown University (Providence)
Buffalo Society of Natural Science
Johns Hopkins University (Baltimore)
Marshall University (Huntington, West Virginia)
Philander Smith College (Little Rock)
Sacramento State College
Southern Methodist University (Dallas)
State University of New York at Buffalo
University of Arkansas (Little Rock)
University of Minnesota (Minneapolis)
Washington University (St. Louis)

♦ **Smithsonian Institution** (Washington, D.C.): A matching grant was made for support of "Explorations," an exhibition assembled by M.I.T.'s Center for Advanced Visual Studies and held at the National Collection of Fine Arts in Washington from April 4 to May 10, 1970. ($10,000)

♦ **Something Else Press (New Means Foundation)** (New York City): A matching grant was made to support the production of two books—*Fantastic Architecture,* a selection of works by artists Claes Oldenburg, Allison Knowles, Richard Lippold, Daniel Spoerri and Richard Hamilton, composers Philip Corner and John Cage, and poets Ken Freedman and Emmet Williams; and *Stanzas for Iris,* a poetry book by Jackson MacLow. ($10,000)

♦ **Whitney Museum of American Art** (New York City): A matching grant was made for a program that brings students from colleges and universities throughout the country for a semester of study at the Whitney. ($10,000)

♦ **Works of Art in Public Places:** In Fiscal 1967, the National Council recommended a continuing program to encourage the acquisition of works of contemporary art for placement in prominent urban areas throughout the country. Grants are made on a matching basis and involve the commissioning of artists recommended by panels of experts mutually acceptable to the city whose application is approved, and the Endowment. Matching grants of $45,000 each were made to Grand Rapids, Seattle, and Wichita for sculpture projects. Grand Rapids commissioned a stabile, *La Grande Vitesse,* by Alexander Calder, dedicated in June 1969; *Black Sun* by Isamu Noguchi was placed in Volunteer Park adjacent to the Seattle Museum in September 1969. (Total: $135,000)

♦ **American Association of Museums** (Washington, D.C.): A Fiscal 1969 non-matching grant was made for salaries, travel, administrative costs, publications, and application of new technologies for the purpose of coordinating museum efforts and resources on a State, regional, and national basis. ($10,000)

♦ **The American Federation of Arts** (New York City): A 1968 program, matched by the Roy R. and Marie S. Neuberger Foundation, provided scholarships for a workshop in art criticism, offered in unison with the New School for Social Research, under the direction of art critic Max Kozloff. ($10,500)

♦ **Andreas S. Andersen:** A study grant enabled Andreas Andersen, Director of the Otis Art Institute (Los Angeles), to survey contemporary instruction in design at British and European public and private schools. A report on this study, illustrated with slides, will be made available to professional art schools and college and university art departments in this country. ($3,500)

♦ **Aperture, Inc.** (New York City): A matching grant assisted *Aperture,* a photography publication, to expand its size and readership while maintaining his high quality, and to print two books, one on the work of Alfred Stieglitz and the other on that of Minor White. ($20,000)

♦ **The Artists Technical Research Institute, Inc.:** Matching grants, $15,000 in Fiscal 1967 and $10,000 in Fiscal 1969, enabled the Artists Institute in New York to conduct research on the uses of new materials in visual arts and to disseminate the results to artists, schools and museums. (Total: $25,000)

♦ **Archie Bray Foundation** (Helena, Montana): Matching grants, $5,000 in Fiscal 1967 and $10,000 in Fiscal 1969, have supported a summer program for creative development in the field of ceramics. (Total: $15,000)

♦ **Contemporary Art Workshop** (Chicago): A matching grant was made for operating expenses and scholarships enabling promising young artists in the area to work and receive instruction at the Workshop. ($12,000)

♦ **Experiments in Art and Technology, Inc.** (New York City): A matching grant was made for support of operating expenses of this new national service organization, designed to promote collaboration among artists, scientists, and engineers, on projects to explore and expand artists' use of the new technology. ($50,000)

♦ **Penland School of Crafts** (North Carolina): A non-matching grant was made to provide individual grants enabling professional craftsmen to reside and work at the Penland School, the oldest craft school in the United States. ($50,000)

♦ **Philadelphia City Planning Commission:** A matching grant was made for the acquisition of sculpture for the central Philadelphia area to enhance urban design. The City has acquired a sculpture by Seymour Lipton entitled *Leviathan* and a stabile by Alexander Calder entitled *Three Discs, One Lacking.* ($30,000)

♦ **Photographic Studies:** A grant was made in Fiscal 1968 to Bruce Davidson for a detailed study of the people, life and environment of a select area in New York's Spanish Harlem. ($12,000)

♦ **Print Workshops for Artists**

Gemini Limited (Los Angeles): A Fiscal 1968 grant enabled Kenneth Tyler, Director of Gemini Limited, to conduct research and experimentation in new print materials and techniques. ($20,000)

Universal Limited Art Editions, Inc. (Long Island): A Fiscal 1967 grant enabled Tatyana Grosman, Director of Universal Limited Art Editions, to implement the development of original works of graphic art by outstanding contemporary American artists for exhibitions by educational institutions and other nonprofit organizations. ($15,000)

♦ **Venice Biennale:** A matching grant was made by the Endowment to provide a United States exhibit, assembled by the National Collection of Fine Arts of the Smithsonian Institution, at the September 1966 Biennale in Venice. ($32,480)

♦ **Vermont Council on the Arts:** A non-matching grant enabled the Endowment to co-sponsor with the Vermont Marble Company America's first international sculpture symposium during the summer of 1968. Ten internationally-known stone sculptors worked outdoors carving from the raw Vermont marble during the two-month symposium; an estimated 100,000 visitors were able to view the works-in-progress. An exhibition of the works was held at the close of the symposium after which the sculptors elected to leave the collection intact as the nucleus of a growing Sculpture Park in Proctor, Vermont. ($10,000)

♦ **Washington Gallery of Modern Art:** A Fiscal 1968 matching grant enabled the Gallery (now the Corcoran Gallery–Dupont Center) to exhibit *66 Signs of Neon*, a group of assemblages made from artifacts found after the Watts riots. ($3,200)

♦ **WPA Art Projects:** A study grant enabled Francis O'Connor of the University of Maryland to investigate and evaluate Federal art projects in the 1930's and their relevance to current Federal arts programs. The completed study has been published by the New York Graphic Society and is titled *Federal Support for the Visual Arts: The New Deal and Now.* ($42,853)

◆ **American Association of University Women** (Des Moines, Iowa): A matching grant was made for support of an Iowa Arts Festival, to be held in conjunction with the Iowa State Fair in August 1970. ($6,570)

◆ **Appalachian Region Exhibit:** A Fiscal 1968 matching grant ($5,000) to the Charleston, West Virginia Section, National Council of Jewish Women, enabled an open, juried exhibition of arts and crafts by residents of and students enrolled in institutions located in the 13-State Appalachian Region. The exhibit, entitled "Appalachian Corridors," opened in the spring of 1968 and was subsequently sent on an extended tour, continuing into 1969. In Fiscal 1970, the Endowment made a matching grant ($4,500) to assist "Appalachian Corridors/Exhibition 2" which opened in Charleston on April 4, 1970. States included, either wholly or in part, in both exhibits were Alabama, Georgia, Kentucky, Maryland, Mississippi, New York, North Carolina, Ohio, Pennsylvania, South Carolina, Tennessee, Virginia, and West Virginia. (Total: $9,500)

◆ **Agnes de Mille:** A grant from the Endowment is assisting Miss de Mille to provide fees for artists and administrative personnel on a project to develop a lyric history, "America, 1630–1776," which explores the shaping forces of American character and will be aimed primarily at college audiences. ($10,000)

◆ **Federation of Rocky Mountain States:** A Fiscal 1970 matching grant was made for support of the Federation's program which assists professional arts organizations to tour communities in Colorado, Idaho, Montana, Nevada, New Mexico, Utah and Wyoming. The companies included in the touring program are: the Utah Symphony, Denver Symphony, Ballet West (formerly Utah Civic Ballet), Montana Repertory Theatre and the Repertory Dance Company of the University of Utah. ($75,000)

◆ **Lubbock Cultural Affairs Council** (Texas): A matching grant supported a pilot project involving community cooperation on arts programming between the Lubbock Chamber of Commerce, local arts organizations, and Texas Technological College. ($5,314)

◆ **National Touring Program:** Two series of matching grants have been awarded under a program initiated in Fiscal 1969 enabling performing arts groups to distribute a limited number of performances, in addition to their normal schedules, to cities or areas which they might otherwise be unable to visit. Grants totalling $356,576 have been made to date to the following 19 groups:

Alaska State Council on the Arts (Harkness Ballet)	$ 4,800
Ballet West	3,000
Baltimore Symphony	1,500
Federation of Rocky Mountain States	35,000
Illinois Arts Council (Toby Show)	6,000
Kansas City Philharmonic	4,600
Maine State Commission on the Arts and Humanities (Portland Symphony)	10,000
Maryland Arts Council (Center Stage)	15,000
Minneapolis Theatre Company/Tyrone Guthrie Theatre	75,000
Minnesota Orchestra	13,500
Montana Repertory Theatre	10,000
New Orleans Philharmonic Symphony Orchestra (2 grants)	14,426
Phoenix Symphony	12,600
Princeton Chamber Orchestra	8,300
Seattle Opera Association	8,000
St. Louis Symphony	9,100
Studio for New Music (St. Louis, Missouri)	750
Utah Symphony Orchestra	25,000
Western Opera Theater/San Francisco Opera	100,000

◆ **Oakland University Audience Development Program** (Rochester, Michigan): A matching grant ($45,500) in Fiscal 1968 assisted Oakland University in the first year of a four-year community audience development plan for theatre and music. Second ($22,700) and third ($21,611) matching grants in Fiscal 1969 and 1970 are continuing the Endowment's support for this program, administered by the University in cooperation with local arts and business organizations as well as the United Automobile Workers and the Amalgamated Clothing Workers of America. (Total: $89,811)

◆ **Performing Arts Council of Los Angeles Music Center:** A matching grant was made to partially cover administrative costs of a program to expand the Center's audience to include people who would not ordinarily attend. ($15,120)

◆ **Special State Projects:** Two series of matching grants, in Fiscal 1969 and Fiscal 1970, have enabled 27 State arts agencies to undertake special projects in addition to those implemented under the Endowment's Federal-State Partnership Program. All States are invited to submit proposals; recommendations on choice of grantees are made by a special panel. Grants of up to $6,700 in Fiscal 1969 and up to $10,000 in Fiscal 1970 were made to the following States and special jurisdictions: (Total: $211,731)

Alaska (2 grants) ($16,700)	Hawaii ($5,000
Arizona ($10,000)	Indiana ($7,500)
Colorado ($6,700)	Kentucky (2 grants) ($11,700)
Connecticut ($6,400)	Massachusetts ($6,500)
Guam ($4,400)	Michigan (2 grants) ($16,700)

New Jersey (2 grants) ($11,700))
New Mexico ($3,500)
New York ($6,700)
Oklahoma ($6,614
Oregon ($6,700)
Minnesota ($6,700)
Missouri ($4,000)
Montana (2 grants) ($10,300)
Nebraska ($6,500)

Puerto Rico ($3,350)
Rhode Island ($2,500)
South Dakota (2 grants) ($13,667)
Texas ($6,700)
Vermont (2 grants) ($3,600)
Virginia ($6,700)
Washington ($6,700)
West Virginia (2 grants) ($14,200)

♦ **AFL/CIO Council for Scientific, Professional and Cultural Employees (SPACE):** A Fiscal 1968 grant of $20,000 assisted a project coordinator, Harlowe Dean, to begin work with union representatives and local arts organizations in New York, Buffalo, Minneapolis and Louisville on the development of a Demonstration Arts Project, in cooperation with local AFL/CIO central labor organizations. A second grant ($20,000) continued Endowment support for this project during Fiscal 1969. (Total: $40,000)

♦ **Alaska '67 Centennial Exposition:** A matching grant assisted in making professional theatre available for the first time in Alaskan history during the time of the Centennial celebration. ($5,000)

♦ **American Theatre Laboratory:** A 1967 project created an experimental theatre laboratory in New York for professional actors, musicians, writers and dancers, under the direction of Jerome Robbins. ($292,797)

♦ **Artists' Rights:** A study grant enabled Melville B. Nimmer, Professor of Law at UCLA, to explore laws applying to the arts and the legal rights of artists. His completed study has been well received and will, in a modified form, be published and distributed. ($24,218)

♦ **Arts and Disadvantaged Areas:** A grant to Julian Euell enabled him to research the use of the arts to benefit disadvantaged persons and areas. ($8,764)

♦ **Associated Councils of the Arts (ACA):** A matching grant was made to assist this New York-based national service organization's program of consultation, information, and other technical assistance to hundreds of State, city and community arts councils in North America. ($75,000)

♦ **Associated Councils of the Arts (ACA):** A grant assisted ACA to compile, publish, and distribute a reference booklet concerning State and national arts programs. Entitled "Directory of State Arts Councils 1969–70," it has been released and is currently available from ACA. ($4,000)

♦ **Center for Inter-American Relations** (New York City): A program was established to stimulate Inter-American artistic activities in the United States and to assist American artists to translate and adapt important Latin American writings. The program was launched by the

Inter-American Foundation for the Arts ($74,556) which was absorbed by the Center for Inter-American Relations ($75,444). (Total: $150,000)

♦ **Common Ground of the Arts** (Detroit): A matching grant was made in Fiscal 1968 for three-year operating expenses of this multi-studio art center for architects, urban designers, painters, sculptors, photographers, print makers and craftsmen. ($13,800)

♦ **Conference for State Arts Agencies:** A matching grant enabled the Federation of Rocky Mountain States (Denver) to conduct a two-day conference in 1967 which offered directors of new State arts agencies technical assistance and consultation on solutions for budgetary, administrative and legislative problems. ($3,000)

♦ **Foundation Giving in the Arts:** This project explored national and local foundation support for the arts. ($13,300)

♦ **Historical Costume Exhibit:** A matching grant was made to the Metropolitan Museum of Art for a comprehensive exhibition of 100 historical and 65 contemporary costumes reflecting the characteristics of our environment. The exhibition was held from October 1967 to January 1968 and resulted in publication of an illustrated catalogue of excellence in this field of design. ($25,000)

♦ **Inner City Summer Arts Program:** A program in cooperation with the President's Council on Youth Opportunity supported Inner City arts programs during the summer of 1968. Matching grants of $25,000 each to 16 cities were made possible by donations to the Endowment from private sources amounting to $200,000, matched by $200,000 from Endowment funds. Each of the cities, in turn, matched its grant on a two-for-one basis, so that a $200,000 Federal funds investment resulted in $1.2 million for arts programming involving thousands of Inner City residents across the country. The cities included were: Atlanta, Baltimore, Boston, Buffalo, Chicago, Cleveland, Detroit, Los Angeles, Milwaukee, Minneapolis, Newark, New York, Philadelphia, San Francisco, St. Louis, and Washington, D.C. (Endowment funds: $200,000; private funds: $200,000)

♦ **Institute of American Indian Arts:** A matching grant was made for the 1966 Festival of Performing Arts of the American Indian in Washington, D.C. ($29,000)

♦ **Jackson Mississippi Folk Art Festival:** A matching grant made to the Community Service Association of Jackson, Mississippi, assisted in establishing nine-week workshops during the summer of 1968 in a number of categories, including the American Negro and the American Indian Folk Cultures in Mississippi. ($10,000)

♦ **National Folk Festival Association:** A Fiscal 1967 matching grant ($39,500) helped the Association plan for an annual national folk festival, encourage regional festivals, and study, collect and publish data on the origin of various forms of American folklore. A Fiscal 1970 matching grant ($39,000) provided general support and assisted the 32nd annual National Folk Festival which was held in October, 1969. (Total: $78,500)

♦ **Rocky Mountain States Audience Development:** A Fiscal 1968 matching grant to the Federation of Rocky Mountain States sponsored an experimental audience development project to assist communities with limited facilities to sponsor concerts, plays and dance performances of professional quality, with special emphasis on areas usually by-passed by touring groups. (The States involved were Arizona, Colorado, Nevada, New Mexico, Texas, and Utah.) ($30,000)

♦ **U.C.L.A. Arts Administration Conference:** A non-matching grant supported a feasibility study and conferences held in Los Angeles and New York in January 1969 regarding the establishment of a permanent Arts Administration Institute at the University of California at Los Angeles. ($10,000)

♦ **University of Wisconsin—Idea Theatre—Rural Arts Program:** Matching grants were made to the University of Wisconsin, College of Agriculture's Wisconsin Idea Theatre for a three-year experimental pilot program in five small rural communities which explored methods to increase public receptivity to cultural programs and to give people who have not had the opportunity a chance to participate in the arts. The first two years of the project were spent mainly on setting up programs in small communities in Wisconsin; the final year of the project included a thorough evaluation of the program and its relevance for arts activities in rural areas throughout the country. (Total: $203,767)

Federal-State Partnership Program
October 1965 through April 1970

The Federal-State partnership program, specifically authorized by the National Foundation on the Arts and the Humanities Act of 1965, and launched in 1967, has resulted in the birth and growth of the State arts councils movement in the 50 States and five special political jurisdictions (American Samoa, District of Columbia, Guam, Puerto Rico, and the Virgin Islands).

Two million dollars were appropriated for matching grants to the States during each of the Fiscal Years 1967 and 1968, and, encouragingly, the funds appropriated by the State legislatures for Fiscal 1968 increased 43 percent over the previous year. In addition, many of the State agencies have been able to stimulate substantial private support as well, thus indicating the tremendous potential to be realized from greater Federal appropriations.

The projects under this program involve all art forms, with major emphasis on performances and exhibitions in smaller communities of the States, thereby affording to many their first opportunity to participate in the arts.

In Fiscal 1968, 46 State arts agencies received Endowment grants of up to $39,383 each, and launched approximately 1,100 projects, conceived and directed by the agencies themselves with their own particular knowledge of their States' cultural resources and needs. As a direct result of the cutback in funds appropriated for this program for Fiscal 1969 (1.7 million), the amount available to each State agency was reduced to a maximum of $30,909. This represented a reduction of more than $8,000 from the previous year grants, and the number of projects undertaken by the agencies consequently dropped to around 715.

In Fiscal 1970, $2 million was appropriated for the Federal-State partnership program. Matching grants of $36,363 each have been made to 54 State arts agencies.

The following is a breakdown of the Endowment's grants to State Arts agencies as of April, 1970:

	Fiscal 1967	Fiscal 1968	Fiscal 1969	Fiscal 1970
Alabama	$37,053	$39,383	$30,909	$36,363
Alaska	35,943	38,799	30,810	36,363
American Samoa	**	**	**	**
Arizona	37,053	39,383	30,909	36,363
Arkansas	37,053	39,383	30,909	36,363
California	49,222	39,383	30,909	36,363
Colorado	37,053	39,383	30,909	36,363

	Fiscal 1967	Fiscal 1968	Fiscal 1969	Fiscal 1970
Connecticut	46,861	39,383	30,909	36,363
Delaware	37,026	25,472*	**	36,363
District of Columbia	49,175	39,254	30,838	36,363
Florida	37,053	31,985	30,909	36,363
Georgia	36,867	8,538	30,909	36,363
Guam	15,376	38,128	30,909	36,363
Hawaii	32,972	38,747	30,909	36,363
Idaho	25,000	14,947*	26,406	36,363
Illinois	37,053	39,383	30,909	36,363
Indiana	16,581	39,383*	**	36,363
Iowa	24,608	30,976	30,136	36,363
Kansas	37,053	39,383	30,909	36,363
Kentucky	50,000	39,383	30,909	36,363
Louisiana	36,800	39,383	30,909	36,363
Maine	25,000	39,383	30,909	36,363
Maryland	37,053	39,383	30,909	36,363
Massachusetts	34,971	35,173	30,476	36,363
Michigan	50,000	39,383	30,909	36,363
Minnesota	37,053	39,383	30,909	36,363
Mississippi	25,000	37,270	30,909	36,363
Missouri	50,000	39,273	30,909	36,363
Montana	23,798	38,945	30,195	36,363
Nebraska	34,133	30,275	30,159	36,363
Nevada	,000	19,453	30,909	36,363
New Hampshire	37,053	39,383	30,704	36,363
New Jersey	46,713	39,383	30,909	36,363
New Mexico	34,893	39,083	30,909	36,363
New York	49,719	39,383	30,909	36,363
North Carolina	36,873	34,240	30,909	36,363
North Dakota	21,908	13,175	29,173	36,363
Ohio	36,907	39,383	30,909	36,363
Oklahoma	35,978	39,383	30,909	36,363
Oregon	25,000	38,883	30,909	36,363
Pennsylvania	37,053	39,383	30,909	36,363
Puerto Rico	48,247	39,383	30,909	36,363
Rhode Island	50,000	39,383	30,909	36,363
South Carolina	25,000	24,500	30,909	36,363
South Dakota	25,000	10,000	30,909	36,363
Tennessee	25,000	39,383	30,909	36,363
Texas	37,053	39,383	28,613	36,363
Utah	37,053	39,383	30,909	36,363
Vermont	36,363	37,537	30,880	36,363
Virgin Islands	25,000	39,383	30,909	36,363

	Fiscal 1967	Fiscal 1968	Fiscal 1969	Fiscal 1970
Virginia	43,000	39,383	30,744	36,363
Washington	50,000	39,116	30,909	36,363
West Virginia	46,400	35,580	30,909	36,363
Wisconsin	37,053	39,278	30,909	36,363
Wyoming	37,053	39,383	30,909	36,363

*Granted to State, State unable to meet provision of the grant.
Delaware received none
Idaho received none
Indiana received none
**No application submitted.